DATE DUE

THE SUN DOES SHINE

THE SUN DOES SHINE

HOW I FOUND LIFE AND FREEDOM
ON DEATH ROW

Anthony Ray Hinton

with Lara Love Hardin

and a Foreword by Bryan Stevenson

ST. MARTIN'S PRESS NEW YORK

www.stmartins.com

Designed by Steven Seighman

The Library of Congress Cataloging-in-Publication Data is available upon request.

ISBN 978-1-250-12471-5 (hardcover)
ISBN 978-1-250-12472-2 (ebook)

Our books may be purchased in bulk for promotional, educational, or business use. Please contact your local bookseller or the Macmillan Corporate and Premium Sales Department at 1-800-221-7945, extension 5442, or by email at MacmillanSpecialMarkets@macmillan.com.

First Edition: March 2018

10 9 8 7 6 5 4 3 2 1

For my mother, Buhlar Hinton.
May we all learn to love as unconditionally as she did.

CONTENTS

Foreword by Bryan Stevenson ix

1. Capital Offense 1
2. All American 15
3. A Two-Year Test Drive 26
4. The Cooler Killer 37
5. Premeditated Guilt 49
6. The Whole Truth 55
7. Conviction, Conviction, Conviction 67
8. Keep Your Mouth Shut 77
9. On Appeal 86
10. The Death Squad 98
11. Waiting to Die 110
12. The Queen of England 119
13. No Monsters 129
14. Love Is a Foreign Language 139
15. Go Tell It on the Mountain 148
16. Shakedown 157
17. God's Best Lawyer 166
18. Testing the Bullets 173
19. Empty Chairs 183
20. Dissent 203
21. They Kill You on Thursdays 215
22. Justice for All 224
23. The Sun Does Shine 230
24. Bang on the Bars 237

Afterword: Pray for Them by Name 243
Acknowledgments 253

FOREWORD

On April 3, 2015, Anthony Ray Hinton was released from prison after spending nearly thirty years in solitary confinement on Alabama's death row. Mr. Hinton is one of the longest-serving condemned prisoners facing execution in America to be proved innocent and released. Most of us can't possibly imagine what it feels like to be arrested, accused of something horrible, imprisoned, wrongly convicted because we don't have the money needed to defend ourselves, and then condemned to execution. For most people, it's simply inconceivable. Yet, it's important that we understand that it happens in America and that more of us need to do something to prevent it from happening again.

Mr. Hinton grew up poor and black in rural Alabama. He learned to be a keen and thoughtful observer of the harsh realities of Jim Crow segregation and the way racial bias constrained the lives of people of color. He was taught by his remarkable mother to never see race or judge people because of their color. He resisted mightily the notion that he was arrested, charged, and wrongly convicted because of his race, but he ultimately couldn't accept any other explanation. He was a poor man in a criminal justice system that treats you better if you are rich and guilty than if you are poor and innocent.

He is blessed with an extraordinary sense of humor, which he relies on to overcome the racial barriers that condemn so many. He lived with his mother until he was in his late twenties and worked as a contract laborer. He had never been accused of a violent act before his arrest.

One night while he was locked in a supermarket warehouse cleaning floors in Bessemer, Alabama, a restaurant manager fifteen miles away was abducted, robbed, and shot by a single gunman as he left work. The victim survived and later misidentified Mr. Hinton as the person who'd robbed him. Despite the fact that Mr. Hinton was working in a secure facility with a guard who recorded everyone's arrival and departure, miles from the crime scene, police went to the home of Mr. Hinton's mother, where they retrieved an old .38 caliber pistol. Alabama state forensic workers asserted this recovered gun was not only used in this recent robbery and attempted murder but also two other murders in the Bessemer area where restaurant managers had been robbed and killed at closing. Based on this gun evidence, Mr. Hinton was arrested and indicted for both murders, and State prosecutors announced they would seek the death penalty. Mr. Hinton passed a polygraph examination administered by police that confirmed his innocence, but State officials ignored this information and his alibi and persisted in obtaining two convictions and death sentences.

At trial, Mr. Hinton's appointed lawyer failed to obtain a competent expert to rebut the State's false claims about his mother's gun. For fourteen years, he could not obtain the legal help he needed to prove his innocence. I met Mr. Hinton in 1999, and he made quite an impression. Thoughtful, sincere, genuine, compassionate, funny, it was easy to want to help Anthony Ray Hinton, although it was worrisome to think how difficult it might prove to win his freedom.

I worked with my staff at the Equal Justice Initiative to engage three of the nation's top firearms examiners, who all testified that the gun obtained from Mr. Hinton's mother could not be matched to the crime evidence. It took fourteen more years of contested litigation and a rare unanimous ruling from the U.S. Supreme Court before Mr. Hinton was released in 2015. During his time on Alabama's death row, Mr. Hinton watched fifty-four men walk past his door on their way to be executed. The execution chamber was thirty feet from his cell.

Mr. Hinton was sustained during his long years on Alabama's death row by a childhood friend who never failed to visit him over the course of nearly thirty years. Lester Bailey insisted that Mr. Hinton never feel alone or abandoned. Mr. Hinton learned to engage those around him and create an identity on death row unlike anything I've ever seen. Not only did he shape the lives of dozens of other death row prisoners but also those of correctional officers who sought Mr. Hinton's advice and counsel on everything from marriage and faith to the struggles of day-to-day life.

While his case created years of disappointment and frustration for Mr. Hinton and cost me many sleepless nights after each adverse legal ruling, we both could be frequently seen bowled over with laughter in the visitation room at Holman State Prison. Such is the extraordinary power of Ray Hinton and his remarkable spirit.

I've visited countless prisons and jails to see hundreds of clients during the course of my career. I'm usually ignored or merely tolerated by correctional staff during these visits. There have been times when I have been harassed or challenged by prison staff who seem to resent incarcerated people getting legal visits. Visiting Ray Hinton was unlike any other legal visit for me. Never have more guards, correctional staff, and prison workers pulled me aside to offer assistance or question me about how they could help than during the many years I have worked with Ray. I have never experienced anything like it.

I have represented scores of condemned prisoners during my thirty years of law practice. Many of my clients were innocent people wrongly convicted or condemned. However, no one I have represented has inspired me more than Anthony Ray Hinton, and I believe his compelling and unique story will similarly inspire our nation and readers all over the world.

Reading his story is difficult but necessary. We need to learn things about our criminal justice system, about the legacy of racial bias in America and the way it can blind us to just and fair treatment of people. We need to understand the dangers posed by the politics of fear and anger that create systems like our capital punishment system and the political dynamics that have made some courts and officials act so irresponsibly. We also need to learn about human dignity, about human worth and value. We need to think about the fact that we are all more than the worst thing we have done. Anthony Ray Hinton's story helps us understand some of these problems and ultimately what it means to survive, to overcome, and to forgive.

Since his release, Mr. Hinton has become an extraordinary public speaker, and he has had a life-changing impact on the audiences who hear him. He is rare in his ability to mix humor, deep emotion, and compelling storytelling to move people to share his agonizing but ultimately triumphant journey.

His message of forgiveness is transformative, and I've seen him inspire groups of people as diverse as hardened police chiefs and prosecutors to young at-risk teens and students.

His story is one of forgiveness, friendship, and triumph. It is situated amid racism, poverty, and an unreliable criminal justice system. Mr. Hinton presents the narrative of a condemned man shaped by a painful and torturous journey around the gates of death, who nonetheless remains hopeful, forgiving, and faithful. This book is something of a miracle, because there were many moments when I believe both of us feared he would never survive to tell his story. We should be grateful that he did survive, because his witness, his life, his journey is an unforgettable inspiration.

Bryan Stevenson, attorney

THE SUN DOES SHINE

| I |

CAPITAL OFFENSE

But more so than the evidence, I have never had as strong a feeling in trying any other case that the defendant just radiated guilt and pure evil as much as in the Hinton trial.

—PROSECUTOR BOB MCGREGOR

There's no way to know the exact second your life changes forever. You can only begin to know that moment by looking in the rear-view mirror. And trust me when I tell you that you never, ever see it coming. Did my life change forever the day I was arrested? Or did the life-changing moment happen even earlier? Was that day just the culmination of a whole series of fateful moments, poor choices, and bad luck? Or was the course of my life determined by being black and poor and growing up in a South that didn't always care to be civil in the wake of civil rights? It's hard to say. When you are forced to live out your life in a room the size of a bathroom—a room that's five feet wide by seven feet long—you have plenty of time to replay the moments of your life. To imagine what might have happened if you had run when they came chasing you. Or if you had gotten that baseball scholarship. Or married that girl when you had the chance. We all do it. Replay the horrific moments of our lives and reimagine them by going left instead of right, being this person instead of that person, making different choices. You don't have to be locked up to occupy your mind and your days trying to rewrite a painful past or undo a terrible tragedy or make right a horrible wrong. But pain and tragedy and injustice happen—they happen to us all. I'd like to believe it's what you choose to do after such an experience that matters the most—that truly changes your life forever.

I'd really like to believe that.

Jefferson County Jail, December 10, 1986

My mom sat on the other side of the glass wall that separated us, looking out of place in her ivory gloves, green-and-blue flowered dress, and her wide blue hat rimmed in white lace. She always dressed for jail like she was going to church. But a nice outfit and impeccable manners have always been used as weapons in the South. And the bigger her hat, the more she meant business. That woman wore hats taller than the pope's. Looking at my mama in this visiting room, you would hardly guess in her own Southern way she was armed to the teeth and ready for battle. During the trial and even on visiting days, she looked a bit dazed and bewildered by it all. She had been like that ever since my arrest a year and a half ago. Lester said he thought she was still in shock. Lester Bailey and I have been friends since he was four years old and our mothers told us to go out and play together. I was six then and far too old to play with a four-year-old. But even though I had tried to lose him that first day, he stuck with me. Twenty-three years later, he was still sticking with me.

During every visit, it was as if my mom couldn't understand why I was still in jail. Three months earlier, I had been found guilty of robbing and murdering two people. Three months since twelve people decided I was no longer of value and this world would somehow be a better place if I weren't in it. Their recommendation was that I be murdered. Oh, the sanitized way of saying it is "sentenced to death." But let's call it what it is. They wanted to murder me because I had murdered.

Only they had the wrong guy.

I was working the night shift in a locked warehouse when the manager at a Quincy's restaurant fifteen miles away was abducted, robbed, and shot. I was mistakenly identified. The police claimed an old .38 caliber pistol owned by my mother was the murder weapon. The State of Alabama claimed this gun was not only used in the Quincy's robbery and attempted murder but also two other murders in the area where restaurant managers had been robbed at closing time, forced into coolers, and then murdered. That old gun my mom owned, I don't think it had been used in twenty-five years. Maybe longer. I had never even been in a fight, but now, I was not only a killer but the kind of cold-blooded killer that would hold a gun to your head and pull the trigger for a few hundred bucks and then just go about my business like it was nothing.

God knows my mama didn't raise no killer. And during those months of waiting for the official sentencing from the judge, her demeanor hadn't changed from before I was convicted. Did she know I was one court date away from the death chamber? We didn't speak on it, and truly I wasn't sure if she was pretending on my account, or I was pretending on her account, or we were both just so caught up in this nightmare that neither of us really knew how to face what had happened.

"When are you coming home, baby? When are they going to let you come home?"

I looked at Lester, who stood behind her, one hand resting on her left shoulder while she held the phone up to her right ear. He usually came alone to see me, and my mom came with my sister or the neighbor. Every week, Lester would be the first in line on visiting day, stopping in on his way to work to say hello and put some money on my books so I had the essentials. He had done that for the last year and a half, like clockwork every single week. He was the first one there no matter what. He really was the best, best friend a guy could have.

Lester looked back at me and shrugged and then shook his head a little. My mom always asked when "they" were going to let me come home. I was the baby of the family—her baby. Up until my arrest, we were together every day. We went to church together. Ate our meals together. Laughed together. Prayed together. She was my absolute everything, and I was hers. I couldn't think of any big moment in my life when my mom wasn't right there by my side, cheering me on. Every baseball game. Before exams and school dances. Graduation. When I got home from work in the coal mine, she was always there waiting to hug me no matter how dirty I was. When I went to my first day of work at the furniture store, she was up early to make me breakfast and pack me a lunch. And she was there every day of my trial. Smiling up at everyone in that courtroom in her best dress with the kind of love that can just break a man's heart into a million pieces. She believed in me—always had, always would. Even now. Even though a jury had found me guilty, she still believed in me. I could feel the lump form in my throat and my eyes start to sting. She and Lester were probably the only people in the world who knew what I knew: I was innocent. They didn't care that the press made me out to be some kind of monster. The fact that these two people never doubted me for a second—well, let's just say I hung on to that like my life depended on it. But even if I were guilty, even if I had murdered those two people in cold blood for a little cash, my mom and Lester would have still loved me and believed in me. They would have still been right where they were. What does a man do with a love like that? What does a man do?

I looked down until I could get control. I had tried my best to keep my feelings and emotions in check throughout the trial because I didn't want to upset my mom. I didn't want her to see me cry. I didn't want her to feel my fear or my pain. My mom had always tried to protect me, to take away my pain. But this pain was too much for even a mother's love to contain. I couldn't do that to her. I wouldn't do that no matter how hard they pushed me. It was all I had left to give.

After a few moments, I looked back up and smiled at my mom. Then Lester and I locked eyes once more.

He shook his head again.

When you've known a guy as long as I have known Lester, you have a kind of unspoken language. I had asked him not to let anyone talk to my mom about my sentencing. My sister had wanted to sit her down and make her understand that they could put me to death and that I was never coming home. Make her face it and deal with it. Lester put a stop to all that talk. I would come home someday. I didn't want my mom to lose her hope. There's no sadder place to be in this world than a place where there's no hope.

When Lester came to visit alone, he and I could talk freely—well, as freely as two guys can talk when their every word is being recorded. We had a sort of code. But since my conviction, it didn't seem to matter much anymore. Time was running out, so we had talked about my options openly.

I put my hand up on the thick glass that separated me from my mom, and I readjusted the phone's handset against my ear. She leaned forward and stretched her arm out so that her hand was pressed against the other side of the wall that separated us.

"Soon, Mama," I said. "They're working on it. I plan to be home soon."

I had a plan. Lester knew it. I knew it. God knew it. And that was all that mattered. Now that I had blocked out all the sadness, I could feel the anger rising up through me and fighting to get out. It had come in waves ever since my conviction. Tonight I would pray again. Pray for the truth. Pray for the victims. Pray for my mom and for Lester. And I would pray that the nightmare I had been living for almost two years would end somehow. There was no question how my sentencing would turn out, but I would still pray for a miracle and try not to criticize it if the miracle didn't look like what I expected.

It's what my mama had always taught me.

Jefferson County Courthouse, December 15, 1986

It was nothing less than a lynching—a legal lynching—but a lynching all the same. The anger I had tried so hard to stuff down and pray away was back in full force. My only crime was being born black, or being born black in Alabama. Everywhere I looked in this courtroom, I saw white faces—a sea of white faces. Wood walls, wood furniture, and white faces. The courtroom was impressive and intimidating. I felt like an uninvited guest in a rich man's library. It's hard to explain exactly what it feels like to be judged. There's a shame to it. Even when you know you're innocent. It still feels like you are coated in something dirty and evil. It made me feel guilty. It made me feel like my very soul was put on trial and found lacking. When it seems like the whole world thinks you're bad, it's hard to hang on to your goodness. I was trying, though. The Lord knows I was trying. I had been all over the Birmingham newspapers from the time of my arrest and then throughout the trial. The press had judged me guilty from the second I had stepped out of my mama's yard. So had the police detectives and the experts and the prosecutor—a sorry-looking man with a weak chin, saggy jowls, and a pallor that made it look like he had never worked a day outside in his life. Now, if I had to judge anyone as evil in that courtroom, it would have been Prosecutor McGregor. There was a meanness that came out of his small, close-set eyes—a hatred that was hard and edgy and brittle. He looked like he could snap at any moment. Like some sort of rabid weasel. If he could have executed me right then and there, he would have done so and then gone about having his lunch without further thought. And then there was Judge Garrett. He was a large man; even in his loose black robe, he looked overstuffed and uncomfortable. He had a ruddy color to his cheeks. He preened and puffed and made a big show out of everything, but it was all a farce. Oh, sure, they all went through the motions. For almost two weeks, they paraded out witnesses and experts and walked us through the chain of custody and exhibits A to Z, all of which I guess gave legitimacy to what was already a foregone conclusion. I was guilty. Hell, as far as the police and the prosecutor and the judge and even my own defense attorney were concerned, I was born guilty. Black, poor, without a father most of my life, one of ten children—it was actually pretty amazing I had made it to the age of twenty-nine without a noose around my neck. But justice is a funny thing, and in Alabama, justice isn't blind. She knows the color of your skin, your education level, and how much money you have in the bank. I may not have had any money, but I had enough education to understand exactly how justice was working in this trial and exactly how it was going to turn out. The good old boys had traded in their white robes for black robes, but it was still a lynching.

"Your Honor, the State rests."

"All right, any witnesses for the defense?"

I watched incredulously as my attorney declined to question the second bailiff who had just lied about me under oath. I never told either bailiff that I knew how to get one over on a polygraph test. I had spent almost two years waiting for my trial—purposefully not talking to anyone about anything to do with my case—and now supposedly in the hallway outside the courtroom, I had confessed to a bailiff that I had cheated to pass my polygraph, a polygraph the State wouldn't allow to be admitted because it had proven that I was innocent? It didn't make sense. None of it made sense.

My attorney turned away from the judge and looked at me. "Do you want to testify?"

I could see the bailiff smirking as he got out of the witness stand. Did I want to testify? They were about to sentence me to death, and nobody was speaking up on my behalf. There were things that needed to go on the record. My wrists were shackled and cuffed together, a heavy chain linking them to the leg irons around my ankles. For a moment, I imagined wrapping that chain around all their necks, but then I unclenched my fists and placed the palms of my hands together as if to pray. I wasn't a murderer. Never had been, never would be. I looked over at the jury, at McGregor, who stared back at me with hatred and self-righteousness, at the judge, who looked overheated and bored. I had spent a good many years testifying for God in church, and now it was time to testify for myself in this courtroom.

I nodded at my attorney. "Yes," I said, a bit louder than I meant to. Inside my head, I was screaming, *Hell yes,* and I accidentally banged my chains against the table as I stood up from my chair.

"Is there any way he can have these handcuffs removed, Judge?"

My attorney was finally doing something right. Fighting a little. I knew at this point it was more about saving face and winning something than about believing in me. When he was assigned to my case and told he would get paid $1,000, I heard him mutter, "I eat $1,000 for breakfast." He was going through the motions, but I knew his heart wasn't in it. He either thought I was guilty or he didn't care much one way or the other. I was just another file in a big stack of files. We had been together for almost two years, but he didn't know me. Not really. Not in the way you would want someone to know you when he holds your life in his hands. Still, I needed him. He knew that, and I knew that. So I was polite and respectful. If today went the way everyone knew it would go, I would still need him.

I held my wrists out to the bailiff. He smirked again as he unlocked my cuffs. Out of the corner of my eye, I could see my mom in the second row. Lester sat on one side of her, and my sister Dollie sat on the other. Our neighbor Rosemary was also there. I looked all the way over my shoulder as the handcuffs came off, and she gave me a little wave. I glanced at Lester and he gave me a quick nod. We had an endgame in mind.

I walked up to the witness stand and turned around and looked out over the courtroom. I was happy to be able to see my mom and face her eye to eye. She smiled at me, and I could feel my heart tighten. God, how I was going to miss her. No matter how big her smile, I knew she was scared, and all this legal mumbo jumbo might as well have been a foreign language. When she had left after that last visit, it had made her smile to hear me say I would be home soon sitting at our table and eating one of her Sunday afternoon cakes. She could bake a cake so good it would make the devil himself confess his sins and beg for mercy just to have a bite. Sometimes, late at night, I would close my eyes and see her red velvet cake with buttercream frosting so clearly in my mind, I swear I could actually smell all that butter and sugar. My imagination has always been both a blessing and a curse. It helped me get through some rough times growing up, but it had also gotten me into some trouble. Nothing like the trouble I was in now.

Every day since they had arrested me, I had thought, *Today will be the day. They'll know I was at work. They'll find the guy that really did it. Somebody will believe me.*

It was all some bad dream that I couldn't wake up from.

I smiled back at my mom, and then I looked over at McGregor. He had been glaring at me for two weeks. It was a famous tactic of his. Stare at the defendant until he cowers. Show him who's the alpha dog. Well, I wasn't a dog, and I wasn't about to cower. On the inside, I was scared to death. I wanted to go home. I didn't want to die. But on the outside, I had to be strong. For my mom. For my friends. Martin Luther King once said, "A man can't ride you unless your back is bent." So I sat with my back as straight as possible in that courtroom, and when McGregor stared at me, I straightened my back even more and stared right into his eyes. He was trying to ride me, all right, trying to kill me. And I wasn't going to make it any easier for him, or for any of them, than it already was.

"Judge," my attorney began, "let me make aware to the court that Mr. Hinton has requested the opportunity to testify. I have no particular idea of the subject matter of testimony, so there's no way of questioning him. I don't see how it could make any difference if he just testifies."

He didn't know the subject matter? The subject matter was this court just convicted me of two cold-blooded murders without any evidence. The subject matter is my attorney just let them find me guilty of two capital offenses based on a third attempted murder that happened while I was at work. The subject matter was my attorney hired a ballistics expert who could hardly see and who was crucified on the stand. The subject matter was the State of Alabama wanted to strap me to Yellow Mama and murder me for crimes I didn't commit. The subject matter was somebody was trying to kill me and I was fighting for my life. That was the subject matter.

I took a deep breath, closed my eyes, and said the same prayer I had prayed in my head a thousand times. *Dear God, let them know the truth of things. Let them see into my mind and my heart and find the truth. Bless the judge. Bless the DA. Bless the victims' families who are in pain. Dear God, let there be justice. Real justice.*

"First of all, I did not kill anybody. It is important to me that the families know this. Believe this. I wouldn't want anyone to take the life of someone I loved. I couldn't even imagine that pain. I know what it is like not to have a father, to be brought up with that missing in your life, and I wouldn't cause it to happen for anyone. There is a man up above who knows I didn't do it, and one day, I may not be here, but he's going to show you that I didn't do it. I wouldn't dare ever think about killing, because I can't give a life and, therefore, I don't have a right to take a life."

I could hear my voice shaking a little, so I took another deep breath, and I looked directly at the widow of John Davidson. "And if you . . . if the family's satisfied that they've got the right man, I'm sorry, but if you really want your husband's killer to be brought to justice, get on your knees and pray to God about it, because I didn't do it."

I looked up at Judge Garrett. "Do with me what seems good to you, but as sure as you put me to death, you bring blood upon yourself and upon your hands. I love all people. I've never been prejudiced in my life. I went to school and got along with everybody, never been in a fight. I'm not a violent person."

My mom was nodding. Smiling at me like I was in a school play or giving a recital. I kept going. "I've been praying to God for the DA, for this judge, and especially for the victims. You got to give an account for what you done, and it don't matter to me, because if I can recall, Jesus was prosecuted, accused falsely for things he didn't do, and all he did was try to love and save this world, and he died and suffered. If I have to die for something I didn't do, so be it. My life is not in this judge's hands. My life is not in your hands, but it's in God's hands."

I spoke to the bailiffs who had just lied on the stand. I told them that I would pray for the Lord to forgive them. *Forgive them, for they know not what they do.*

"You all sent an innocent man to prison. You kept an innocent man locked up for two years, and I begged, I pleaded with you to give me anything that you believe in. Truth serum, hypnosis, anything. I have nothing to hide."

I saw McGregor shake his head and roll his eyes and then give a half snort, half laugh.

I looked directly at him. "I'm praying for you," I repeated. "I'm praying that God will forgive you all for what you have done, and I hope that you have enough wisdom to ask God to forgive you. You're going to die just like I'm going to die. My death may be in the electric chair, but you're going to die too. But one thing—after my death, I'm going to heaven. Where are you going?" I looked at the judge and the bailiffs and the district attorney and the police detectives. "Where are you going?" I asked again. "A lie should not carry in God's sight. When the police came and arrested me, I had no idea what they were arresting me for. And I want the family to know that if I had killed somebody, you wouldn't have found me in my mama's backyard cutting grass. I had nothing to hide, and I didn't know anything about these murders."

My attorney was looking down, scribbling on his notepad. I was rushing to get everything out. God only knew if I was making sense.

"Since I been in jail, I've read the paper every day, and hardly a day goes by where people haven't been forced in a cooler, and you going to read about it again. Somebody's going to get killed. Maybe by then, you're going to realize you got the wrong man. But I pray to God it don't happen that way. I just pray that the man that really did it—I just hope the Lord will put enough burden on their heart where they can just come and tell you. But then, I'm not convinced you going to want to believe them. But when God is in the plan, I ain't worried about what you believe. I don't want to be electrocuted, but whatever way the Lord have me go, I'm ready to go. And you know I looked and I've seen prejudice in this courtroom. You people don't want the truth. You people don't want the right person. All you wanted was a conviction.

"I never, ever committed such a violent crime. Yes, I got off on the wrong track, and I stole and I wrote some bad checks—but I didn't try to hide it. I admitted it, and I paid for that. How long do I have to pay for that? I'm not up here trying to reopen this case, but I think every one of you, you got some doubts. You got some doubts. I'm sorry we don't live in a just world. My Bible tells me every knee must bow and every tongue must confess."

Rosemary yelled out, "Amen!" and I watched my mom pat her on the arm.

I looked directly into McGregor's eyes. "I don't think *the people* really care who's innocent. I'm just one black man, and that don't mean nothing to you. I don't know what color God is, but I can tell you he loves me just like he loves you. You might think you're superior in this world, but you're not. I had a life just like everybody else had a life, and I don't hate you. Mr. McGregor, I don't hate you. But for a slight moment during the trial, I was beginning to hate you, I really was, but I thank God that it came to me that I can't make it into heaven hating nobody."

"Amen," I heard again.

"I love you. You might think I'm crazy for telling a man that I love him that's done prosecuted me and is trying to send me to the death chair, but I love you."

"Amen." Rosemary was holding her hands up like we were in church and there was a good sermon going on. My sister had her eyes closed. Mom was just smiling and nodding, and Lester looked grim.

"You know, I haven't told many people this, but when I was coming up, I took business law in school, and I loved it. And I wanted to be a judge, thought perhaps of going to college and being a DA or something, but you know, I'm glad that I didn't do that. I'm glad because we don't really know when a person is innocent or guilty. You have proven that."

I closed my eyes then. If I could put my heart in the judge's heart, he would know I didn't do it. He would know I wasn't violent. I have always cared about all people—white, black, green, purple—if you needed help, I would help you. It's how I was raised, and it's who I am. I knew right from wrong. And what happened in this courtroom was wrong. It was all wrong.

"You people got a joy out of prosecuting me," I said.

I wasn't sure how to say this exactly, but there was an excitement to it. During the whole trial, it had felt like McGregor and the detectives and the State's experts were enjoying themselves—like taking away my life was some sort of sporting event.

"Everybody that testified for me testified the truth. I can't say that about the people you called. They got to give an account for that, and you reap what you sow, believe me. And I feel sorry for those twelve people that found me guilty. I feel real sorry for them, but I ain't mad at them. If you happen to see them, tell them I ain't mad. I'm always going to pray to God that he forgive them, and in my heart, I know he is a forgiving God. There's no doubt about it.

"Might sound crazy, but I got joy—even with leg irons on me. The joy I got—the world didn't give it to me, and the world can't take it away. That's a fact. Your Honor, I thank you for letting me have my say. Mr. McGregor,

I'm praying for you real hard. Ever since I seen you, you've been constantly in my prayers, and I'm going to continue to pray for you. Wherever they send me, God can hear my prayers. Now, what would really make me worried is if you could isolate me from God, but you can't do that. You took me from my family, but you can't take me from God.

"You know, I'm proud to be black. I would be proud if I was white. And it's sad when a police officer that is supposed to uphold the law tells you you're going to be convicted because you're black, and you got a white jury and you got a white DA. You know, that's sad. It's sad—real sad. If you talk to Lieutenant Doug Acker, tell him I'm praying for him also.

"Now, I look at those little kids back there, and that's a sad thing to know that their father won't be around no more. I know what it's like. I know what it's like."

I looked again at Lester sitting next to my mom. He would take care of her for me. That gave me some peace. But I worried that if this could happen to me, it could happen to him. Or one of my brothers. Or any black man in Alabama. Or any black man anywhere.

"The only harm I'm guilty of is I looked like somebody. And you know what y'all always say—we all look alike. But it's a funny thing—we all look alike, but you can positively identify us in that time of trouble. You know what Lieutenant Acker told me? 'Take this for your rap, because if you didn't do it, one of your brothers did it because y'all always helping one another, so take this.' And that's sad."

I paused and took one more deep breath.

"The saddest thing of all is that you're ready to close the case. This judge is glad it's over. The families are going home thinking the man's been brought to trial. The police case is closed. But God ain't closed the case, and he ain't about to close it. He's going to reopen it. It might be a year from now, it might be tomorrow, it might be today—he's going to reopen it."

Lester nodded at me, and I nodded back at him. This case was going to get reopened by God, but Lester and I were going to do everything we could to give God a little help.

It was time for the judge to sentence me. This was my fate from the second they arrested me. Someday they would know I didn't do it. And then what? What do you say to a man when you find out he didn't do it? What would they all say then? I sat up as straight as I could. I wasn't going to beg for my life.

"I'm not worried about that death chair. You can sentence me to it, but you can't take my life. It don't belong to you. My soul, you can't touch it."

It was a brief recess. Just three hours until they were bringing me back into that courtroom of rich wood and white faces for the last time. I listened as my attorney made one last attempt to object to them trying me for two capital offenses that were only related to each other by circumstance and not related to me by any evidence whatsoever. Somehow, the State of Alabama was able to consolidate the cases, relate them to a third, and put the death penalty on the table. This was the real capital offense.

The judge banged his gavel. Cleared his throat.

"It is the judgment of the court that the defendant, Anthony Ray Hinton, in each of these cases is guilty of the capital offense in accordance with the verdict of the jury in each of these cases. And it is the judgment of the court and the sentence of the court that the defendant, Anthony Ray Hinton, suffer death by electrocution on a date to be set by the Alabama Supreme Court pursuant to Alabama Rules of Appellate Procedure 8-D (1).

"The sheriff of Jefferson County, Alabama, is directed to deliver the defendant, the said Anthony Ray Hinton, into the custody of the director of the Department of Corrections and Institutions at Montgomery, Alabama, and the designated electrocution shall, at the proper place for the electrocution of one sentenced to suffer death by electrocution, cause a current of electricity of sufficient intensity to cause death and the application and continuance of such current to pass through the body of said Anthony Ray Hinton until the said Anthony Ray Hinton is dead."

I dropped my head. Judge Garrett banged his gavel, and my attorney said some things about an appeal, but my stomach was in my throat and there was a buzzing in my ears like a swarm of bees had been let loose in that courtroom. I thought I heard my mom crying as if in pain, and I looked back to see Dollie and Rosemary circled around her. The bailiffs were leading me toward the door that led out the back of the courtroom, but I turned and started to walk toward my mom. One of the bailiffs grabbed my arm below the shoulder, and I could feel each of his fingers digging in hard. There was no going to her. There was no way for me to comfort her. They would kill me if they could. I couldn't let them. I needed to get back to my mom, and she needed to get me back. I was her baby. Dear God, I was her baby, and I was innocent. I watched as if underwater as Lester and my mom both stood. I saw the tears on Lester's face, and my mom reached her arms out to me just as they pulled me through the door. It was all too much for one man to bear.

Dear God, please let the truth be known.

Dear God, do not let me die this way.

Dear God, I am innocent.

Dear God, protect my mom.

I am innocent.

I am innocent.

As they hurried me through the back hallway behind the courtroom, I remembered the grim look in Lester's eyes as I had testified. He knew what I knew. What every poor person tangled up in the legal system knows. McGregor may have won, but I don't think he or the judge realized that by sentencing me to death, they were giving me the only shot I had at proving my innocence. Now that I was sentenced to die, I would be guaranteed an appeal and guaranteed some representation by my attorney. If I had been sentenced to life, I would have had to hire an attorney to appeal.

The best chance for my life was to get sentenced to death. There was no money to prove my innocence. I was headed to Holman Prison. The House of Pain. Dead Man Land. The Slaughter Pen of the South. It had a lot of names. I was terrified, but I knew the only way to fight this injustice would be from inside.

God have mercy on my soul.

| 2 |

ALL AMERICAN

Do any of you have any bias or prejudice that would influence your verdict if you were selected to serve as a member of this jury?

—HONORABLE JAMES S. GARRETT

West Jefferson High School, May 1974

I blocked out all the noise and ground my left foot a little deeper in the dirt. Even with my helmet on, I swear it felt like the May sun was burning a hole right through the top of my head. I took a few practice swings, looking the pitcher right in the eye. He met my gaze and then spit over his left shoulder. I heard the catcher mutter something behind me, and the umpire gave a little snort, but I didn't care what he said or what the umpire thought was so funny. I had been called names before and I would be called names again, but I just let the names roll off me like water rolling over a rock.

I watched as if in slow motion while the pitcher lifted his left leg and cocked his right arm back. I knew this guy. We had been here before. Season after season we had faced each other down. He didn't take it well when he lost. He liked to throw his glove. Or his hat. Or kick the fence alongside the dugout. I was taught to remain calm. When you win, you stay calm. When you lose, you stay calm. Now, don't get me wrong, I wanted to win. Nobody likes to lose in baseball or in anything. But my mom always taught me that if you have a tantrum out there on the field and let the other team know they've upset you, it's like losing twice. "They may beat you now and then," she used to say, "but that don't mean they have to break you. You don't change who you are and how you was raised for anyone. And I didn't raise no child to have a tantrum in the middle of a baseball field or anywhere."

So I stared the pitcher down, and I let the catcher and the umpire roll off my back like water because I was a hundred times more afraid of my mom than I was of any of these three jokers.

I never took my eye off the ball, and while I wanted nothing more than to swing and to swing hard, it was an out-of-control curveball that just barely landed into the catcher's glove far outside of the plate.

"Strike!"

I looked back at the umpire. Had he lost his mind?

"Let's go, boy," he said, and this time, the catcher laughed.

So that's how it was going to be.

I looked up and around at the stands. It was a sea of white faces, and no one seemed to be overly concerned or protesting the call. I looked over into the dugout, but Coach Moore had his back turned to me as he talked to our first baseman. When this county finally gave in and integrated its schools, we were bussed from Praco to the white school. Over the past four years, it had pretty much been just like this—people either completely ignored us or they muttered slurs under their breath when we walked by. The white boys were braver when they were in a group. Because both Lester and I were big guys, no one ever called us names to our faces. They were afraid of us, which was funny, because both Lester and I had been raised to be afraid of them. Before the first day I got on the bus to go to West Jefferson High, my mom had sat me down and told me not to talk to any white girls. "Don't even look their way," she warned. "You study. You keep your head down. You keep your eyes down. And when the teachers talk to you, be polite and follow the rules. You go to school, and then you get home. Fast."

"Yes, ma'am." I had heard this before, but I knew better than to mention that to her.

"I'm not playing about those white girls," she added. "You pretend they don't even exist." I nodded, but inside, I was laughing. My mom was no fool, and she knew that not only were girls *my* weakness, I was *their* weakness as well. Girls loved me. Grown women loved me. I was almost eighteen and I had always been tall for my age, so the girls around Praco and in church had started noticing me right around seventh grade, and it had only increased the older I got. I wasn't looking to mess around with any white girls, though. They may have cheered me on in basketball and occasionally in baseball, but that was as far as it ever went. One thing I had learned in my new school—the better a season you had, the less racist everyone around you would become.

I was graduating soon, but Lester still had two more years to go. I worried about him walking home without me. It was almost five miles, and neither of our moms knew how to drive. Even if they had known, it wasn't like we could afford a car. My mom had a hard enough time earning the $44.29 she paid every month for our house.

I hadn't seen Lester before the game, but I knew he was around somewhere, watching and waiting for me. The bus took us to school, but if you played sports, you had to get yourself home at night. Sometimes walking home felt like being in the middle of a war. You had to be on alert at all times—ready to defend yourself or take cover. It was barely tolerable if you had someone with you, but if you had to make that walk alone, it felt like you were watching a horror movie the whole time, just waiting for the killer to jump out from behind the door. Lester always had my back on that walk, and I always had his.

I looked around Tiger Field, which was brown and dirty and not much to look at compared to most big high school fields in Alabama. The dugouts were made out of thick, gray cement blocks, and you felt like you were in a prison when you sat in them and looked out at the old chain-link fence surrounding the field. Our field wasn't even at the school; it was a couple of miles away. This was the "Home of the Tigers." And it did feel a little bit like you were in a cage when you played.

Rumor had it there were some college scouts from Georgia at our game. The last scout who had come to a game had talked to me after and told me he was impressed with my .618 batting average, but he needed someone with more speed. I was a power hitter, and nothing felt as good as setting a ball free from Tiger Field. Sure, I would've loved a baseball scholarship, especially if Auburn called me up or maybe a school out in California. USC, UCLA, Cal—I would happily sit on the beach out there—but graduation was a month away, and it didn't seem like I had that many chances left to impress the scouts. I knew I was at least in the top ten of all high school baseball players in the state, if not the top five, but nobody in my family had ever gone to college. I was the youngest of ten children, and after they had graduated high school, pretty much every one but two of my sisters had gotten the hell out of Alabama. Lots of folks were leaving the South for Cleveland,

and my brothers and sisters were no different. In Cleveland, white people weren't bombing the churches or bombing the black neighborhoods like they had been in Birmingham since I was born. The whites lived in Birmingham, the blacks in Bombingham. The people here had no problem letting the dogs loose on kids. I had grown up hearing the adults talk about it. Four little girls killed at a church bombing. Almost a thousand kids put in jail. People living on Dynamite Hill having to hide in their bathtubs because bombs were being thrown into their houses. People refusing to serve you if you were black. Hell, I couldn't even go to Woolworth's in Birmingham and sit at the counter and order a cheeseburger and shake until a couple of years earlier. Even now, you could tell people were only serving you because they had to. They were not happy about it. And 1974 wasn't too different from 1954 or 1964.

I was seven when Martin Luther King was locked up in our jail, and I remembered when the church was bombed and how my mom made all us kids stay home that day. It was the only Sunday I can remember that we didn't go to church. She told us to run if any white men in a car pulled up next to us. We sat up on the dirt hillside overlooking Praco and talked about what we would do if they came for us. My brother Willie said he would fight, and my sister Darlene said she would run into the woods and hide. Lester and I sat shoulder to shoulder. He was only five, so I watched out for him most of the time. The Hintons and the Baileys. There were sixteen kids total, and neither family had a dad at home, so we liked to think we were our own little army keeping guard over the town. We never figured out what we would do if they came for us that day, but up on our hill, at the edge of a forest of turkey oaks and longleaf pines we could run to if we needed, we were brave and strong and ready to defend what was ours.

Everyone who lived in Praco either worked in the coal mines or for the mining company in some way. The coal mining company owned our town. Owned our houses. They had a store—a commissary—where we bought our groceries, our clothes, and anything else we needed. If our roof had a leak, the company sent someone over to fix it. We had a church, and really, except to go to school, we never had to leave town if we didn't want to. My dad had worked in the coal mines until he got hit in the head and had to go live in an institution. Then my mom was in charge of the ten of us and had to pay the rent and feed us and buy our clothes and keep us together. Lester's dad was gone too, although I never asked him why or what happened. We were all the same in Praco. The blacks lived up on the hill, and the whites lived down below in the flat areas. The company owned everything, and the only difference was that the white houses had indoor plumbing and real kitchens and bathrooms. We had an outhouse and a number-three tub in the backyard for our baths. Our house had four rooms, one of which was a kitchen where we ate and did our homework and watched television. We would sleep three or four kids to a bed in each room. Two of my sisters would sleep with my mom. We were happy in Praco. We ate good food our mothers cooked for us. We played outside until dark. And we went to church. Everybody had the same, so nobody felt like they were better or worse off than the next person. Our community was close, and we all loved each other, like a giant family. Any adult could tell any kid what to do and he did it. Everybody watched out for everyone. If you got in trouble three streets away, your mom would know about it before you could even get home to tell her. The adults handled adult business, and if two adults were talking, you were supposed to make yourself scarce. We used to hide out and listen when we could, but mostly we just played and ran around and didn't know too much about how the outside world was operating except for what we saw on television.

And then they integrated the schools.

Now, a senior in high school, not a day went by that I didn't hear someone yelling "Nigger!" in my direction. It didn't matter if I was just walking down the road or standing at my locker or even if I was playing baseball and helping the team win. I was about to graduate, and what I'd learned most in four years besides biology and arithmetic was just how much people can hate you because of the color of your skin. People can want to hurt you for no good reason other than you look different or talk different or live different. Oh, I got an education by going to the white school, just not the kind of education the politicians and lawmakers had planned on.

"That's my baby!"

I heard my mom yelling and saw her standing outside the chain-link fence next to the bleachers. I had no idea how she had managed to get from home to the ball field. She cleaned houses to make money, but there was never enough time or a car to get her to my ball games. She waved a white handkerchief at me and yelled again.

"Go, baby! That's my baby!"

I smiled. It didn't matter that I weighed in at 230 pounds and towered over her. I was her baby. I would always be her baby. I eyed the pitcher and took another practice swing. Maybe there really was a scout around watching today, but unless he said, "I'm going to pay for your college education, drive you there, and then come back to help your mom get to the store and do her chores while you're gone," it didn't look like I was going anywhere but into the coal mines come graduation.

But then again, I did have the best batting average in all of Birmingham and maybe even in all of Alabama. Hank Aaron was from Alabama. So was Willie Mays—he was from right here in Jefferson County. And I was raised to believe in miracles.

I watched the pitcher shake his head at whatever signal the catcher had given him for the next pitch. They didn't want me to hit the ball, and it didn't seem like the umpire was going to call it fair, but that didn't bother me. I had been playing baseball as long as I had been walking. We used to get pieces of cardboard and paper from behind the commissary and mash them together, then wrap black electrical tape around the clump until it was the size of a baseball and almost as hard. For a bat, we would use an old broom handle, and the bases would be a shoe or someone's shirt or more old cardboard if we could get it. They could play by the rules, or we could play us some street ball. It didn't matter to me. One way or another, I was going to hit that ball. I was going to make my mom proud. She had come all this way to see me, and I wasn't going to let her down. Sure, I cared what a scout thought, but I cared what my mom thought more.

The pitcher spit again and began his windup dance. What was it going to be? Curveball? Fastball? Knuckleball? I could hit them all. I was going to swing and hit it whether it was outside, low, inside, it didn't matter. Street ball never had the nuances of organized baseball. You had rules, but you didn't argue the small stuff. If a pitch made it anywhere close, you swung and you swung hard. Playing in the dirt in Praco, we never waited for the perfect pitch to take a swing. You swung at the pitch you were given, and you made the best of it.

I was more than ready. I could feel the weight of the bat in my hands, smell the ashy pine odor of the wood. I checked the bat to make sure the Louisville Slugger name was straight up, because this meant the sweet spot—the place where the grain of the wood was the strongest—was facing the pitcher. He finished his windup, and I kept my eye on the ball as it released.

It felt like the bat was vibrating in my palms, and I couldn't hear the crowd or my mom or the cheating ump or the catcher. It was just me and my bat and the ball. I watched as the ball came closer and closer, and I pulled the bat back a little so I could let it rip even harder, but the next thing I knew, the ball was heading right toward my face. I dropped the bat and then flew back and down as fast as I could, but I swear I still felt that ball skim across my cheekbone. I landed on my left hip into the dirt, and I put my palm down to catch my fall, and it felt like a drill went straight from my wrist to my shoulder. The catcher laughed as he turned to retrieve the wild pitch, and I could only hope that the ump wasn't bigoted enough to call that one a strike as well.

"Ball!" he yelled as I stood up and brushed the dirt off my pants. My arm hurt bad, but I didn't say anything.

"Come on, baby!" I heard my mom yell.

The pitcher was smirking as I got back in my stance and pulled the bat back. He could smirk all he wanted, but if he got that ball anywhere near the plate, it was gone. If he threw the ball at my head again, I would fall down, but I would still get back up. No matter what, this was going to end the same. He was going to hit me or I was going to hit the ball—either way, I was going to get on base.

The next pitch was a changeup. I knew it even as he released it. Most people would have thought fastball, but I can read a changeup a mile away. I brought my weight back, and I paused. Most guys miss the changeup by swinging too soon. They can end up swinging themselves in a complete circle from missing a changeup. Nothing funnier than that, but I was done being a source of amusement today. I waited and I waited, and I put all my weight into my swing, and I swear I saw the moment that ball slowed down and I swung for my team, and for my mama, and for Lester, and for every kid in Praco who was going to be called a name today, and I heard the only sound that a batter wants to hear. It's that sweet and sharp sound of the ball hitting the bat right where you want it. I've had dreams with that sound so loud and clear, it's woken me up. It sounds just like thunder on a hot day in August. I didn't even look to see where the ball was going when I heard that sound. I just dropped the bat, kept my head down, and began running.

"That's my baby! That's my baby!"

I rounded first, and out of the corner of my vision, I saw my mom waving her arms in the air. On my way to second, I looked up as the ball soared up, up, and out over the center-field fence. That's when I slowed down. I don't think there's ever a reason to hurry when you got a bunch of white people cheering you on. I planted my foot on second base and took my sweet time rounding to third. The shortstop muttered something when I went by, but I couldn't tell what it was, and I didn't care. These were the moments you lived for. I liked to hear the applause, hear the kids call me "Homer." Sometimes they even chanted it. "Ho-mer! Ho-mer! Ho-mer!" One time in basketball season, we were at an away game in the town of Good Hope, when I scored thirty points in the first half—a record for the school—and I walked off the court to the sound of the crowd chanting, "Hin-ton! Hin-ton! Hin-ton!" I couldn't understand why all the Good Hope fans were chanting my name too or why when I sat on the bench none of the guys on my team were smiling or high-fiving me.

My coach went out to center court and started yelling at the crowd. "That's enough now! You stop that!"

I turned to our point guard, who was sitting next to me, and said, "What are they saying?" He just shook his head, so I asked him again. "What are they saying?"

"Man, they are saying, 'Nig-ger! Nig-ger!'" He hung his head.

That's what the crowd was chanting. I thought it was "Hin-ton!" My pride went to shame in a split second. No one was cheering for my record-breaking half. When we got on the bus to make the hour-long drive home, our coach made us sit on the floor in the middle of the bus until we were outside of town. It wasn't safe to sit by the windows if you were black.

When I crossed home plate, I looked over to see the pitcher throw his glove in the dirt, and for some reason, this made me smile more than the home run or the crowd chanting for me. *They can beat you, but they can't break you.* I guess his mama hadn't taught him the same things my mama did.

I hit a triple and another home run, and we ended up winning the game, 7–2. It turned out there was a scout at the game, but he must not have been looking for a third baseman or a power hitter, because he didn't ask to talk to me or my mom before she had to leave. When I came out of the locker room back at the school, Lester was waiting outside for me. The sun was just beginning to dim a little in the sky as we began our walk back to Praco.

"Tough game."

I looked at Lester and nodded. The team won, but it was a tough game for me. I could feel the soreness in my hip and shoulder starting to turn into real pain.

Lester slapped me on the back, and we both just started walking.

Flat Top was a two-lane road, and running alongside it was a ditch that bordered the woods for most of the way. Lester watched ahead, and I looked behind so that we could see any car that was coming even before we could hear it. If it was someone we knew, we flagged it down and caught a ride into Praco. If it was a car we didn't recognize, we would jump into the ditch and hide the best we could. We would have to hide four or five times during the hour-and-a-half walk home.

I hoped someone we knew came by soon. I just wanted to get home to my mom's cooking.

Lester and I didn't talk too much on the walk. We were both busy scanning the road in two directions. If you got to talking, you could get distracted and then be surprised by a car coming up behind you. There weren't many houses on this road, and there wasn't anyone to help if we met trouble.

I heard the car before I saw it, but when it came into view, it was bright red. No one we knew drove a car that red.

"Car!" I yelled, and Lester and I both turned right and headed into the brush alongside of the road. The car was coming too fast, so we both kind of leaped the last foot and ended up on our sides in the deep culvert that ran next to the road. I think my foot might have kicked him in the head on the way down, but somehow we landed shoulder to shoulder. I held my breath because if someone was going to stop, you could usually hear the brakes kick in if you were quiet enough. We stayed quiet until the car went rushing past.

My heart was beating fast.

"You okay?" I asked Lester.

"Yep. You?"

I thought about it for a second. Was I okay? Here I was in the dirt again for the second time that day. I might even be in it again a few more times before we got home. I could feel a sharp rock pressing into the back of my head. I had scraped my arm against something with thorns—maybe it was a devil's walking stick or another tree with spikes we called the toothache tree. If only I had a car, I wouldn't have to be lying in the dirt with my eyes down like some disobedient dog that's so scared he's about to piss himself. And what was Lester going to do next year when I was graduated and he had to make this walk himself? I wasn't okay. He wasn't either. Nothing about this was okay. But here we were. Again.

"You know what's strange?" I asked Lester.

"Besides us lying in this ditch?"

"Yeah, besides the obvious."

"Besides your hair?"

I laughed. "Yeah, besides my hair and my big feet and all that."

"Okay, then. What's strange?"

I looked up at the sky. It was just that perfect shade of in-between. When it goes from the bright blue of the day to the black blue of the night. I wish I knew the name for that color. It was like an ending and a beginning. Whatever you called that color, it always made me sad and happy at the exact same time. Like when everyone sang "Amazing Grace" at church. It's a song that made a guy hopeful but also reminded him that he was a wretch that needed to be saved.

"It's strange what you can get used to."

Lester grunted in his Lester way. I knew it meant he agreed with me. Lester wasn't a big talker.

"There's some things a body shouldn't have to get used to," I said.

Lester turned his head toward mine and gave his chin a little lift in agreement. We could both hear another car coming in the distance, and we knew it wasn't time to get up out of the dirt. Not yet.

I took a deep breath. I knew I had a choice. Looking up at that sky, I knew I could get angry or I could have some faith. It was always a choice. I could easily have been angry, and maybe I should have been angry. This was God's country, and I chose instead to love every single shade of blue that the sky wanted to show me. And when I turned my head to the right, I could see what looked like ten different shades of green. This was real and true, and it reminded me that even when you are flat on your back on the ground, there is beauty if you look for it. I took another deep breath. The dirt smelled a little bit like burned sugar. I knew my mom was waiting at home with some grits and turkey neck and a sweet piece of cobbler. I had just played a great baseball game, and even if the scouts and the coaches and the colleges didn't want to pay attention, I knew I could hit like nobody else. Hell, even in the dirt, I had my best friend at my side. Things could have been worse. They could always be worse.

I listened as the car came closer. It had that whine and deep throttle noise that was more old truck than sedan. I closed my eyes as it passed by, and we waited. I didn't hear brakes, and I didn't hear any other cars. I could only hear my breathing and Lester's. I wanted to protect him. Protect myself. Protect my mom and my sisters and brothers. Protect everyone in this whole world who couldn't walk down a street without feeling some kind of fear. The soil of Alabama was full of the sweat and tears and blood and fear of guys just like us. Guys who were forced to the ground just because of the color of their skin.

This was something that I didn't want to get used to.

This was something that should never be normal.

"Let's get going," I said, and with that, we climbed out of the ditch and continued our long walk home.

| 3 |

A TWO-YEAR TEST DRIVE

If you are big and brave enough to throw a rock, you'd better be big and brave enough not to hide your hands behind your back when you get caught. You show your hands, and you own up to what you done.

—BUHLAR HINTON

Mary Lee Mine No. 2, 1975

There was blood everywhere. I could feel it on my face, taste it as it rushed like a waterfall into my mouth, over my chin, and down the inside of my shirt. I wanted to spit, but it was like my lips didn't work, so I just tried to turn my head so I wouldn't choke on the blood or get sick from the coppery, sweet taste of it. The pain was sharp and hot, and it felt like my whole head had been split right in two. I could feel something hanging below my lip, but as much as I wanted to run my hands over my face to hold it together, I knew that whatever was bleeding wouldn't be helped by the toxic filth of the Mary Lee getting into it.

I never really believed I would end up working the coal mines, but it was the only place I could get a decent wage right out of high school. There weren't many options for me after graduation. No scholarship. No college. No opportunities other than those I could make for myself. Hell, we didn't even have ten dollars extra to pay for my class ring when I graduated. The mines were the best-paying job around, and as much as I had sworn I would never work them, I wasn't going to turn my back on a decent job. Good jobs were few and far between, and there were long lines of men trying to get on at the mines. I had a leg up because we lived in Praco, because my dad had been a company man, and because I knew a few of the white guys from high school who put in a good word for me with the superintendent. My ability to get along with the whites also helped, and I didn't have any reputation from school or from town for causing trouble.

I was responsible for installing the long steel bolts that supported the roof and kept it from falling. Whether it was whole roofs that caved in and crushed miners or heavy rocks falling loose from between the bolts, death came from above in a mine. You could literally be knocked senseless like my dad, or have your skull bashed in by a loose boulder or sliced open by a razor-sharp piece of shale raining down from forty feet above. Pinning, as we called it, wasn't an easy job. No job in the mines was easy. Most days, we were working in small shafts and tunnels where we had less than four feet of height to maneuver in. You ride the elevator down almost a mile, and then you get in shuttle cars that you ride for miles in dark, dank air in a world with no light and no color. It's dark when you go down in the morning, it's dark all day, and it's dark when you get outside at night. It wasn't easy to maneuver the machinery and the bolts, some of them four or eight feet long, and drill holes into solid rock and secure the bolts with steel plates, but it had to be done and done right or men would die. Some days it felt like the best you could do was pray that the roof's weight held.

I hated every second of it.

I wasn't meant to be kept in a small space; I didn't like to be hunched over, to feel like walls were slowly closing in on me and there was no place to run, no place where there was light and air and space for a man to breathe. I didn't know much, but I knew that God didn't make me to live underground or in a small space. It felt like climbing into your own coffin every day. What man in his right mind would do that? I used to imagine I was outside—walking in the woods or driving on a long stretch of highway across the country. I didn't have my own car, but I loved to drive. I would ride that elevator into the mine, but in my head, I was traveling across Alabama and out West. I'd drive through Texas and New Mexico. Some days, I'd make it all the way to the Pacific Ocean, but other days, I'd hang a left in Texas and travel down through Mexico and even make it into Central America, where I'd dance with beautiful women in Honduras and Panama. Other times, I'd go north and visit the Great Lakes before heading to the wide-open skies of Montana and then up into Canada. I was never sure how far north a person could drive—was Greenland up there? Could you actually drive to Alaska or the North Pole? I didn't know, and I didn't care for cold weather like that, so I'd always turn my imaginary car around in Canada. Some days, I would go up to Maine to eat lobster drenched in warm butter, and other days, I would go swimming in Key West, Florida. In my mind, I would travel anywhere but into that black, dark pit where every breath was full of float dust that brought coal and rock and dirt into your lungs where it settled in and took root as if to punish you for disturbing it in the first place. I grew up with old men who hadn't gone into the mines in twenty years but still turned their handkerchiefs black every time they coughed or blew their noses or wiped their foreheads on a hot summer day. I saw other men dying before they even got a chance to retire—watched them struggling to breathe from lungs that were full of a sickness that didn't have a name. I remember my mom making soup and cakes and bringing them to women who had lost their husbands to the mine. So many soups and so many cakes, and so many women and children left on their own. Growing up, it seemed like every month men disappeared from Praco, and I remember thinking that the mine openings were actually the mouths of great big monsters that lived underground, and when the men walked in, they were chewed up and either spit out broken like my dad or they were swallowed and gone forever. I didn't want to die in the mine or sweat coal for the rest of my life or have the mine grow in my lungs until it choked everything out, but what else was a guy to do when he was ready to work and earn his way in the world? Working for minimum wage in a fast-food joint where white people still didn't want to see that a black man might be touching their food didn't set well with me either. The sad truth was, the best way to go up in the world was to go down into the mines. And the more dangerous the job, the better it paid.

The ambulance ride was a blur, but I remember seeing my sister waiting at the top of the mine when they brought me out. She was crying because of all the blood, and I didn't understand why the paramedics said they couldn't put an oxygen mask on my face. I tried to tell them about the monster and how it had chewed me up and spit me out, but there was too much blood in my mouth, and I couldn't move my lips the right way to get the words out, so it seemed easier just to close my eyes and imagine I was back in Panama and there was a beautiful woman in a red dress that left her brown shoulders bare who wanted to dance with me, so I held her in my arms and we danced in slow circles around and around and around while the ambulance sirens played their music.

The rock that virtually sliced off my nose fell down from about twenty feet above me that day. I was lucky that even though it was heavy enough to cause a concussion and sharp enough to slice through my face like it was butter, there was no permanent damage other than a large scar across my nose from the twenty-two stitches it took to put me back together again. I'd like to say that I never went back down in the mine after that day, but then I'd be lying. I worked in that mine for five long years.

There was no big event that caused me to leave the mines. One day, I just woke up late and the sun was shining and I could hear birds chirping and the sky was the brightest blue I had ever seen, and I just knew I couldn't go down in that dark place again. I wanted to be in the sunshine. I was twenty-four years old, and it seemed like all I had on my brain was women, and there were no women at the bottom of that mine.

After high school, I had started a recreational softball league with Lester as my star pitcher. But most of the guys who had played were moving on and getting too busy with work and life to show up on a regular basis, so we had just ended the league. Lester had gone down into the mines too, but he worked over at the Bessie Mine, not the Mary Lee, and he had no plans of giving up a solid job anytime soon. He just shook his head at me when I told him I'd rather be poor in the light than rich in the dark. Lester put his head down, went to work, and didn't complain one way or the other. I admired that about him. But life pulled at me in a different way, and I dreamed of big adventures, beautiful women, and a life where a man could be rewarded for his hard work without putting his life at risk. I imagined going to law school or even business school. I would wear silk suits, and I imagined myself as a CEO or a lawyer who could outargue anyone in a courtroom. Sometimes I even imagined I was a doctor or a firefighter. I didn't dream of baseball anymore; that was still too painful. I knew that if I had been born someone else, I would have gotten a scholarship and gone to college, maybe even been drafted, and that knowledge hurt so much I put that dream away.

During the four years or so we ran the softball league, I had also been dating two sisters on the sly. One of the guys I played against, Reggie, was pretty angry about it because he had asked out the younger sister and she turned him down and confessed that she was dating me in secret. I was openly dating the older sister, but I had the younger one on lock. Reggie was going around town talking some big talk about how he was going to take me down. I wasn't too worried about it, because I had at least half a foot on him and probably about sixty pounds. Reggie was a little guy, with mean eyes that always seemed to be staring my way. We had a lot of friends in common, so I knew what he said about me. I heard everything. He was like a snake slithering around behind my back wherever I went, but I knew he was all hiss and no bite.

I wasn't proud of dating two sisters, and there was no doubt my mom would've skinned my behind if she'd found out, but women were my one weakness. My one true vice. I didn't drink. I didn't smoke or do drugs. But I fell in and out of lust every single day, it seemed. There was no greater thrill than the chase for me. I didn't care if they were married, had a boyfriend, or if I was dating their sister. Maybe it was a gift or maybe it was a curse, but when I was talking with a woman, whether it was for an hour or for a night, she was the only one for me. I wasn't playing a game, and I don't know how to explain exactly how I justified it in my head, but whatever girl was in front of me was absolutely the sole focus of my attention and my love. And my favorite thing was when one of my friends would tell me a girl was out of my league. "Give me five minutes," I would answer. And it never failed. I could sweet-talk any woman until she was weak in the knees. And I meant every word I said to every single one of them. I believed it, so they believed it.

But the minute I was away from them, it was out of sight, out of mind.

Like I said, women were my weakness, my kryptonite, and my Achilles' heel all rolled into one. And on more than one occasion, I left a woman's house right when her boyfriend or husband was coming home. There was no doubt that I was a sinner during the week, but on Sundays, I always went to church with my mom and prayed for forgiveness. Come Monday, though, those women would fill my head again, and while I knew it was wrong, I also knew that in my own way, I genuinely cared about every single one of them.

The one big obstacle to both my work life and my dating life was a vehicle. We had been forced to move out of Praco—Alabama By-Products first closed the store and then officially gave notice that company housing was over. They served final eviction notices right before Christmas 1981, which didn't make the people who were still there too happy. The actual mines that were in Praco had closed up a long time ago, and while we never did get indoor plumbing, I loved Praco and didn't want to move away.

We loaded our house on the back of a truck and moved it to a piece of land in Burnwell, a short ways away from Praco. I was the youngest child and the one who was expected to stay with my mom and help her out. All but two of my siblings had left Alabama altogether. It wasn't an easy place to live. Some had gone north to Ohio. My brother Lewis had gone all the way to California. Staying with my mom wasn't an obligation, though; it was a joy. I loved her more than anything, and I couldn't have lived anywhere else knowing she didn't have anyone to help her out. Her happiness was my happiness and the other way around, and that's the way it had always been and would always be. I also didn't mind her cooking for me. She would cook for me anytime day or night, and that food tasted just like love felt.

Moving out of Praco meant I needed a car more than ever, because there were no neighbors to give me rides anymore, and every time you hitchhiked, you never knew what you were getting into. I had gone from hiding from strange cars on the road to getting into strange cars because I was desperate for a ride. It was a risk, because it wasn't like the world had gotten any safer for a black man. I knew I could defend myself if I had to, and I had places to go, money to make, and women to see. But I couldn't get a job without a car, and I couldn't buy a car without a job, so I was stuck, and I was so tired of being without, of wanting, of struggling to make a dollar outside of the mine. I had always been a hard worker, but you couldn't walk ten or fifteen miles to a job and then back home again. Something had to give.

That *something* gave on a Saturday. I woke up, put on my best church clothes, had breakfast with my mom, kissed her goodbye, and then caught a ride into Vestavia Hills from a friend of mine. I had him drop me off a few blocks away from a car lot I had seen before. I don't want to say what happened next was premeditated, exactly, but it was one of those times when you are looking at yourself doing something and it's like you are watching a movie. Some days you want to be somebody else so much, it's like you really believe you are that imaginary person. And on that Saturday, I wasn't a poor kid from Praco who was struggling to keep a job—I was a guy just out of college who had landed a great corporate position and was shopping for a brand-new car. I walked up and down the rows of cars, and while I had spent many nights imagining myself driving a new Monte Carlo, or Buick Regal, or Pontiac Grand Prix, it was the Cutlass Supreme that caught my eye that day. It was a shiny, sky-blue, two-door beauty, with blue velvet seats so soft they felt like clouds, and four headlights that made it look like the car had a face, and that face was smiling just for me. I stopped in front of it on the lot just long enough for the salesman to take notice and move in for the kill.

"She's a beauty."

I smiled at the salesman. He was a white guy, with long sideburns and brown hair that looked like it was getting a bit thin on top.

"She sure is. A beauty, for sure," I said.

"You can't do any better than the Cutlass."

I shook the hand he held out to me.

"You want to take her for a test drive?"

I nodded. "I'd like that. I'd like to see how she drives."

The salesman smiled, thinking he had his commission in the bag. I watched as he walked into the single-story building and then came back out with a set of keys.

"These belong to you."

He held out his hand, and it felt like I was moving in slow motion, but I watched as my own hand reached out and grabbed those keys.

"Be sure to open her up on the highway. You'll be surprised at what she can do." He opened up the driver's-side door and kept smiling as I climbed in. He slammed the door shut and slapped his hand two times on the roof. I put the key in the ignition and turned it. The velvet seats smelled like a new toy, a new bat, a new pair of shoes, and every other wonderful new thing you could think of all mixed together. It smelled like Christmas morning, and Easter Sunday, and Thanksgiving dinner, and my birthday all rolled into one. I had never breathed in sweeter air than the air inside of that car when I turned the key in the ignition.

I drove out of the lot and took a right. I drove around some of the smaller streets downtown for about twenty minutes. I felt strong and powerful and like there was nothing in this world I couldn't do. And when I finally took the on-ramp and merged onto the highway, I pressed my foot down on the gas pedal and listened to the engine roar. I drove that car south toward Montgomery for more than an hour. And when I turned her around and headed back toward Birmingham, it seemed like nothing at all to pass the exit that led to the car lot and instead head back toward my mama's house, where I knew dinner would be waiting. I couldn't wait to show her my new car. I couldn't wait to tell her that life was really going to be changing for us. In that moment, I felt a hope so big I thought my heart might jump right out of my chest. I knew everything was going to be different, and that's when I decided to really open her up and see what this car could do. She was a beauty. And she was all mine.

I drove that car for two years. I installed a brand-new Pioneer stereo system that I was able to buy because I had a car to drive to my new job at a furniture store. I kept the car in pristine condition, washing and waxing her every single weekend. My mom was happy I could drive her to the store and to run errands. She always sat straight up in that car, with a big smile on her face. I'm not proud that I was riding dirty with my mom, but I never ran a yellow, failed to come to a complete stop, or drove one mile over the speed limit.

Two years after I drove that car off the lot, I would swear that she was in better shape than when I got her. But it had started to gnaw at me. My mom trusted me, and every time I drove with her at my side, I started imagining what might happen if we got in an accident, or broke down on the side of the road, and the police came. What would she think of what I'd done? I wanted to return the car, but I didn't know how to explain that the car was suddenly gone. I felt trapped in a lie that had grown so big I couldn't find my way out of it.

When I heard from a friend that the police were looking for me, I knew I couldn't pretend any longer. I also knew it was time to tell my mom.

I don't think I've ever been more scared to tell anyone anything, but there was no avoiding it. I felt sick to my stomach. I could daydream all I wanted, but there was a guilt living in me that had been growing for years, and now it felt like it was festering and rotting out everything good inside me. The last thing I wanted to do was hurt my mom. She was standing at the sink when I walked up behind her and wrapped my arms around her shoulders. She wasn't a small woman, but she always felt tiny compared to me.

She lifted a wet hand and patted my arm at the hug.

"What's this now?" she asked.

"I need to tell you something. Something serious."

She turned off the sink and dried her hands on a dish towel. "Well, let's have a sit now. You don't talk about something serious standing up."

I sat at the table and waited while she got out two glasses and a pitcher of sweet tea out of the fridge.

"And you never talk about something serious without having a drink," she added. She poured the tea and sat to my left at the table. "Now what's all this fuss about?"

"I did something. I did something wrong."

She looked in my eyes and took a sip of tea. She didn't say anything. My mom could say more in silence than most people could say in a ten-minute speech. She waited. Sipped more tea. Then she nodded at me, and the whole story came out. I told her about the test drive and the wanting to be someone different from who I was and how I had never paid for that car. And how now everything was crashing down and I didn't know what to do next.

She took another sip of tea and looked at me with the saddest eyes I have ever seen. "Are you sorry?"

"Yes."

"Are you going to make it right?"

"Yes, ma'am."

"Well, then, you go make it right. You go to the police station, and you tell them everything, and you face the music. I didn't raise you to take something that don't belong to you, but I did raise you to admit your wrongs. You aren't a boy anymore, and I can't protect you from this. You admit what you did to them police, and then you admit what you did to God. He will forgive you, and so will I. But you need to choose who you are, Ray. You need to choose what sort of man you are going to be. You need to choose now. I know you will choose right. I know you will."

I heard a little hitch in her voice when she said that, and the shame poured over me. This was not who I wanted to be. I was going to choose the right way.

The way that would make my mama proud. She put her hand on my face and shook her head, and I vowed right then and there at that kitchen table I would never do anything to put that look of hurt in my mama's face again. I didn't care if I had to walk everywhere for the rest of my life or if I had to go back to the mines—I was going to only travel the straight and narrow. I was going to be the son my mom deserved and the son she raised me to be.

Lester was at work, so I called another friend to drive me to the police station. It was a relief. I confessed my sins, and I accepted it when they locked me in the jail. I went to court in September 1983. I admitted my guilt, and I was sentenced to a year and a half in prison, but since I was given two days for every one day while I had been waiting for the court to make a deal, I ended up having to spend only a few months in a work release program. I went to Kilby Prison just to be processed, but I was only there long enough for them to get my name into the system.

My mom and one of our neighbors picked me up in Birmingham on the day I got off work release, and I went to see Lester as soon as I could.

"You done with all that nonsense now?" he asked.

I thought long and hard about that kitchen table conversation with my mom, and I knew that being in jail was the best thing that could have happened to me. Prison wasn't for me. There was nothing glamorous about it. The food was horrible. The smell was horrible. The lack of freedom made every cell in my body ache. No car, no money, no job, and no girl was ever worth risking my freedom for. I would be on parole for a year and a half or so, until August 1985. I didn't mind—I could have been on parole for fifty years for all I cared—and I knew I would never, ever do anything that was outside the law. I would never do anything that would take me away from my life or put that look of hurt in my mama's eyes. At night, away from home, I spent a lot of time thinking about who and what mattered in this life.

God mattered.

Lester mattered.

My freedom mattered.

And most of all, my mom mattered.

Everything else in life was just weather that was passing through.

"As God is my witness," I said to Lester and lifted my right hand in the air.

He gave a little snort.

"I'm serious," I said. "As God is my witness, I will never take something that doesn't belong to me again."

Lester stared at me to see if I was going to crack any jokes, and when I just stared back, he finally gave me a grunt of approval.

I waited a beat and then got on my best preacher's voice. "Even if it's the sweetest Corvette you ever did see. Even if God himself comes down from heaven and says, 'This here's your car,' I promise that if I need a car, I will get a car loan. If I write a check, I will make sure I have the money to cover it. If someone hands me car keys, I will hand them right back if they don't belong to me. Unless it's you handing me your car keys. Or unless it's some fine lady who wants me to take the wheel because she's had a little too much to drink. But other than that, I do solemnly swear that I, Anthony Ray Hinton, will never steal again. Even if—"

Lester interrupted, laughing. "I got it the first time; I don't need to hear you talking all day when there's barbecue we could be eating."

| 4 |

THE COOLER KILLER

Every sheriff and police officer in this county knew after Captain D's that there was as cold, as brutal a killer walking the streets of this county as has ever walked these streets.

—LIEUTENANT DOUG ACKER

Birmingham, February 25, 1985

WORKER SHOT IN RESTAURANT HOLDUP DIES

The assistant manager of a Southside restaurant died last night after being shot twice in the head early yesterday morning by a robber.

John Davidson, 49, of 2249 Third Place Northeast was declared brain dead at 10:55 P.M. yesterday in Medical Center East after undergoing surgery earlier in the day.

*In addition to the bullet wounds, Davidson also had been severely beaten.**

I don't know where I was the night John Davidson was murdered. I didn't spend my days developing alibis for my nights. I had never even eaten at Mrs. Winner's Chicken & Biscuits in Southside. But on February 23, somebody robbed the restaurant and forced John Davidson into the cooler and shot him twice in the head. Someone took a son away from his parents and a husband away from his wife. There were no fingerprints. No eyewitnesses. No DNA. Anyone could have done it. The murderer walked away with

---

* Mike Bennighof, "Worker Shot in Restaurant Holdup Dies," *Birmingham Post Herald*, February 26, 1985.

$2,200. What is the price of a life? What is the dollar amount a man will trade his soul for? I don't know the answers to those questions. I've thought about that man—wondered just what it was that led him to such a desperate act. What must he have been thinking as he sat in the dark waiting to rob and to murder? Every desperate act has its price, but I didn't know then that the person who would pay the price was me. Where was I on the night John Davison was murdered? I have no idea. Was I asleep in my bed? Laughing with Lester? Eating with my mom? Visiting a lady friend? My days and nights were pretty unremarkable. I worked at a store assembling and delivering beds six days a week. I had kept my promise to stay out of trouble. And while I can't say where I was or what I was doing on that particular night, I do know I was not out beating and robbing and murdering.

I also know somebody got away with murder.

Birmingham, July 3, 1985

My job at The Brass Works wasn't one I could keep long term, because I just couldn't wrap my head around always having to work on a Saturday. Saturdays were for potlucks at church, barbecues with friends, running errands with my mom or taking her fishing, and college football. Our church didn't have many men in it, and it seemed like every Saturday they had car washes or building repairs that needed to be made, and they always asked for some men to help out. As much as I tried for over six months, I just wasn't happy working on Saturday, and eventually it showed. Monday through Friday, I worked as hard as I could—always showed up on time and gave it my best—but come Saturday, it was like a switch flipped in me, and I knew I wasn't doing my employer justice. I made up as many excuses as I could to get my Saturdays off, and I may have even stretched the truth now and then, but eventually, it became clear that this wasn't the job for me. Every Saturday, it was harder to be the kind of employee they needed me to be. I quit a couple of weeks after my birthday. I left with no hard feelings and made plans to sign on with a company called Manpower, which provided temporary labor to businesses around Birmingham.

I had just turned twenty-nine, and honestly, I still didn't know what I wanted to be when I grew up. Sometimes it felt like life was more a process of elimination than a series of choices. I knew I didn't want to be a coal miner. I knew I didn't want to be in prison. I knew I wasn't cut out to be a deckhand on a tug hauling coal up and down the river. I knew I didn't want to work on Saturdays. I knew I didn't want to leave my mom on her own. But apart from those things, I just wanted to make a living, pay my bills, have a nice car to drive, and find a nice woman I could fall in love with and marry and have children with. I was hoping that woman would be willing to live at my mama's house, but I figured I would cross that bridge when the time came.

Manpower wasn't going to be a whole lot of money, but it was something, and I was optimistic that moving from business to business and doing different jobs would help me learn what it was I wanted to do with my life. You just never knew who you might meet or what might be sparked. I had been out of high school ten years, but I still loved to learn new things. I liked talking to different people and going to places I had never been before and seeing how they operated. I had a good head for business, and I thought about opening up a restaurant where I could serve people the food my mama had been making for me for so long. She taught me to cook everything she made me.

Her cooking lessons always began with, "If it makes you happy, you'd better be able to make it yourself. I don't see no wife on your arm anytime soon."

My mama always had a way of getting her point across.

She made me laugh, she kept me on the straight and narrow, and she never once rushed me to figure things out. She just loved me the same way she had loved me for as long as I could remember—absolutely and unconditionally.

RESTAURANT MANAGER FOUND FATALLY SHOT

A five-year employee of Captain D's was found fatally shot yesterday morning in the walk-in cooler of the restaurant in Woodlawn. He was an apparent robbery victim.

Birmingham police said Thomas Wayne Vason, 25, of 11 Oak St., New Castle, died of a gunshot wound to the head. There were no signs of a struggle. Some money had been taken from the safe but the amount was not known yesterday.

*Homicide Sgt. C. M. Quinn said there are some similarities between Vason's slaying and the murder of an assistant manager of a Mrs. Winner's Chicken & Biscuits restaurant in February. But Quinn said he did not know if the two slayings are related.**

We celebrated the Fourth of July like we did every year—the best barbecue you could imagine, friends from church, and sweet tea by the gallon. There was no bigger holiday in Alabama than the Fourth. You couldn't take a walk down the street without strangers inviting you in to eat something from their table. Fireworks, watermelon, and kids running around while grown-ups squirted them with water from a hose. We may have been separate throughout the year, but something about the holiday brought neighborhoods and people together like nothing else. We weren't black or white, we were American, and we laughed and played and clapped for the parade floats, and it was the one time of year it seemed like all of Birmingham fell in love with each other, and 1985 was no different. Gunnysack races, and egg tosses, and more food than you could imagine. My mom wore her best white hat and her blue dress with red piping at the sleeves. I remember sitting in some folding chairs with Lester and watching her laugh with the ladies from church and feeling a joy so big I couldn't even contain it. I knew that in a couple of months, I would be off parole, and all those mistakes from my past would be put to rest. There was a special new girl I was seeing, Sylvia, and I was hopeful that the Manpower work I was going to sign on for tomorrow would lead to something bigger. I turned to Lester and said, "This holiday feels just like the Pledge of Allegiance."

"Man, what do you mean?"

So I tried to explain it. "You know, one nation under God with liberty and justice for all. Everything today feels like that. Hopeful. Like justice and freedom and anything is possible. You know?"

"I guess so. It kind of just feels like another hot Fourth of July, but I see what you mean."

---

* Kathleen M. Johnson and Mike Bennighof, "Restaurant Manager Found Fatally Shot," *Birmingham Post Herald,* July 3, 1985.

"What if next year one of us is getting married? Or I have a kid? Or who knows what?" I stopped, because in that moment, I felt such a love for Lester and for my mom in her gloves and hat and for Alabama and for hot days in July with sweet tea that cools you from the inside out that I was actually at a loss for words.

"You fixing to have kids anytime soon?" Lester laughed.

"You never know," I said, swallowing a lump in my throat that had come up out of nowhere. "Just feels like change is in the air."

"I don't know." Lester looked up at an overcast sky and laughed. "Feels like thunder to me."

Ensley, July 25–July 26, 1985

I clocked into Bruno's warehouse at 11:57 P.M. I didn't mind working the night shift, and when the clock struck midnight, I stood in a group of about a dozen other temporary workers, ready to get my marching orders for the night. Bruno's was a giant warehouse, and the temporary workers had to be checked in through a guard shack outside and then report to the supervisor. They kept a close eye on us, I guess because being temporary workers meant we might steal something or not work as hard. It never made sense to me—temporary workers wanted permanent jobs, so if anything, we worked harder than regular employees.

My assignments usually involved driving the forklift—typically, I'd use the forklift to bring empty pallets to the back of a truck, where they would get loaded with merchandise by other workers, and then I'd take the loaded pallets up to the high side, which was what we called the part of the warehouse where the racks were the tallest, and store them up on the shelves. It wasn't rocket science, but it was kind of fun to drive a forklift.

My shift began at midnight on July 26. We would stand around for ten or fifteen minutes while the supervisor, Tom Dahl, checked us in and wrote down our names and handed out assignments. My first assignment was to use the forklift to get a pallet loaded with buckets and cleaning supplies and mops and drive that around to all the locations where guys were going to be cleaning. That took about ten minutes, and then my supervisor asked me to go up and clean the bathrooms and scrape all the gum off the bathroom floors. It was amazing how much gum got on those floors during the day. I had no idea why grown men and women were just throwing gum on the floor, but it wasn't my job to ask. My job was to scrape all the gum off and mop and bleach those bathrooms from top to bottom. Not my favorite kind of work—but it was work, and I liked to do a good job no matter what it was. I finished that particular task around 2:00 A.M., got it approved by Dahl, and then took my break for fifteen minutes. After that, I worked outside separating out the broken pallets from the good ones—seeing which of the broken ones could be repaired and which ones were so badly damaged they wouldn't be worth the time it would take to fix them. It was foggy that night—I couldn't even see any stars—but I was glad I had worn a sleeveless shirt, because even at 3:00 A.M., it was in the midseventies and humid. It felt like rain was gathering. Nothing more exciting happened that night. I had my lunch at 4:00 A.M., cleaned out under the Dumpster, and called it a night.

Birmingham, July 27, 1985

ROBBERY-SHOOTING MAY BE TIED TO MURDERS

Police are investigating whether Friday morning's robbery-shooting of a Bessemer restaurant manager is related to the murders earlier this year of two Birmingham restaurant managers.

All three managers were shot in the head during late-night robberies at their restaurants. But the assistant manager of the Quincy's Family Steak House at 1090 Ninth Ave. SW in Bessemer survived his wound and police have questioned him.

Sidney Smotherman of 3341 Berry Drive, Hueytown, was listed in good condition in Carraway Methodist Medical Center in Birmingham on Friday night, a hospital spokesman said. Police said Smotherman was shot in the head and one hand.

Bessemer Capt. J. R. Pace said Friday that police originally believed one bullet "had done all the damage" to Smotherman, but that they now believe there could have been two shots fired.

Pace said Smotherman also was injured in the chest, although the source of that injury was undetermined.

All three robberies took place after the restaurants had closed and each manager was forced to the back of the establishments, where they were shot.

Police have worked since February trying to solve the robbery-murder at Mrs. Winner's Chicken and Biscuits at 737 29th St. South in which John Davidson, 49, of Center Point was shot twice in the head and left for dead inside the restaurant.

Because of blood stains in the rear of the restaurant, detectives believe Davidson, an assistant manager, was forced into the walk-in cooler and shot there.

On July 2, Thomas Wayne Vason, 25, night manager of the Captain D's at 5901 First Ave. North, was found dead in the restaurant's cooler when employees opened for business.

Pace would not elaborate on facts of the Bessemer case, but read the statement Smotherman made to police.

According to Smotherman's statement and other Bessemer police accounts, the Friday morning robbery and shooting at Quincy's unfolded this way:

At about 12:30 A.M., Smotherman and four other people left Quincy's in separate vehicles on their way home after the restaurant closed. Smotherman was alone in a 1985 Pontiac Fiero and stopped at a grocery store along the way.

After leaving the grocery store, Smotherman said he stopped at the intersection of Ninth Avenue and Memorial Drive and was bumped from the rear by a black Chevrolet or Buick.

When Smotherman stepped out of his car to check the damage, the driver of the sedan pulled a gun on him, told him to get back into the Fiero and the gunman joined him in the car.

The gunman told Smotherman to drive to Fourth Avenue and Memorial Drive, where they left the Fiero parked on the side of the street and went to the gunman's sedan.

The gunman drove Smotherman back to Quincy's, where he forced him to open the door and go inside.

Once inside, the robber ordered Smotherman to open the safe and then pulled a plastic garbage bag from a trash can and filled it with the money.

At that point, the gunman ordered Smotherman into the cooler. But

Smotherman talked him out of it, saying it was too cold. The gunman then told Smotherman to go into the storage room and as Smotherman turned to do so, the gunman shot him in the head.

Smotherman fell to the floor, where he purposely lay motionless until his assailant left. Once the gunman was gone, Smotherman made his way to the Motel 6 next to the restaurant and sought help.

Smotherman described his assailant to police as black, 5-foot-11, 190 pounds, with a mustache and wearing blue jeans and a red checkered shirt.

Pace said Friday that his department has discussed the Quincy's robbery with Birmingham detectives. "But we are investigating our own incident down here," he said.

Birmingham Homicide Sgt. Howard Miller, who is investigating Vason's murder at Captain D's, said he had talked with a Bessemer detective Friday morning and "we are working with Bessemer."

Smotherman had worked at Quincy's about three years, said his daughter, Mrs. Martie Hamilton of Atlanta. She said he began as a manager trainee at the restaurant.

Mrs. Hamilton said her father was in "very good condition and in very good spirits" Friday night.

*"We all know he was lucky. It just wasn't his time to go," she said. "We just hope they catch him (the gunman) and that this doesn't happen to anyone else."**

Burnwell, July 31, 1985

July is always hot in Alabama, even when it's cloudy out, so when my mother asked me to mow the lawn, I didn't want to do it. In fact, it was the last thing I wanted to do. I was thinking about seeing my girl, Sylvia, later, and I was thinking about the revival we were going to at church. And the last thing I wanted to do was get all hot and sweaty cutting the grass. I had already washed my car, a sweet, red Nissan that we had put in Sylvia's name because I was

---

* Peggy Sanford and Kaye Dickie, "Robbery-Shooting May Be Tied to Murders," *Birmingham News,* July 27, 1985.

still cleaning up the mess I had made of my credit when I was younger. The heat was settling in, and all I wanted to do was drink something cool in the shade of my mama's living room.

"I'll cut that grass tomorrow," I said, settling down on her worn couch.

She just looked at me in that quiet way she had that meant business. "Now I'm trying my best to see how you get to 'I'll cut it tomorrow' from my telling you to cut it now."

You don't raise ten children on your own by putting things off until tomorrow, and all of us kids had grown up knowing that once you were told to do something, you rarely got out of doing it. But if anyone had a chance of sweet-talking Mama, it was me.

Not today.

I cranked up the old lawn mower and started running through Bible verses in my head. I had to pick something to recite later at church, and I wanted to look good for both God and Sylvia. As I went back and forth across the front lawn, I finally settled on one that seemed perfect for the day—Philippians 2:14–15. I knew it would make my mama smile to hear me read the beginning of the verse: "Do all things without grumbling or disputing."

I don't know what made me look up right then to see the two white men standing on the back porch. They were staring at me, and neither was smiling. I cut off the lawn mower as the rest of the verse ran through my mind: "So that you will prove yourselves to be blameless and innocent children of God, above reproach in the midst of a crooked and perverse generation, among whom you appear as lights in the world."

"Anthony Ray Hinton?" One man took a step toward me, yelling my name, and I noticed that both men each held a hand over the gun at his side. "Police!"

I had no idea why there were two policemen on my mama's porch, but I wasn't afraid. We had always been taught if you haven't done anything wrong, you have no reason to fear and certainly no reason to run. I hadn't done anything wrong since I'd gotten out, and I checked in regular since I had been paroled. There was nothing to be afraid of.

I walked to the top of the driveway.

"We need to talk to you." They flanked me on both sides and sort of nudged me down the driveway to their car. It was then that I felt a little twinge at the back of my shoulder blades, and my stomach felt like it does when you ride over the top of a hill real fast in a car.

"Am I going to jail?"

They patted me down and cuffed my hands behind my back.

"I didn't do anything," I said. My voice was a little loud, a little sharper than I wanted it to be. One guy started to open up the back door of their car. "What's this about?"

"They will tell you when we get you to Bessemer."

"Can I go in and tell my mom that I'm leaving?" Whatever this was about, I knew it would get cleared up fast. I hadn't done anything wrong.

They walked me up to the side door, and I yelled for my mom. She opened the door, and the three of us took a step in.

"They are arresting me. Taking me to jail. Don't worry. I didn't do anything. Don't worry." I said it fast because I could see the confusion on her face, and I didn't want her to start yelling at the police or to start crying. Just like that, they turned me around and walked me back to the car. A sergeant named Cole introduced himself and read me my rights.

"Is that your car?" The other man pointed to my red Nissan.

"Yes. My girlfriend leased it for me. It's in her name, but it's my car."

"Do you mind if we search it? And your bedroom?"

I didn't mind. Maybe that would get these cuffs off me and I could avoid a trip to jail for no reason. "Sure. I want you to. Please search them both." The sooner they searched, the sooner they could get out of here and I could finish cutting the grass and get to the revival and Sylvia. I knew my mom would probably help them search my room. She would want to help the police fix whatever mistake was made that had me sitting in the back of a police car in handcuffs.

I sat with Cole in the car while the other guy, Sergeant Amberson, searched my car and my room. He walked back out to the car with nothing in his hands. They hadn't found anything. I was hoping this meant I could go.

My mom walked out the back door, following him.

"Let's go!"

Suddenly, Sergeant Amberson was back in the car, and the doors slammed shut while the ignition turned on, and I could see my mom walking toward the front of the car, and she started yelling just like she used to do during one of my baseball games.

"That's my baby! That's my baby!"

Only she wasn't cheering, she was crying, almost sobbing, and my hands were behind my back, so I yelled as loud as I could as they swung the car out at the bottom of the driveway.

"It's okay, Mama! It's going to be okay."

They started down the road, and I swiveled my head back to see my mom standing at the bottom of the driveway with her arms stretched toward me. She was crying and yelling, and I saw our neighbor's front door open, so I knew someone would go to her.

It felt like my heart was going to crack in two pieces.

"It's okay," I mumbled. "It's all going to be okay."

I watched the trees go by and felt the rumble under me as we crossed over the railroad tracks at the end of the street. This was all going to work itself out. I hadn't done anything wrong. That was the truth, and the truth would set me free so that I could go back home and put my arms around my mama. She didn't like to be alone at night, so I just hoped that whatever this was could be cleared up in a few hours.

I closed my eyes as we continued the drive into Bessemer. These guys weren't saying anything else and neither was I until somebody told me what this was about. Once they told me, I would clear it up, and I would be out of these cuffs and back home.

Home.

I just wanted to go home.

Birmingham, August 2, 1985

HOLDUP SUSPECT CHARGED WITH SLAYINGS

Capital murder warrants were issued yesterday charging a suspect in a Bessemer robbery and shooting with the slayings of two Birmingham fast-food restaurant managers.

Anthony Ray Hinton, 29, of Burnwell near Dora in Walker County was being held without bond yesterday. He is charged with the slayings of John Davidson on Feb. 23 and Thomas Wayne Vason on July 2.

Both men were shot in the head and left to die in the walk-in coolers of their restaurants. . . .

Hinton also is being held in Sunday's robbery of Quincy's Family Steakhouse. . . .

Smotherman survived to give police their first description of the robber, and later to identify Hinton as the man who shot him. . . .

Authorities also recovered from Hinton's home the .38-caliber pistol used to fire the shots that killed Vason and Davidson and wounded Smotherman, Birmingham Homicide Sgt. C. M. Quinn said.

"We had the bullets matched with each other already," Quinn said. "All we were lacking was the weapon they were fired from, and we (got) that yesterday and took it directly to ballistics. They worked on it a good portion of the night and gave us the results."

*He was transferred from the Bessemer City Jail to the Jefferson County Jail.**

---

* Nick Patterson, "Holdup Suspect Charged with Slayings," *Birmingham Post Herald*, August 3, 1985.

| 5 |

PREMEDITATED GUILT

Equal and exact justice to all men of whatever state or persuasion.

—WORDS ETCHED INTO THE JEFFERSON COUNTY COURTHOUSE

When I stepped out of the car at the police station in Bessemer, I saw nothing but flashes of bright light. I ducked my head down and tried to keep my eyes closed because the light and the noise and the shouting were disorienting and confusing. I don't know who called the press or what they had been told, but I had watched enough television to know this was a perp walk and I was the perp. I was annoyed at this point, or somewhere between annoyed and angry. *How embarrassing,* I thought. For me and for the police when they had to tell the press they made a mistake.

They brought me into a room at the police station, and three more officers—Vassar and Miller and Acker—were waiting along with a man who didn't say anything but who I found out later was David Barber, the district attorney of Birmingham. They read me my rights again. Acker put a blank piece of paper in front of me and asked me to sign it.

"What's this?" I asked.

"Just sign it, and we are going to type up your Miranda rights on it so everyone knows we read you your rights."

"You know what? I'm an honest person, so if anyone asks me—whether it's a judge or another police officer or anyone—I will tell them that you read me my rights," I said.

The detective put the pen on top of the paper. "We're going to take the cuffs off you, and then you can sign the paper and have a drink, and we'll get this all sorted out right quick."

I knew I hadn't done anything wrong, but I wasn't a fool. There was no way I was going to sign a blank piece of paper. I looked up at the men around me. They looked happy, excited. Maybe even a little jumpy, like you do when you have a big secret you are just dying to tell. In that moment, I felt the first real twinge of fear. Why did they want me to sign a blank piece of paper? That wasn't right. None of this was right.

"I'm not going to sign that paper."

I said it firmly, and I saw them all look at each other. One of the other detectives picked up the paper. I didn't really know who was who. They started firing questions at me.

"Where were you on the night of February 23?"

"I don't know that. How am I supposed to know that?"

"What about the night of July 2? Where were you on the night of July 2?"

I thought about it a bit. I had gone to Atlanta on the night of the third with Sylvia to drop off my nieces. For the life of me, I couldn't remember what I had done the night before.

"I was probably home on the second. I don't remember doing anything else. I was probably home in February too. I don't go out much," I said. "I would have been home with my mom those nights."

"Can you prove it?" the detective said quietly, and I felt a shiver go up my spine.

"I can't prove it. Man, could you tell me where you were on some random day in February? Seriously."

"I'm not the one under arrest here."

"Well, I shouldn't be under arrest either. I haven't done nothing wrong. Whatever this is, you guys got the wrong guy." I folded my arms up around my chest, trying to look cool and calm, but I could feel my heart pounding against my folded arm.

"Where were you on the night of July 25?"

I thought about it hard—I should be able to account for a week ago. I started walking backward through my week. And then it hit me, I absolutely knew where I was on the twenty-fifth.

"I was at a friend's house a couple of miles from my place. This was on Thursday, right?"

One of the detectives wrote something down in a notebook.

"What's the name of your friend?"

I gave them her name.

"What time were you at her house?" I thought back to that night. I had dinner with my mom and then went by my friend's.

"I got there about 8:00 P.M. or so, and I left at 11:15."

"And where were you after 11:15?"

"I drove to my job out in Ensley, and I was at work all night. I worked the night shift. Midnight to 8:00 A.M. Bruno's Warehouse. Although sometimes we got off earlier if we finished the work. I think I got off around 6:00 A.M. that day. That would be the twenty-sixth."

There was nothing but silence after that.

They put me behind bars, and that's when I realized I was going to be spending the night. It's not easy to get comfortable when the bunks aren't meant to fit a big man, so after a sleepless night, they transported me to the county jail in Birmingham. Lieutenant Acker rode with me.

"What am I under arrest for, exactly? The other guys said robbery. Who did I rob?"

"You want to know why you're under arrest?"

"Yes, I do."

"You're under arrest for first-degree kidnapping, first-degree robbery, first-degree attempted murder."

"Man, you got the wrong person."

"*Man,* we're not even done with you yet. There's going to be more charges." Acker turned around and looked me in the eye for the first time since I had told him I was at work on the twenty-fifth. "You know, I don't care whether you did or didn't do it. In fact, I believe you didn't do it. But it doesn't matter. If you didn't do it, one of your brothers did. And you're going to take the rap. You want to know why?"

I just shook my head.

"I can give you five reasons why they are going to convict you. Do you want to know what they are?"

I shook my head, no, but he continued.

"Number one, you're black. Number two, a white man gonna say you shot him. Number three, you're gonna have a white district attorney. Number four, you're gonna have a white judge. And number five, you're gonna have an all-white jury."

He paused and smiled at me then.

"You know what that spell?"

I shook my head, but I knew what he was saying. You couldn't be raised in the South and not know what he was saying. My whole body went numb, like I was under an ice-cold shower in the middle of winter.

"Conviction. Conviction. Conviction. Conviction. Conviction." He pointed to each finger on his left hand and then he held up the number five and turned his palm toward me.

I leaned my head back up against the seat and closed my eyes. Since the age of four, I could remember my mom teaching all of us kids to respect authority. She respected authority—almost blindly so. "Tell the truth," she always said, "and you've got nothing to fear." Even when I had gotten in trouble before, she told me, "Even if it hurts you, you tell the truth. What's done in the dark will always come to light." In my mom's world, there was no gray area. The police were who you ran to when you were in trouble—you never ran from them. They were always there to help. That's why I had let them search my car and my room. That's why I had told them my mom had a gun when they asked me earlier. You told the truth. The police were there to help. There was nothing to be afraid of.

I remember her sitting me down after graduation. "Listen, there are going to be people that dislike you just because of the color of your skin. Some going to dislike you because you black; some people going to dislike you because you light-skinned. You going to have people dislike you because of whatever reason they find to dislike you. That's just how the world is. But you have to be knowing that you are responsible for how you treat others, you're not responsible for how they treat you. Do you understand? I don't care what people say about you—you don't drop down to their level. You always treat someone better than what they treat you. Always."

I thought of her at home alone. She must be scared. I hadn't been offered a phone call. Hopefully the neighbors were with her. I knew Phoebe, Lester's mom, would be at my mom's side just as soon as she could. Lester should be out of the mines by now. I wondered if he had heard. He would make sure my mom was okay, just like I would have done for his mom. That was the only thought that brought some comfort. This would get cleared up.

First-degree robbery and attempted murder and kidnapping? Hell, I felt like I was the one being kidnapped. They would see I was at work. Talk to my friend. I didn't know about those other nights. I couldn't remember, but I had to believe that they would believe me. I hadn't done anything wrong, and the more I cooperated and helped them investigate whatever this was, the sooner I would go home. I didn't care what Acker said. No one was going to convict me for something I didn't do. I was innocent, and it would get sorted out in the morning.

The press was out front of the Birmingham jail as well, and they paraded me around and inside. I was read my rights again and processed into the jail with fingerprints and mug shots and was told they were also charging me with murder. Two murders. They had evidence, they said. The gun at my house matched the bullets. They found the murder weapon. Someone saw me. It was over. I should confess. None of it made sense. I refused to speak. I just wanted a moment to clear my head and sort this out in my mind. I needed to talk to my mom. I was given green-and-white-striped scrubs to change into, and it was all a blur until they took me up to the seventh floor—C block. I was given a thin, one-inch mattress, a plastic razor, a plastic mug, a toothbrush, and my very own roll of toilet paper. I set my stuff down on my bunk. All I wanted was to lie down and sleep for a week.

"Stand outside your cell with your back against the wall."

I lined up with everyone else and watched as the guards did roll call. I counted the names in my head as they yelled them out. There were twenty-four of us altogether. I looked around. Most were black; some were white.

When the guard was done, I turned to go back into my cell.

"Hinton!"

I turned toward the guard.

"You can't go back in your cell until the day's over. Everyone has to be in the common area."

The common area had metal seats and tables bolted to the floor, and all of them were arranged so that they faced a small television mounted to the wall. I just wanted to call my mom and Lester and see if they could straighten out this mess somehow. And then I wanted to close my eyes and sleep and wake up at home in my own bed and have the last twenty-four hours be some sort of bad dream.

I sat down on one of the cold, rounded seats and nodded at the white guy who sat down across from me. He had bright red hair, and he gave me a big smile that looked half-friendly and half-serial-killer-clown.

"Welcome to C block," he said. "It's where all the capital murder kids come to play."

| 6 |

THE WHOLE TRUTH

It is the opinion of this examiner that the subject told the truth during this polygraph examination.

—CLYDE WOLFE

They sent me to Kilby Prison to finish out the weeks I had left on my parole when they arrested me. It was a way to buy some time, I guess, get their ducks all in a row. I barely had a moment to speak to my mom and to Lester; the phones were never free, and collect calls were expensive. "This is all a mistake," I said when I finally got hold of them. "We will get this sorted out. Once I have an attorney and explain everything, they will realize they have the wrong person and let me go." I was reassuring them and reassuring myself. At least, I thought, when this was cleared up, I would be totally free once and for all. No more parole. No more checking in every month. No more chance they could just swoop me out of my house because I was in the system. I did my few weeks at Kilby and returned to Jefferson County to wait for my time to go before the judge.

I was indicted by a grand jury on November 8, 1985. My face was in all the local newspapers. People wanted to string me up. Shoot me outright and save the taxpayers some money. And this was all before I had even stepped foot in a courtroom. Before I had been appointed a public defender. And before I was even able to say, "Not guilty," at an arraignment.

My case was assigned to a judge on November 13, 1985—his name was Judge James S. Garrett. I met my court-appointed attorney, Sheldon Perhacs. He was only a little shorter than I was, around six feet or so, but he was lean and muscular. He wore his hair slicked back like he was some sort of Italian mobster or maybe even a boxer. I had seen all three *Rocky* movies, and the fourth one was just about to come out. At my arraignment, he barely looked at me. He was officially assigned my case, and I heard him mumble, "I didn't go to law school to do pro bono work."

I cleared my throat, and he looked me in the eye for the first time. Even though I was handcuffed and chained, I held out my hand to shake his.

"Would it make a difference if I told you I was innocent?"

"Listen, all y'all always doing something and saying you're innocent."

I dropped my hand. So that's how it was going to be. I was pretty sure that when he said "all y'all," he wasn't talking about ex-cons or former coal miners or Geminis or even those accused of capital murder.

I needed him, so I had no choice but to let it slide. I had to believe that he believed me. He was my Italian fighter. He was Rocky, and I was Apollo Creed—not like in the first movie but in later movies, where they are allies, friends even. I had only seen the trailer for *Rocky IV,* and I wanted to think of Perhacs training early in the morning, running up the courthouse steps, drinking raw eggs while he read through tall stacks of case files and left no stone unturned in his investigation. It gave me comfort to think of him this way—to pretend that he believed he was in the fight of his life fighting for my life.

It wasn't until about ten years later that I actually got to see *Rocky IV.* It made me glad that I hadn't known that Apollo Creed died in the movie while Rocky stood by and watched.

The judge set a trial date of March 6, 1986.

I turned to Perhacs before they took me back to C block. "Give me a lie detector test. A truth serum. Hypnotize me. Whatever you have to give me that will show them I'm telling the truth. I don't care what it is, I'll take it, I'll do it. This whole thing is a mistake. I'll take any test they have to prove it."

He just stared at me, and then he waved his hand in the air like he was swatting away a fly. "I'll come see you at the jail soon. We'll talk about your case. I promise."

I held on to that promise like a drowning man hangs on to whatever he can grab that he thinks will save him.

CONFIDENTIAL

DATE: 5/13/86

SUBJECT: ANTHONY RAY HINTON

SSN: XXX-XX-XXXX

Mr. Sheldon Perhacs
Attorney at Law
Suite 1414
City Federal Bldg.
2026 Second Ave. N.
Birmingham, Ala. 35203

At your request ANTHONY RAY HINTON was given a polygraph examination to determine his truthfulness in a case of Kidnapping, Attempted Murder, and Murder. Standard polygraph procedure was exercised throughout the examination.

RESULTS:
During the pre-test interview ANTHONY RAY HINTON stated that his address is XXXXXX XXXX, Burnwell, Ala., and that he was born 6/1/56 in Jefferson County, ala. Subject is a 29 year old male, 6′2″ tall, 220 lbs., with black hair and brown eyes. Subject said he has a high school education, is single and has no dependents.

Subject said he was convicted in 1982 in Bessemer, Ala., of Theft of Property; also was convicted twice in Bessemer, Ala. in 1982 of Auto Theft, and was sentenced to 15 months and placed on 1½ years of probation for these three convictions. Subject said he has been convicted in Bessemer, Ala. of several worthless checks and has paid the fines.

The subject went on to say that he has never shot anyone and has never robbed Quincy's, Captain D's or Mrs. Winner's. The subject insists that he had nothing to do with the crimes in question and doesn't know who committed the crimes.

The subject was then asked the following relevant questions:

TEST I

Q Do you plan to try to lie to any of these questions?
-no
Q Have you told me the whole truth about this matter?
-yes
Q Did you ever commit an armed robbery?
-no
Q Did you ever point a gun at anyone?
-no
Q Did you ever shoot anyone with a gun?
-no
Q Are you trying to withhold any information about this matter?
-no

TEST II

Q Did you know Mrs. Winner's was going to be held up?
-no
Q Did you plan to hold up Mrs. Winner's?
-no
Q Did you ever point a gun at anyone in Mrs. Winner's?
-no
Q Did you ever shoot anyone in Mrs. Winner's?
-no
Q Have you told me the whole truth since we've been talking?
-yes
Q Did you purposely try to lie to any of these questions?
-no

TEST III

Q Did you know Mrs. Winner's was going to be held up?
-no
Q Did you plan to hold up Mrs. Winner's?
-no
Q Did you ever point a gun at anyone in Mrs. Winner's?
-no
Q Did you ever shoot anyone in Mrs. Winner's?
-no
Q Have you told me the whole truth since we've been talking?
-yes
Q Did you purposely try to lie to any of these questions?
-no

TEST IV

Q Did you plan to rob Quincy's?
-no
Q Did you tell Mr. Smotherman to open the safe?
-no
Q Did you point a gun at Mr. Smotherman?
-no
Q Did you shoot anyone in Quincy's?
-no
Q Have you told me the whole truth since we've been talking?
-yes
Q Did you purposely try to lie to any of these questions?
-no

TEST V

Q Did you plan to rob Quincy's?
-no
Q Did you tell Mr. Smotherman to open the safe?
-no
Q Did you point a gun at Mr. Smotherman?
-no
Q Did you shoot anyone in Quincy's?
-no
Q Did you shoot Mr. Smotherman at Quincy's?
-no
Q Have you told me the whole truth since we've been talking?
-yes
Q Did you purposely try to lie to any of these questions?
-no

TEST VI

Q Did you know Captain D's was going to be robbed?
-no
Q Did you point a gun at anyone in Captain D's?
-no
Q Did you rob Captain D's?
-no
Q Did you shoot anyone at Captain D's?
-no
Q Have you told me the whole truth since we've been talking?
-yes
Q Did you purposely try to lie to any of these questions?
-no

TEST VII

Q Did you know Captain D's was going to be robbed?
-no
Q Did you point a gun at anyone in Captain D's?
-no
Q Did you rob Captain D's?
-no
Q Did you shoot anyone at Captain D's?
-no
Q Have you told me the whole truth since we've been talking?
-yes
Q Did you purposely try to lie to any of these questions?
-no

CONCLUSION:
It is the opinion of this examiner that the subject told the truth during this polygraph examination.

POLYGRAPH EXAMINER,
CLYDE A. WOLFE

I knew I had passed the polygraph. I heard a female guard talking to the examiner while I waited to be brought back to C block.

"How'd he do?"

The examiner hadn't said much to me, but he spoke to the guard. "If I could go by this test, he would walk out of here with me right now. He showed no signs of deception. He didn't do it. He doesn't know anything about these murders, I can tell you that for a fact."

She sort of grunted in agreement. "You know, I've been doing this for twenty-seven years, and I've seen a lot of killers. He's no killer."

I went to sleep that night with new hope. I didn't know how my mom had been able to come up with $350 for the polygraph test, but I knew that as soon as I was out and could get to work, I would earn enough money to pay it back. Every day felt like being in the middle of a bad dream. I kept thinking they would catch the person who really did it. It was like the police and the judge and the prosecutors and even my own attorney were in on some bad practical joke, and I was just waiting for them to tell me they had been punking me.

When the guard next called me out for a legal visit, I thought Perhacs was finally there to tell me I could go. It was straight out of John 8:32—"And the truth shall set you free." He had only visited me a couple of times in jail, but he had given me his phone number and said I could call him whenever I wanted. That was more than most guys in C block got from their court-appointed attorneys. He and Bob McGregor had made an agreement that whatever happened with the polygraph, whatever the results, either side could use the test to argue their case. If I failed, McGregor could use it to convict me, and if I passed, Perhacs could use it to prove my innocence and show them once and for all they had the wrong guy. I hadn't worried about making that deal—I knew what the results would be.

"They're not allowing the polygraph. Bob McGregor nicked on the deal."

I watched as Perhacs's mouth kept moving, but it sounded like a swarm of bees had gathered in my head. I couldn't hear anything he was saying. Betrayal felt like ice under my skin. I went cold and numb, and then it felt like those bees in my head were stinging every part of my body. This was real fear. I thought of Lester and me diving into the ditches when we walked home. I thought that was what fear felt like—your heart pounding and your breath going fast, but this was different. This was ice and steel and a thousand blades carving you up from the inside out. I couldn't make sense of what was happening. They knew I didn't do it, but they were still going to take me to trial? They were willing to let the real killer go and pin this on me?

I had Perhacs walk me through it all again, slowly.

All the bullets from the two murders and from the Quincy's robbery matched my mom's gun. I knew this was impossible, because that gun hadn't been fired in twenty-five years. Our neighbor had been there when the police went back to get the gun from my mom, and she had seen the detective put a cloth inside the gun, and when he pulled it out, he said that it was full of dust and hadn't been fired in a long time.

Smotherman had picked me out of a photo lineup and said I was the guy who robbed him and shot at him. I was at work when this happened. I was signed in. I couldn't understand how they were just ignoring this. There was no way I could have left work at the beginning of my shift and robbed someone. I was with other people. My supervisor gave me assignments all night long.

"How could I be in two places at once?" I asked Perhacs. "What are they thinking? That's not even possible. There was a guard. I had to check in and out!"

"They are going to say you snuck out. You drove to Quincy's and you robbed him." Perhacs rubbed his hand through his hair.

"That's impossible. When we're at trial, can we ask the judge to have the jury drive the route exactly at midnight and see that the time frame won't work? I can't be in two places at once. Did you drive the route? It's not even possible for me to clock in and get my assignment and get back to Bessemer in a few minutes. It takes at least twenty or twenty-five minutes to get there. Drive the route. Can you get an expert to drive it? Clock it? That'll prove it." My voice was getting louder than I wanted, but I needed him to see this logically. I couldn't be in two places at once. There was no way they could say I clocked in to work and ten minutes later was a half hour away robbing somebody. "We can show them there's a fifteen-foot fence I would have had to have climbed. And show them where the guards are at and how you have to log in and account for your time the whole shift."

"So what, now I have a lawyer for a client?" Perhacs said this slowly, and I got the message loud and clear. Let him figure it out. Let him put on the defense. I was just supposed to sit back and be a good boy and not make trouble.

What choice did I have?

I laughed it off, but I had to say just one more thing. "I've been reading the papers. You see that there's been other holdups? Other managers getting robbed at closing? I definitely can't be doing that when I'm locked in here."

"Yeah, I'll look into it. They're only paying me $1,000 for this, and hell, I eat $1,000 for breakfast." He laughed, but it wasn't funny.

The other big obstacle was finding a ballistics expert. We needed someone to look at the gun and the bullets and get up there and testify. I knew the State was lying about the bullets and my mom's gun, but it wasn't like a judge or a jury was going to believe me. Perhacs had told me that the only thing keeping me from a good defense was money, and then he asked me if

I had anyone who could pay him $15,000 to do the work. Nobody had that kind of money. I had been shocked my mom came up with the lie detector money. I told him that much, and then I pleaded with him.

"I promise you that once you prove that I didn't do this and I get out, I'll pay you. You have my word on it. If I have to work night and day and holidays and weekends, I will pay you. Please?" I was begging, but it didn't matter.

"Anthony, it just don't work like that. What proof do I have you will pay me? You don't have money to hire me, and besides, I was appointed this job by the court. *You* can't pay me."

He had been struggling over finding a ballistics expert. The court was only allowing him $500 for each capital case to hire an expert, and he couldn't find anyone to do the work for $1,000. He had until August to find an expert, and it wasn't looking good.

It turned out that $15,000 was also the number that would get me a good expert. Everything depended on those bullets, since they had no other evidence against me. No fingerprints. No DNA. No witnesses. Because I had no alibi for the nights of the murders—because I couldn't account for where I was—that made me guilty. That and the bullets. They weren't even charging me for the Smotherman case, only using it to prove I had done the other two because it was of similar plan and design. That was the magic phrase. But I read the paper every day. There were robberies of similar plan and design happening every week in Birmingham.

Perhacs made it clear that my only shot was an expert who could counter the State's experts. I hadn't wanted to, but I called my oldest brother, Willie, in Cleveland and asked him for the money.

"Can your attorney for sure get you off if you hire an expert?"

"I don't think he can say for sure."

"Well, I need to talk to him. I would need some assurance the money would put an end to this. I need him to give me a guarantee so I'm not wasting my money."

He didn't say yes and he didn't say no, so that was something.

I tried not to dwell on the fact that if things were reversed and I had the money, well, I would have given it no questions asked.

Perhacs couldn't give him that guarantee. Who in their right mind could make any guarantee like that? I knew my brother was raised like I was—raised to trust the police, the lawyers, and the judges. He was an upright citizen, never had any trouble and never wanted any. I'd like to think he didn't help because he knew I didn't do it and believed the courts would provide everything I needed. My heart broke when Perhacs told me that Willie wouldn't give the money. I would have moved heaven and earth to help him or to help any of my siblings in the same situation. That's what you do when you are a family. It's what you should do. It would be almost thirty years—without seeing or hearing from him—before I would come to accept the truth. My older brother must, in some small place within him, have believed that I was a killer. There are families of sinners and families of saints, and all are deserving of love and help. The sinners even more than the saints. It hurt inside to not have his help. It was like everything good was being taken away, one small chunk at a time. Belief. Family. Truth. Faith. Justice. I wondered who I would be when this was all over—how could I be the same person? Would there be anything left after this trial? And what if they actually found me guilty? What then? Nobody believed me, and some days it felt like the whole world, except for Lester and my mom, was conspiring against me. Sometimes late at night, I would lie in my bunk and think about the trial to come and imagine the jury. Were they going to be against me too? Would they really be fair and impartial? I could feel the paranoia seeping around the edges of my mind, fighting to get in like a poison gas slipping in through the vents. I willed myself to think of other things, but there was a darkness pushing up against my hope that I couldn't keep at bay.

I knew my last and only and best hope was going to be my attorney. He held my life in his hands, because it became clear that this wasn't about them having the wrong guy. They weren't making a mistake. They were setting out to send an innocent man to death row. And they were willing to lie to do it.

I made sure to call Perhacs later that week just to tell him how much I appreciated him and how great he was doing. He was my only voice. And I needed his voice to get loud in that courtroom. I needed him to show that jury the truth. Show them who Anthony Ray Hinton was—a boy who loved his mama, who grew up in a community that loved him, a man that had never had a violent moment in his life. I was a lover. I was a joker. I was a man who would help anyone who needed help.

Not a man who would hide in the dark to take your money and your life.

Not a cold-blooded killer.

I wasn't that man.

I wasn't.

| 7 |

CONVICTION, CONVICTION, CONVICTION

He is cloaked in innocence, and you should not consider him anything but innocent until and unless the State of Alabama proves beyond a reasonable doubt to you the facts alleged in these indictments.

—PROSECUTOR BOB MCGREGOR

Jefferson County Courthouse, September 12, 1986

It's amazing what money and revenge will do to people—it can change them from the inside out. Make their ugly shine through in ways that God himself would be ashamed of. I watched Reggie up on the stand, and I wondered how rejection by one girl could make a man so small-hearted and mean. Lord knows, if I could go back in time and not date two sisters at once, I would. If I had known that it had created in him such jealousy and rage that he was willing to lie and frame me for murder—actually put me to death over it—well, I would have paid for them to go out on a date myself. He worked at Quincy's and had told Smotherman that he knew a guy who fit the description of the man who robbed him. At least now I knew how my name had come up in all this mess. And I also knew what my life was worth to Reginald Payne White—$5,000—the amount of the reward I heard he was getting for cracking the case and helping to catch a killer. I imagine this was just icing on the cake for Reggie. The snake was finally ready to strike after all these years.

DEFENSE TESTIMONY TO BEGIN IN RESTAURANT SLAYINGS TRIAL

*The first person to identify Hinton as the robber was Quincy's employee Reginald White. White, who has known Hinton since 1979, said that two weeks before the robbery Hinton questioned him about how good Quincy's business was, and the time the restaurant closed.**

The lawyers had argued about Reggie taking the stand when the jury was out of the room. My lawyer lost. I'd like to believe that the reason Reggie wouldn't look at me while he testified was because he had a conscience and wouldn't have been able to lie as well if he'd had to do so while looking into my eyes. Did he know they wanted to kill me? Did he understand what he was saying? Did he know how much bigger this was than any girl he wanted to date when we were kids? Or was he, like every other young and poor black man in Jefferson County, just trying to get a little extra scratch to make it through? I couldn't understand how a life could mean so little. We weren't friends, but until that day, I had no idea we were mortal enemies. I watched him on the stand, feeling important, maybe for the first time ever.

"State your name, please, Mr. White."

"Reginald Payne White."

"Where do you live? What county, that is?"

"Jefferson County. Bessemer."

"Where do you work?"

"Quincy's Family Steak House."

"How long have you worked there?"

"Nine years."

After baseball ended, I had seen Reggie at Quincy's. My mom and I liked to go there sometimes, for the salad bar mainly. The brother of the sisters I was dating also worked at Quincy's. I hadn't been to that Quincy's in years, not since it came out I was dating the sisters. Their brother didn't want to see me. Neither did their mom. Because of me, that family was torn apart for a while, and I regretted the harm I had caused. I had put all

* Nick Patterson, "Defense Testimony to Begin in Restaurant Slayings Trial," *Birmingham News,* September 15, 1986.

that behind me, as had the family, but it must have stayed fresh in Reggie's mind. He and I had run into each other at the beginning of July, a few weeks before I was arrested. We had a harmless conversation, but Reggie was taking that little bit of truth and creating a whole drama out of it. My stomach turned over. I wondered if anyone had ever thrown up in open court before.

"Directing your attention to the month of July 1985. Sometime during that month, did you have an occasion to have a conversation with a man named Anthony Ray Hinton?"

"Yes, sir."

"And do you see Anthony Ray Hinton in court today?"

"Yes, sir."

"Where is he?"

"Right there." He pointed at me, but made sure his gaze went over the top of my head.

"The man sitting at the end of the bench, the defendant?"

"Yes, sir."

"How long have you known Anthony Ray Hinton?"

"Maybe a total of about six years."

I watched Reggie fidget as they asked him about running into me. I had been waiting for Sylvia to get off work, and he had driven up and parked near me. We said hello, talked about what we were doing. He told me he still worked at Quincy's, and I asked if the brother still worked there and the manager that I knew. Then I went on my way, and he went on his way. A chance encounter. A bit of chitchat at the end of a hot day in the middle of summer. And now he said I was there waiting for him, as if I knew he would be there, and he was so scared when he saw me he reached for his gun he kept in the car? I could feel my legs begin to shake as he testified. He was making things up. Straight-up lying under oath.

"All right, anything else?"

"Then he asked me about how was business. I told him it was normal, and then he asked me did we still close at the same time, and I told him yeah we closed at 10:00 through the week and 11:00 on weekends."

"He asked you what time you closed at Quincy's?"

"Yes, sir."

"Did you tell him anything about any personnel at Quincy's?"

"I told him about Sid—Mr. Smotherman. I didn't call him no name. I told him we had a nice old manager. He had just bought a new Fiero."

"You told him that you had a what now?"

"A nice old manager that had just bought a new Fiero."

"You told him the type of car?"

"Yes, sir."

So that was it. I had used Reggie to find out when the place closed and what kind of car. I looked at Perhacs. Was he catching this? Say this craziness were true, did it make sense that Reggie told me they closed at 11:00 but I had chosen a night when I started a work shift at midnight behind a razor fence with a guard and locked doors to sneak out, rob, and murder a man, and then sneak back in? Did they think I was the Terminator? Why wouldn't I have just robbed him on a night I had off? It couldn't be for an alibi, because I certainly hadn't been clever enough to set up alibis for myself on the other two murders. All of this ran through my head, and I wanted to stand up in court and become my own lawyer. Walk the jury through it. There was no logic to the story they were creating. It was like they had picked me as the killer and then went about twisting reality to make me fit into the plot they were creating. Why wouldn't I have just gotten there early and waited for Smotherman to leave like I was supposed to have done at the first two murders? Why would I follow him around a grocery store and then carjack him in the road while in my car? I didn't sound like the cleverest, coolest killer to walk these streets—I sounded like the dumbest criminal in the world. Somehow I had missed him at point-blank range with my gun but had been amazing at scaling fences, switching cars, traveling at supersonic speed, and making it back over the fence, past the guard, through the locked doors, all in time to scrape gum off the bathroom floor. Where was the money? Where were my bloody clothes? Where were the snags on my clothing from climbing over a fifteen-foot razor-wire fence? Where was the heavy, dark sedan with which I had carjacked Sid Smotherman? Where did I get it from, and when did I switch from my small red Nissan? Was I a superhero? Was I James Bond? I must have been to accomplish all of this and still clean out under the Dumpster when my supervisor asked me to.

I don't know if what was going through my mind started showing on my face, but Perhacs cleared his throat and put a hand on my shoulder as he got up to question Reggie.

"Mr. White, how're you doing?"

"How're you doing?"

"Mr. White, you know my client. You and he used to play softball together, didn't you?"

"Yes, sir."

"Not on the same team, though?"

"No, sir."

"And you also knew him because you know a man named Quinton Leath."

"Yes, sir."

"Got a bunch of . . . Quinton's got a bunch of sisters?"

"Yes, sir."

"He dated one, and you saw one?"

"Yes, sir."

"Now we're talking back in '79 and '80, aren't we?"

"Yes, sir."

"And this is a gentleman with whom you have spoken on a friendly basis off and on for years, haven't you?"

"Yes, sir."

"When you meet him, you're friendly to him, aren't you?"

"Yes, sir."

"And when you and he have met, he's been courteous in front of you?"

"Yes, sir."

I could hardly sit there and listen to this. Perhacs just moved on to the next topic from the sisters, and he didn't even get it right. I had told him everything about Reggie. What had happened, what he used to say about me. I had given Perhacs Reggie's motive for lying, but he was acting like he was asking him about the weather.

"Now, in this conversation that you had with him in Hoover, it was you who told him about who was working out there, wasn't it?"

"Yes, sir."

"He wasn't taking any notes with any pad or pencil either, was he?"

"No, sir."

Perhacs went on to ask him if he was married or about to be. I didn't know what that was about. It didn't even make sense.

"All right, and that's all the conversation consisted of, wasn't it?"

"Yes, sir."

"You left and went about your business?"

"Yes, sir."

"He walked off?"

"Yes, sir."

"That's all I have."

And that was that. No mention of the reward money. No catching him in his lies. No showing that he'd had it in for me for years. Nothing but the kind of talk you'd hear on my mama's porch any old afternoon.

I went back to my cell every night after trial and replayed the day in my head. They had traced all the bullets—they called it *chain of custody*—from the victims, to the hospital, to the police, to the crime lab. The police testified about arresting me. They didn't mention the blank piece of paper they wanted me to sign or the fact that they said the gun hadn't been fired in a long time. Anything true that didn't make me a killer was left out or just plain lied about. My only hope was our ballistics expert. Perhacs had hired him, and he had done the tests and concluded that the bullets didn't match the gun. I knew they couldn't have, but the State's experts said they had. They were either bad at their job or lying, and it was hard for me to truly wrap my mind around the fact that all these people would just lie to put me to death. What had I done to them? Why me? The questions kept me up all night. I thought back to when I was arrested. I replayed that last afternoon over and over again in my head. Would I have walked to the porch if I had known what was going to happen? Or would I have run? Innocent men don't run. Except sometimes innocent men need to run. This is true in Alabama and everywhere. If you're poor and black, sometimes your best and only chance is to run. I imagined running up into the woods that bordered our backyard or down the street toward the highway. But where could I have run to? Everything I was and loved and cared about was in a few miles' radius of that house. Would they have shot me? Probably. Sometimes I played the movie out in my head—me running and getting shot in the back—my mom crying, Lester showing up, and Sylvia, the neighbors all gathered around my body as I breathe my last breath. There was no good end to the running in my mind, but there were nights when it seemed like dying on the pavement would have been a whole lot easier than proving my innocence in a courtroom. I shouldn't have had to prove I was innocent—they were supposed to prove I was guilty—but not in this courtroom.

I missed my mom and I missed Lester, and I hated that they had to sit in this courtroom and hear the lies. I had broken up with Sylvia about a year ago—told her to move on because I didn't know how long I was going to be caught up in this mess. Sylvia was a good girl, and I knew her family wouldn't want her with me until my name was cleared. I didn't want her hanging on when I didn't know myself when this nightmare would end. I had been in this county jail for what felt like forever, and I couldn't even begin to think about what would come next if I was found guilty. My mind would just shut down when I tried to think on it. I had to believe that a miracle would happen. God never fails. Hadn't my mom said as much to me since the time I could walk? God never fails. I needed them to catch the guy who had done it. I needed my ballistics expert to get on that stand and prove that there was no way my mama's old gun could have killed anybody.

He was my only hope.

Wednesday, September 17, 1986

DA HITS TESTIMONY DEATH BULLETS NOT FROM GUN AT HINTON HOUSE

Prosecutors today challenged the testimony of a defense witness who said the bullets used in the 1985 slayings of two restaurant managers and the shooting of a third were not fired from the gun found at Anthony Ray Hinton's house near Dora.

"He didn't know what in the world he was talking about," said Deputy District Attorney Steve Mahon during closing remarks this morning.

Andrew Payne, a retired Army colonel, is a professional witness who will come into court and testify about almost anything, Mahon said.

Payne said he is a consulting engineer and has testified in about 1,000 court cases. Two of those cases involved firearms identification, he said.

Mahon called Payne's report "the height of irresponsibility."

*The firearms evidence is the main link prosecutors have to the murders.**

Andrew Payne never had a chance.

He did a great job with Perhacs, walking him through all the ways that the bullets didn't match the gun. He was an expert, although a bit socially awkward and too nerdy for the jury to really relate to, but he did his job. His findings proved I was innocent. For a minute, I felt like a huge weight had lifted off my chest. I turned and sent a quick smile to my mom and Lester. And then it was the State's turn to cross-examine. Mahon started out easy, nice almost, but it was a setup right from the start.

"It's your testimony, sir, that you have used comparison microscopes in excess of a thousand times?"

"I would say yes, sir, about a thousand times."

"And you were familiar with that comparison microscope that Mr. Yates has?"

"Well, not familiar with it. It's the first time I'd ever used or seen an American Optical."

"American Optical is a pretty obscure brand?"

"Well, I wouldn't say it's an obscure brand but just that I had never operated one before."

"As a matter of fact, when you were looking at the Smotherman projectile there at the laboratory of the Department of Forensic Sciences, you had to ask Mr. Yates how to cut on the light source for the comparison microscope, did you not?"

"Very possible. In fact, probably did, yes."

"And as a matter of fact, after he told you how to do it, you reached over to your immediate right and threw the switch on an electric inscribing tool that was on a shelf next to the microscope, did you not?"

"Very possible, yes, sir."

"You did that, didn't you?"

It went from bad to worse after that. It turns out he didn't even know how to use the microscope after he found the light. And then he didn't know whether

---

* Kathy Roe, "DA Hits Testimony Death Bullets Not from Gun at Hinton House," *Birmingham News,* September 17, 1986.

or not there were controls to raise the glass up and down or how to switch the magnification lenses. He tried to ask the State's experts for help? He dropped the bullets? I looked over at Perhacs—this was his fault. Didn't he know all this? He looked surprised. Had Payne not told him how it went at the lab?

"Well, let me ask you this: Did you say, 'I don't seem to be able to see the bullet. I can see the mirror, and I can see my finger fine'?"

"It's very possible that I said that. That would be one of the problems you would have when you were trying to locate the higher-power glass, and that's why I asked for instructions."

I took a deep breath. My expert was whining and complaining on the stand that the other experts wouldn't help him. Things only got worse when they showed that some of his slides came straight out of a firearms book they held in their hands. A book that was from 1956. Mahon asked him to refer to page 6 in Payne's book.

"Page six? Did you say six?"

"Yes, sir."

"Go ahead."

"Wherein that paragraph at the bottom of the page begins with the title 'The Charlatans.'" Mahon started reading from the book. "'Following the invention of photographic and plastic impressions was a heyday of charlatans. Very few judges knew anything about firearms. They had heard rumors of marvelous developments. The world was willing to accept anything said to be specific, almost any . . .'"

"I think that word's *scientific* rather than *specific*."

Now Payne was helping the prosecutor read correctly the text that called him a charlatan? I think I even heard someone in the courtroom gasp.

"Yes, sir, *scientific*. I'm sorry. 'Almost anyone was permitted to testify in court as an expert. Many had little knowledge but a natural core presence and a great deal of gall. For fifty dollars a day, a lot of money in those days, they would go cheerfully into court and swear to most anything. Would appear of outside calipers, an ordinary hand magnifying glass and a steel gauge and that was the third instrument you took—'"

"I think that's a steel scale, if you will look at it more carefully."

"You have your scale you took with you on the twenty-ninth of July with you today, do you not?"

"Yes. Sure."

"Hold it up for the jury."

I watched as Payne held up the scale that the prosecutor had just described as one of the hallmarks of a charlatan. Was this going over his head? Did he not see what everyone else in that courtroom saw?

"Sure. You know without trying to be facetious at this particular time, because this is such a serious matter that I hate to use any levity, but mine must be twice as good as the one they're talking about in the book, because mine is graduated in sixty-fourths."

Mahon ignored the attempt at humor and just kept reading.

" 'They would cheerfully swear away the life of an innocent man or free, for further depredations against society, the most atrocious criminal.' "

"Sure."

"Mr. Payne, do you have some problem with your vision?"

"Why, yes."

"How many eyes do you have?"

"One."

"That's all."

I could do nothing but lay my head down in my arms and cry. I knew at that moment, I was going to be convicted of murder. I was innocent. And my one-eyed expert had just handed the prosecution a guilty verdict.

Nothing mattered anymore.

It took the jury two hours to find me guilty.

It took them forty-five minutes to determine my punishment.

Death.

In that moment, I felt my whole life shatter into a million jagged pieces around me. The world was fractured and broken, and everything good in me broke with it.

Two months later, right before Judge Garrett affirmed and read aloud the official death sentence, I told them what I hoped to be true—God would reopen this case, and if not, they could take my life, but they could never, ever touch my soul.

| 8 |

KEEP YOUR MOUTH SHUT

Dead men tell no tales.

—PROSECUTOR BOB MCGREGOR, CLOSING ARGUMENTS

Birmingham, December 17, 1986

It's strange when life can move so fast and so slow at the same time. I can't tell you exactly what happened in the twenty-four-hour gap between when the judge sentenced me to death and when they came for me. I was officially a condemned man, and none of the guards or the other inmates would meet my eye. It was like the death penalty was a contagious disease and everyone thought they could catch it from me. I was still in shock, and I could feel a rage inside me bubbling below the surface. I was now the worst of the worst. A human not fit for this life. A child of God who was condemned to die. I couldn't wrap my brain around it. How did I suddenly become the most dangerous person in the jail?

My cell in county had been home for the past year and a half. The guys in C block who had money seemed to come in and go out a lot faster than the guys like me who were poor. If you had a court-appointed lawyer, like Perhacs, your case always seemed to be delayed, trial dates moved back, hearings postponed. Some guys who came in after me had already been tried and gone up to death row in Holman, and others were given life sentences. Hardly anyone was found innocent. The van for death row came on Mondays and Thursdays, so I figured it would be the following Monday before I left. I wanted to talk to my mom and Lester. I hadn't been able to use the phone since my sentencing, and I wanted to make sure my mom was okay and tell her I was okay so she didn't worry.

I wasn't okay, though. For the thirty-six hours since I left that courtroom, I had been replaying every word of the trial and sentencing in my head. I hadn't slept, and I hadn't eaten, and I hadn't talked to anybody. Perhacs had told the judge and prosecutors that he had gotten a call at his office and at his home from a guy saying he was the real killer, and nobody had tracked that down. We had a discussion about it with the jury out of the room, but nobody cared. Nobody had hunted that man down. McGregor had told the jury that I killed those people because I knew if I got caught, I would get life without parole because of my earlier trouble with the car theft. I wasn't evil. I wasn't a cold-blooded killer. I wasn't any of the things he made me out to be, and every time I thought of him, I felt this boiling black hatred start to rise. Why had he picked me to railroad? How was he sleeping tonight? I thought about him high-fiving the other DAs, maybe the judge, maybe my own attorney—"We got another nigger off the street, boys, and sent to die!" Were they all in on it? How did they get people to lie for them? The bailiffs lied. Reggie lied. Clark Hayes, a grocery clerk I didn't even know, had lied when he said he saw me following Smotherman around Food World. The State's firearms experts, Higgins and Yates, lied or they just plain got it wrong—there was no way those bullets matched my mom's gun. I thought about poor Payne—he was destroyed on that stand, humiliated, mocked, and made to look like a liar himself. Around and around and around, the scenes from the trial played out in my head. Why hadn't Perhacs put up my mom and Lester and my neighbor and the people from my church to tell the jury who I was and what I was about? He just let the jury sentence me to death without any discussion or testimony. I didn't understand. I hoped Perhacs did better with my appeal—I was innocent—and I know he knew it. The lie detector test proved it. Maybe Lester and my mom could come visit before they came for me, and we could plan what lay ahead. I couldn't think too much about death row yet—I couldn't even wrap my brain around what that was going to be like. I wanted to go home. I wanted to cut my mom's grass and sit with her outside at sunset. I wanted to take her fishing. God, why didn't I go fishing with her more when she loved it so much? How was she going to get around? Who was going to help her keep up the house? Lester would, but it wasn't the same. I wanted to do it; it was my job. I missed Sylvia. I missed her sweet kisses and her skin that smelled like spring flowers after the rain. I hadn't smelled anything good in a year and a half. Only the sweat of men forced to wear the same clothes for weeks at a time. I wanted to feel the rain on my neck, the sun on my face. I wanted to take a walk at sunrise. I wanted to play baseball and basketball. I wanted to drink sweet tea and eat my mom's grits, and, Lord, I wanted some of her cobbler. I hadn't had real food in so long. I wanted my simple life back. I wanted my own bed and a hot shower and a pillow so soft I could sink my face into it. I wanted to feel carpet under my feet, and grass, and anything soft. God, how I missed soft things; sweet-smelling, soft things. I wanted to drive. I wanted to get in my little car and drive to all the places I used to imagine driving to. I wanted to see somewhere other than Alabama. I had never been anywhere more than a few hours away from home. I wanted to see the West Coast, and go to Hawaii, and visit England, and travel to South America. I wanted to get married and have children and show them the same kind of love I had as a kid. I wanted to go back to being able to laugh and joke with people. I wanted my life back. I wanted Praco. I wanted my freedom back. I didn't want to be locked up like some rabid animal in a cage. I didn't want to be told what to eat and when to eat it. I didn't want people watching me shower and watching me shit. I wanted my dignity. I wanted my freedom. I wanted to cut the fucking grass in my own backyard without the police showing up to haul me away. I wanted justice.

I wanted to kill McGregor.

The knowledge hit me like a sucker punch to my gut and brought me out of my swirling thoughts. It scared me. This wanting to kill. I wanted to murder him the way he had murdered my life. I wasn't a murderer, but I knew if he walked into my cell I could wrap my hands around his neck and enjoy watching the life leave his staring, lying eyes. I imagined it. I held my hands in the air in the night and imagined his neck between my fingers. What would he say? Would he cry and beg for his life the way he had wanted me to cry and beg for mine? Would he confess his lies, his sins, and beg for a mercy that he didn't have?

I could feel his neck in my hands, and in the dark, I began to squeeze so hard that I could feel his bones crunch and snap against my skin. I pressed harder until his eyes bulged and his tongue rolled out of his mouth and he turned blue. I squeezed and squeezed and squeezed until every last breath from his lying, hateful, racist body was gone. I squeezed until he no longer struggled. I squeezed so he could never hurt another person again. I squeezed until every last lie he had in him died with him.

I hadn't come into this jail a murderer, but if that's what they said I was, that's who I would be.

"Hinton, all the way! Hinton, all the way!"

The intercom jolted me upright, and I swung around to put my feet on the floor. I heard the automatic lock click on my cell door as it opened. *All the way* meant to pack everything up. I couldn't believe they were taking me so soon. It had to be around 4:00 A.M. I wasn't ready to go to Holman. I hadn't talked to my mom. The intercom blared again.

"Hinton, all the way! Get a move on!"

I packed up some legal papers and a few pictures. I didn't know what else I could take, so I left my commissary behind for whoever wanted it. When the other guys woke up, they would be all over my cell like vultures to take whatever I had left behind. Let them have it. Let them have all of it.

"Let's go, Hinton."

I walked through the dayroom and stood at the outside door with my stuff. I was supposed to roll up my mattress and bring my sheet and blanket, but I just left it there. I wasn't going to follow the rules anymore. I had done that, and look where it had gotten me. I was the worst of the worst, so maybe it was time I started acting like it.

They put me in a holding cell and gave me a breakfast of congealed eggs and a hard biscuit and jelly. I put the food in my mouth, but it had no taste. How was it possible to take away all the taste in food? I was strip-searched, made to bend over and spread my ass cheeks while the guards laughed and joked. They wrapped extra-heavy chains around my waist and attached them to the metal cuffs on my wrists and ankles. I could barely walk, and I wondered who had sat around and said to himself, *I should invent something that will chain a man like an animal and make those chains so heavy he can't hold up his arms or move his legs.* I wondered who that bastard was, because I had a hatred for him as well. The guards who walked me out to the van tried to chitchat with me, but I said nothing. They looked uneasy. I had been nice to them since I'd been there, and cooperative. But no more. Why should I make their jobs any easier? I let myself go limp when they tried to hoist me up the first step of the van. I weighed over two hundred pounds. Let them lift me. Let them feel the weight of me as they carted me off to my death. I was somebody. I was a person. Let them feel it.

Their struggling brought me no joy, so eventually I climbed into the van and inched my way across the back seat. I didn't say a word. I wasn't going to speak to them or to anyone ever again. When no one believes a word you say, the best thing to do is stop talking.

We rode for over three hours. I had never been this far south before. It felt like we were driving to the end of the world. They didn't let me call anyone before I left, I guess so I couldn't plan an escape. I wanted to say goodbye to my mom and to Lester. I hated them even more for not giving me that chance. Two guards sat up front, and there was a mesh cage separating us. The windows had wire mesh over them as well, but I could see out. The guards were joking and laughing up front, and I watched the countryside I loved pass by me. Would I ever feel grass again? I always said this was God's country, but where was God now? I was chained and shackled like a slave being taken to auction. I was cargo. I was less than human. I thought of my mom always reacting to good news in our neighborhood by saying, "God blessed this family. God did this for our neighbor. Praise be to God for looking out for that family." If God blessed people, then did he also punish people? I wanted to know why God was punishing me. Why had God blessed that person but put me in the back of a van, wrapped in chains? What did I ever do to God?

I imagined the van crashing and rolling over and over again so that my chains came off and I could climb out of the van. I would run and run and run until there was no death penalty and I wasn't a condemned man. I would keep running until I was out of Alabama and in some place where freedom was real and my life couldn't be taken away from me.

I spent another hour just staring out the window. It had been a long time since I'd seen cars and people and open road and open sky. I tried to capture pictures. There was a little boy looking bored in the back seat of a station wagon. There was a pretty girl driving a blue car. There was a restaurant with a Closed sign. There was a family laughing in that car. There was a flash of leg on a woman with a short skirt in the passenger side of that red car. There was a whole world out there enjoying a Wednesday morning, without fear. They were free to do what they wanted, and I wondered if they understood what that meant. I saw a black man, about my age, drive by in a Buick. "Watch out," I murmured out loud. "They're going to come for you too."

"Hey!" I yelled up to the guards.

"What?"

"I have to go to the bathroom."

One of the guards mumbled something I couldn't understand, and the other guy laughed.

Eventually, we pulled into a store with a gas station out front. We parked around the side, and one guard took me into the bathroom while the other went and filled up with gas. I could see some black kids outside the store staring at me like I was a strange animal in the zoo. Let them stare. Let them see what a black man looks like chained from head to toe. Let them remember.

We pulled up to Holman Prison, and I saw inmates outside the building. A tall wire fence separated them from the parking lot outside the fence and the road beyond that. Two guards opened a big gate for us, and we drove through. They brought me in through a heavy door and took the chains off but cuffed my hands.

"He's all yours," the county guard said and turned me over to a corrections officer. He was a short, squat man with long sideburns and a comb-over. They sat me down in a chair and asked me for my name. I said nothing.

"What's your social?"

I just shrugged.

The guard read it off a paper. "Is that your social?"

I nodded. I wasn't going to talk to them. I wasn't going to make this easy.

"We're gonna send you to the infirmary to get checked out, and then you'll get a real physical at another time. You gonna put these whites on, and then you'll be escorted to your cell."

I didn't say a word.

I changed into a white prison jumpsuit that said *Alabama Department of Corrections* on the back. I was given my inmate number—Z468. The infirmary weighed me. Asked me if I took any medication. Asked me if I was on drugs. If I had any medical problems they needed to know about. I shook my head to everything they asked but still didn't speak.

After medical, I was brought down a hall. There were some other inmates in the hall, but they were told to turn and face the wall with their noses on it. I could feel the tension in the guards when we passed the other inmates. I couldn't understand why they did this, but then I saw one of the guys look up at me from the wall, and I saw fear in his eyes.

The guard started yelling at the other inmate. "Don't look at him! You can't look at him! On your knees! On your knees, hands behind your back, nose against the wall! All of you!"

I had no idea what was going on or why the guard reacted that way. The guy was about my age, white, and I realized they all thought I might attack. The regular inmates were being protected from the death row inmate. I was the scariest person in that prison.

I was taken to another guard—the captain of the guards. He told me he was in charge of death row.

"I didn't ask for you to come here, and I have but one job, and that's to keep you here. As long as you are at Holman Prison, you are going to see these blue uniforms and you are going to respect them. You will abide by the rules and regulations and do anything these blue uniforms tell you to do. Is that clear?"

I nodded.

"Now, you can make it easy on yourself or you can make it hard on yourself. However you decide to do it. You are on ninety-day probation. You will be cuffed at all times when you are out of your cell. If we get no trouble, you can have the cuffs off when you shower and when you walk. You walk fifteen minutes a day in a cage on the yard. The rest of the time, you are in your cell. We don't want no trouble. Okay?"

I kept my eyes down and nodded again.

"Sergeant, take him to his cell."

We walked down a long hall and through a doorway that said *Death Row* at the top. We walked up a flight of stairs, and the guard started yelling out row numbers. Finally he stopped in front of cell number 8.

"Number 8!" he yelled.

I heard a voice call the number back, and then there was a loud clank and the door opened. Inside was a small, narrow bunk with a thin plastic mattress. Another guard walked in and put a sheet, blanket, towel, and washcloth on the bed. He also set down a brown bag of my stuff from county. It had my Bible and some letters and legal papers from my trial. I could hear guys yelling, and I saw some mirrors sticking out of the other cells so the inmates could see what was going on, who the guards were bringing in. From somewhere far off, I could hear a man screaming. Another man was laughing. Another one just kept saying, "Hey! Hey! Hey!" over and over again.

I walked into the cell, and the guards stepped out.

"When we close the door, stick your hands out through here and we'll take off the cuffs." I didn't say anything, and the guard looked at me like maybe I was stupid. "It's too late for you to order a Christmas package this year, but maybe next year."

Christmas? The last thing I was thinking about was Christmas. I didn't want to order a Christmas package, and I didn't want to celebrate Jesus's birthday.

The door slammed shut, and the sounds began to echo in my head. My mouth tasted like metal, and I wondered if I was going to throw up. I could feel my stomach doing flips, and my knees began to shake. I stuck my hands through the small slot so the guards could take off my cuffs. I flexed my wrists and turned back around to face my cell. It was five feet wide and about seven feet long. A metal toilet with a sink on top, and a shelf and the bed. That was it.

I sat down on the edge of the bed and looked in the bag of my stuff. I pulled out the King James Bible.

There was no God for me anymore. My God had forsaken me. My God was a punishing God. My God had failed and left me to die. I had no use for God. *Forgive me, Mama,* I thought to myself as I threw the Bible under the bed. I had no use for it. All of it was a lie.

I didn't bother making my bed. I just lay down and closed my eyes. I didn't get up when they tried to pass dinner through the slot in my door. I wasn't going to talk to anyone or take anything from anyone.

I was completely alone.

I was full of a hate too big for that little cell.

I would find a way to escape, and I would find a way to put right all that had been made wrong. I would prove my innocence. I would get my revenge.

I lay there for hours and I must have drifted off, because when I woke up, it was dark except for a light coming from outside my cell.

The only other sound was someone on death row screaming out in the darkness.

"No, no, no, no, *noooo*!"

I pressed my pillow against my ears, but the screaming never stopped.

9

ON APPEAL

Representation of a death row prisoner is unlike any other kind of case because the client's life literally depends on counsel's effort. A capital case demands and deserves from an attorney, and others working on the case, his or her most careful, conscientious and committed effort.

—*ALABAMA CAPITAL POSTCONVICTION MANUAL,* 4TH EDITION

There is no *Welcome to Your Appeal* brochure that you get after you are condemned. Nobody sits you down and explains what you have to file and how much time you have to file it. You are guaranteed a direct appeal to the State appellate courts—the Court of Criminal Appeals and the Alabama Supreme Court—but that's really it. The State of Alabama does not want to make it easy on you, and they offer zero assistance to death row inmates. Unfairly convicted? Prejudiced at trial? Confession coerced? Constitutional rights violated? Your attorney sucked? Good luck with that. There is no postconviction help once you are condemned. You are on your own, and the State does everything it can to make it difficult—a one-year statute of limitations, attorneys general who create the laws that control the process and keep federal reviews from happening later, and a host of other obscure procedures and rules that seem to prevent you from revisiting anything once a court has ruled on it. And in Alabama, judges are elected based on how many people they send to death row, not on how many people they let off.

I called Perhacs's office whenever I could, and his secretary assured me he was working on my appeal and promised to give him the message I had called. Every week it seemed like I would read about another robbery in Birmingham that fit the same description as Quincy's, Mrs. Winner's, and Captain D's. The Cooler Killer hadn't slowed down at all, and the times when there was a suspect description, it was the same as Smotherman's—black male, five foot eleven, 180 pounds. It hadn't mattered that I was six foot two and 230 pounds, and it didn't matter that I was locked up and the same crimes kept happening. I thought about the victims' families. Were they reading the paper? Were they seeing the similarities? Did they ever wonder if the State had convicted the wrong man? I sent Perhacs a note along with every crime report I found in the paper. "Just trying to help," I wrote. "Thank you so much!"

I wondered if it ever kept him awake at night. What was it like for him knowing I was innocent and sleeping on death row? Did he feel anything? I didn't know at the time that my mom had started writing Perhacs letters, pleading and begging for him to save my life. Asking him to protect her boy. She wasn't happy with what was said about me in court. I was her baby, and listening to the lies had been a strain on her. Our neighbor Miss Wesley Mae brought my mom to see me at Holman after my ninety-day probation was over and I was allowed a visit. These two old ladies had never driven so far, alone, and had gotten lost trying to find their way to Atmore. They showed up on a Friday night, two hours after visiting time was over—but the warden had some sympathy for them in their Sunday best making their way to the prison, so he let me have a visit for about twenty minutes.

I hugged my mom as long as I could—another thing that wasn't usually allowed. She smelled like laundry soap and rose water, but she looked tired. There were dark circles under her eyes, and I could see new lines around her mouth that weren't there a few months ago. "God will fix this," she kept saying. "God can do everything but fail, baby. God is going to fix this right up for you."

"Yes, Mama," I said, and I could see one of the guards look surprised at hearing me speak. I didn't have the heart to tell her that I was done with God. God didn't live in this place. If there was a God and he thought it was okay to send me to hell while I was still alive, well, then, he wasn't my God. Not anymore. Not ever again.

"You come with Lester next time. I don't want you two driving all this way alone. You got that?"

"You okay, baby?" My mom reached her hand out and touched my cheek.

She wasn't the only one with new lines on her face and circles under her eyes. I could see her eyes fill with tears.

"I'm okay, Mama. Don't you be worrying about me. This place is fine. They are treating me real fine." I knew it was wrong to lie to her, but I believe that lies told to ease pain or protect someone's heart are lies that need to be told. She already had to live apart from me. If Alabama had its way, she was going to have to live through them putting me to death. I was going to comfort her every single moment that I could, even if it meant telling a million lies. "Now, we only have a few minutes. Don't spend them crying. I'm just fine, but I could use some of your cooking. I could use a nice, juicy hamburger right now."

My mama laughed, and I tried to memorize that sound in my mind. I wanted to hang on to that laugh and hear it in my head instead of the endless moaning I heard all day every day on the row.

"Your attorney sent me a couple of letters. He's going to get you out of here. He's working real hard."

She carefully unfolded two letters she had brought in. They were addressed to her. I hadn't heard from Perhacs yet, but when I called his office, his secretary said that he had filed a motion for a new trial.

I looked at the first letter. It was dated a few weeks before my sentencing.

"Mama, this first letter is from before I came here."

"Well, I been writing him so he know who you are. I wanted to tell him that what they said at your trial was a lie. They lied on your name. My son is no killer." She dabbed at her eyes with a white handkerchief.

"It's okay. It's okay." I patted her hand. "Let me have a look." The letter had *Law Office of Sheldon Perhacs* at the top and my mom's address below.

November 25, 1986

Re:

Dear Ms. Hinton:

Thank you for your letter dated November 17, 1986. I want you to know that I will continue to do everything I know how to do to protect your son. His case is going to be appealed, and I think I'm going to win the appeal. The appeal will probably take a couple of years. After that, we will probably have to try his case again. The next time we try it, we will do some things differently. I still think he has a good opportunity to be acquitted of these charges.

I will continue to do everything I know how to do.

Sincerely,
Sheldon Perhacs

I didn't want to sit on death row for a couple of years. I wanted him to get me out now, but there was nothing I could do. He would do some things differently next time? How about getting me an expert with two eyes? I still cringed when I thought about my expert getting crucified on the stand. Would they give us more money for a better expert if they tried me again? It seemed like if you were poor, you were as good as guilty. I picked up the second letter. It was dated just a month ago.

March 2, 1987

Re: Your Son

Dear Ms. Hinton:

I intend to continue to do everything I know how to do to protect your son. The case is in the process of being appealed. The appeal will take quite some time to complete. It is my opinion that we have a good opportunity to win this case on appeal. If we do, we will have a new trial. At the new trial I am going to hire another expert to testify about the bullets.

I also believe that your son is not guilty of killing anyone. I will continue to do everything I know how to do to protect him. I'm sorry that I missed your call when you called the other day, and I am certainly glad that you wrote to me to tell me about it. Please feel free to continue to contact me whenever you need to.

Sincerely,
Sheldon Perhacs

My heart broke at what I read between the lines of his letters—my mom calling him and writing him and asking him to protect me. What I didn't know at the time was that she was also sending him money orders for twenty-five dollars every time she wrote, pleading and begging him for help. *Here is all my money—save my son.* Did he laugh at those little money orders? Twenty-five dollars was nothing to a man who ate a thousand dollars for breakfast. But twenty-five dollars might as well have been a hundred thousand to my mom. Perhacs didn't know what it meant to be poor. To have just enough to make it through a month without a penny to spare. An extra ten dollars needed for an emergency would mean you had no water or no electricity for a month, or maybe even longer than a month, because you had to pay a reconnect fee to turn it back on. I know why my mom never told me about the money—I would have put an end to it, never understanding that she needed to send that money, because she needed the comfort of knowing she was doing everything she could to save her son's life. I would have taken that comfort from her.

I knew my mom felt helpless.

We all felt helpless.

And at the time, I didn't want to think my attorney would take advantage of that helplessness. I couldn't think about that. He was my only chance. I didn't tell my mom that he had told me he would handle my automatic appeal and then he was off my case. It was as if he was already planning to lose. I was hoping he would have a change of heart. I was hoping the man who called him during my trial and said he was the killer would call him again. I was hoping for a miracle but planning my escape.

I hugged my mom and Miss Mae goodbye. My mom promised to come with Lester next time, and I think Miss Mae was relieved. Visiting days were every Friday at first, and then they were changed to once a month for death row visits. No weekend visits for us; they didn't want to make it easy on our families and friends. Lester had to take the day off work, but as soon as he was allowed, he made the seven-hour round-trip drive every Friday. Sometimes he worked the night shift on Thursday and still drove all day Friday. I used to worry about him falling asleep at the wheel, but he was always the first one at the prison waiting to get in. He brought his mom and my mom, and the three of them were the only bit of light in the darkness.

I don't remember those early visits too well, because I was so full of hatred and rage that it was all I could do to smile and chitchat. If they noticed something wrong, they never said, but every once in a while, I could see Lester watching me. He knew me better than anyone, but I don't think he could have known what I was thinking. I had never felt such a darkness in me. I couldn't control my thoughts. Every hour of every day, I imagined how I would kill McGregor. My days and nights were spent watching. And listening. Even at visiting hours, I was memorizing the routines of the guards. There had to be a way out. A moment where I could sneak over a fence, hide in the back of a car, take off running. It wasn't logical, and I didn't have a plan—but I watched and I waited because there had to be a way to escape. There just had to be.

Wouldn't it be better if they killed me while I was trying to escape rather than killing me strapped to a chair? The only hesitation I had was that I didn't want people to think I had run because I was guilty. I wanted to prove my innocence more than anything else. I wasn't a killer, but I wanted to kill. Inside, I was becoming the monster the world thought I was, and I was afraid Lester and my mom would see it, so I lied to them about how things were. *The food is fine. The guards are nice. The other inmates are quiet and keep to themselves.* I lied to them every week. *I'm sleeping just fine. I have everything I need.* I lied and I lied and then I lied some more.

The reality was we had to eat breakfast at 3:00 A.M., lunch at 10:00 A.M., and dinner at 2:00 P.M. And every night, I was hungry. Every day, I was hungry. I weighed 220 pounds when I got there. I had lost ten pounds at county, but I could see losing a lot more than I wanted here. Breakfast was some powdered eggs, a biscuit so hard you could bounce it off the floor, and a little spoonful of what was supposed to be jelly. They had a whole prison to feed, so the death row inmates had to eat early in the morning. At 2:45 A.M., the guards would start screaming, "Breakfast! Breakfast! Breakfast!" If I was lucky enough to have fallen asleep, I would bolt upright in the dark, thinking I was under attack. Lunch was some bland patty of an unknown meat substance. I heard it was horsemeat, but I hoped that was just a bad joke. Dinner was the same formless patty, but at night, it was called a cutlet. On Fridays, there was a soggy fish cutlet. There were canned beans or peas or some other vegetable in a watery liquid that smelled slightly of tin and mold and tasted metallic and bitter. Instant mashed potatoes that would turn into a dry powder in your mouth. I was hungry every day. It was a physical hunger, yes, but it was also a mental hunger. I felt empty and hollow. I hungered for home, for my own bed and my family and my church, and for friends I could laugh with and sit with. I was alone all day with a hunger so big it felt like I was falling with nothing to grab on to. Like when you lean back in a chair and have that moment of panic where you've gone too far and you have to jerk yourself upright so you flail about to try to save yourself. I had that panic of falling all day every day. I was hungry for my freedom. I was hungry for my dignity. I was hungry to be a human again. I didn't want to be known as inmate Z468. I was Anthony Ray Hinton. People called me Ray. I used to love to laugh. I had a name and a life and a home, and I wanted it so bad, the wanting had a taste. I wasn't going to survive here. I felt like eventually I would hollow out so completely, I would just disappear into a kind of nothingness. They were all trying to kill me, and I was going to escape. I had no other choice.

Perhacs's motion for a new trial was postponed for over six months, until finally, on July 31, 1987, it was denied. It was exactly two years to the day that I got arrested.

In Alabama, at that time, you had forty-two days to file a notice of appeal and another twenty-eight days to file a brief. Did I find this out because Perhacs came to death row to visit with me and talk about a strategy for my appeal? No. I found this out by listening to the other death row inmates talking about their appeals.

It was like a legal class going on all day long, and while I still wasn't speaking, I did listen to the other inmates talking to each other.

"Man, you got to call Bryan Stevenson. He'll get you a lawyer in here."

"Bryan Stevenson sent my lawyer from up in Ohio. And another guy came from D.C."

"You have to tell him to read your transcript and see if they prejudiced the jury."

"Tell him about the guy who lied."

It went on all day, and I could hear the other inmates arguing case law with each other and talking about their appeals. I learned that Alabama had just started electrocuting people again in 1983 after taking a break for eighteen years. Now people were afraid they were going to start giving out dates to everyone who had been there a minute and who didn't have an attorney trying to stop the State.

"He's got a bunch of lawyers helping him out. A whole resource center."

"I heard he's watching every single person on the row—tracking everybody. He's like Santa Claus, and he's gonna know if you are naughty or nice."

All day long I heard the name *Bryan Stevenson,* but I didn't care about Bryan Stevenson. I cared about Perhacs and what he was doing for my case. I had an attorney, and for that, I was grateful. It sounded like a lot of the guys were waiting for one to magically show up from the good graces of this one attorney named Stevenson. I didn't believe in God, and I didn't believe in Santa Claus. And I didn't ask any questions, because one thing I had learned from my trial was that if you said anything, people would lie about it if it helped their cases out. I didn't trust the other inmates. I didn't trust the guards. I didn't even trust Perhacs, but he was better than nothing. If I had to ask the guards for something, I wrote it down on the inmate stationery and handed it to them. I don't know if they thought I was dumb or what, but they knew I spoke when I had my visits. I think they were happy I didn't speak—it was one less inmate they had to deal with.

The guards brought me to the shower every other day, sometimes at 6:00 P.M. Other times it would be at midnight. There was no schedule. A guard walked in front of me, and a guard walked behind me. My hands were cuffed for the first three months, and after that I could go to the shower without being cuffed. There was no privacy in the shower, and there were always two guys showering at once and two guards watching. The water would be scalding hot or icy cold—it just depended on the day, or maybe what the guards felt like doing to entertain themselves. You had to soap up and get out fast, in under two minutes. The guards watched us the whole time—even the female guards. There was no pleasure in a female seeing me naked. It was humiliating. We were like farm animals being hosed off outside the barn. Once a day, we were brought out to individual cages in the yard that we could exercise in, or pace back and forth. Nobody had to "walk" as the guards called it, and a lot of guys just stayed in their cells. They didn't want to change or shower or exercise. I always took my fifteen or twenty minutes outside. I was looking for an escape. I could see the prison parking lot from my cage on the yard and the road that led away from Holman. I just needed to get to it. Every moment of every day, I was watching for a weakness in the system—despite what the prosecutors had said, I couldn't scale a fifteen-foot razor-wire fence. And certainly not one with guards and guns trained on it. I thought about digging a tunnel. There were rats and roaches that crawled in and out of my cell through a little vent near the ceiling. If they could get in, I thought, then I should be able to get out. I stared at that vent every day. There was always something lurking there—always an antenna or a whisker peeking through. Every night, I could hear the rats scratching and scurrying across the floors. I imagined the roaches swarming the walls at night and hiding back in the vent during the day to watch me. I was the trapped insect. Those roaches had more freedom than I did. The sounds at night were like being in the middle of a horror movie—creatures crawling around, men moaning or screaming or crying. Everyone cried at night. One person would stop and another would start. It was the only time you could cry anonymously. I blocked out the sound. I didn't care about anyone's tears or their screams. Sometimes there was laughter—maniacal laughter—and that was the most frightening. There was no real laughter on death row. Those that could sleep yelled out in their dreams, as if they were being chased. Sometimes they cursed. I don't think I slept more than fifteen minutes at a stretch ever in those first months and years. It makes you crazy to never sleep. It makes you go to a place where there is no light, and no hope, and no dreams, and no chance for redemption. It makes you think of shadows and demons and death and revenge and of killing before you can be killed.

There was death and ghosts everywhere. The row was haunted by the men who died in the electric chair. It was haunted by the men who chose to kill themselves rather than be killed. Their blood flowed in the cement cracks of the floors like a slow river, until it dried and then split apart under the weight of the creatures that crept over it in the night. The roaches had blood on them, and they carried it from cell to cell. The rats nibbled at the dried blood and carried it back into the walls and vents where it blew around in the air like darkened dust and settled over us all. It was hard to hang yourself in death row but easy to bash your own head open against the cement wall, over and over again, until it splattered the cell red and your pulpy flesh filled in the cracks and divots like spackle and hardened into a stain that would never come clean. The row was haunted by remorse and regret and the deaths of all who had died at the hands of the guilty, and of all those who had not died at the hands of the innocent but wanted justice and for their killers to be found. Freedom was a ghost that haunted us all on the row, but most of all we were haunted by a past we could not go back and change. Loss and grief and a cold madness that defied words floated in the grime and filth that we were all coated in. Hell was real, and it had an address and a name.

Death Row, Holman Prison.

Where love and hope went to die.

In 1988, the Court of Criminal Appeals affirmed my conviction. I didn't hear from Perhacs, but I got a copy of my appeal and the court's response. There were five issues Perhacs raised in my appeal. He said Judge Garrett made an error in combining the two capital cases and not granting his motion to sever. He also said that there were two more errors when there were no test bullets entered into evidence. Finally, he said that the court never proved I was linked to the two murders, because they had no direct evidence I was there, and finally, that we should have been allowed to submit the polygraph test into evidence. The Court of Criminal Appeals disagreed with everything. Perhacs sent me a letter in April of 1989. He was appealing my case to the Alabama Supreme Court. I had been on death row for over two years.

April 11, 1989

Mr. Anthony Ray Hinton, #Z468
Holman Unit #37
Atmore, Alabama 36506
RE: Your case

Dear Anthony:

I presented oral argument for you to the Alabama Supreme Court yesterday. I got the impression that they were interested in the argument that I made, and I think we've got a pretty good opportunity to reverse your convictions to get a new trial. The court has ordered that additional briefs be filed, and that will require approximately 2 weeks. After that they will take the case for their consideration. I'm unable to tell you exactly when to expect an opinion from them, but I've got a good feeling about this case. If the convictions are overturned, then we will have to prepare to defend these cases again. We will also have to prepare to defend the Quincy's cases. I've got a number of ideas about some things that we will do that will be new to each of the cases. All of the cases continue to have very serious legal problems within them, and I expect to take advantage of every legal opportunity that is presented to us.

One of the things that I think we will have to do is hire another expert. Even though our expert was willing to help us, I don't think he was too persuasive with the jury. I thought our presentation to the jury with Mr. Payne was excellent, but he crumbled under their cross-examination. There really are a lot of other things that we can do in addition to getting a new expert.

If the Supreme Court does not order a new trial to you, then I still think that we've got an excellent opportunity to appeal this case to the United States Supreme Court. The appeal I would take to the U.S. Supreme Court is not financed or paid for by anybody. Someone in your family would have to find a way to pay some attorney's fees. Your case is so unique that I think the U.S. Supreme Court would listen to your appeal. I really think that sooner or later we are going to win these cases.

Contact me if you have any questions.

Sincerely,
Sheldon Perhacs

I read the letter at least five times. I did have a question. Why didn't he do all these "other things" the first time around? And what about my innocence? Why didn't my appeal say anything about the fact that they had the wrong guy? The U.S. Supreme Court? That was crazy. And he knew nobody in my family had any money to give him. I had to hope that the Alabama Supreme Court ruled soon and ordered a new trial. I still hadn't found a way to escape, and I still wasn't ready to take my own life.

I wanted to prove I was innocent.

But I didn't know how much more I could take. I had to get out of this place.

One way or another.

| 10 |

THE DEATH SQUAD

I may not be here, but you remember these words. God is going to show you that I didn't do it.

—ANTHONY RAY HINTON

I didn't even realize they had executed Wayne Ritter until I smelled his burned flesh. I didn't know Wayne—I didn't know anyone yet—but in the middle of the night on August 28, 1987, there was the sound of a generator kicking on and then hissing and popping, and the lights in the hall outside my cell flickered on and off. And then through the night, the smell came. It's hard to explain what death smells like, but it burned my nose and stung my throat and made my eyes water and my stomach turn over. I spent the next day dry heaving, my stomach retching and twisting. All up and down the row, you could hear men blowing their noses, trying to get the smell away. There was no real ventilation or air circulation, so the smell of death—like a mixture of shit and rotting waste and vomit all mixed up in a thick smoke of putrid air that you couldn't escape—seemed to settle into my hair and in my throat and mouth. I rubbed at my eyes until they were red and gritty. I heard one of the guys complain to a guard about the smell.

"You'll get used to it." The guard laughed. "Next year or one of these days, somebody's going to be smelling you just the same. What do you think you gonna smell like to everyone? Not too good."

The guard laughed again, and I felt my stomach turn over and heave as I ran to the toilet. I was swallowing Wayne Ritter every time I took a breath, and the nightmare that was death row only got worse.

I wanted to ask how long he had been there. Did they kill people every week? Every month? I wanted to know if Ritter knew they were killing him that day, but I still wasn't talking to anyone. I didn't know when they would come for me. Could they come kill me even though I was on appeal? If Perhacs failed, would they come take me right away—pull me from my cell in the middle of the night and strap me to a chair and electrocute me until I lost my bowels and my heart stopped and the smell of my burning flesh and fried organs drifted up and down the row to remind men of what was to come? I couldn't stop my mind from racing and imagining what it would feel like to be sitting in that chair, and the fear, like a ton of bricks, crushed my chest until I thought I would stop breathing. Everything in me was fighting to run, but there was nowhere to go. It was like when you have a dream where you open your mouth to scream but no sound comes out and you stand there, mouth open and helpless, as danger descends. I wondered if I could get a gun from a guard on my way to the shower and then shoot my way out. Would that be a better way to die than in that yellow chair with nothing but my smell to remember me by?

I spent months thinking about Ritter. I wondered if he had cried or pleaded for his life. I wondered if he had been guilty or innocent. I had never thought about the death penalty too much before being on death row. It was never in my world as something to think about. At trial, McGregor had asked me what I thought the appropriate sentence would be for someone who did what I was accused of doing, and I had said the death penalty would be appropriate. But was it? Who was I to say who was worthy of life or death? How could I or anyone know if someone was guilty or innocent? What happened to Ritter seemed like murder to me, and how was it okay to murder someone for murdering someone? I heard some guys say that after an execution, the cause of death listed on the death certificate was homicide. I didn't know if this was true or not. How could it be true? The thoughts swirled in my head all day and all night—and I waited to see who the guards would come for next.

They started practicing a couple of months before the next execution. They called themselves the Execution Team, but everyone knew what they really were—the Death Squad. The Death Squad would line up, twelve of them in all, and march solemnly down the row. One guard would pretend to be the inmate, and the other would lead him to the holding cell that you stayed in before being executed. The death chamber was only about thirty feet or so from my cell. I was upstairs or 8U as they called it—which stood for Eight Side Up. There was a guy a little younger than I was in the cell below. I had never talked to him, but I knew his name was Michael Lindsey, and I knew he was the next to be executed.

In the month leading up to his execution, he cried every day. He cried on the yard. I had never heard anyone cry like that before, but I remained silent. He cried as the Death Squad practiced marching in front of his cell, and he cried as they went into the death chamber and turned the generator on to test Yellow Mama. He cried as the lights flickered, and he cried at night when the lights went out. The guards practiced their ritual for killing him, and then they would ask him how he was doing and did he need anything—as if they weren't rehearsing his murder. It was gruesome to watch, and it only made Michael Lindsey's terror grow. On the Monday before his execution, you could hear him begging and pleading with a guy named Jesse who had just started something called Project Hope to fight the death penalty from within Holman. Jesse had no power. He was on death row too. But Michael Lindsey begged him to save his life. It was heartbreaking and painful.

In the days leading up to your execution, you were allowed to have visitors all day each day. You were allowed to hug them and hold their hands—things you weren't allowed to do on regular visits. In nearly eight years on death row, Michael Lindsey never had a visitor. He was twenty-eight years old when the Death Squad came for him in May of 1989. He had been convicted of murdering a woman and stealing her Christmas presents. I thought about him crying and begging someone to save his life in those last days—and what it felt like for him to know there was nobody to save him, and the guards who were suddenly being so nice to him were going to be the same people who strapped him to the electric chair, shaved his head, and put a black bag over his face so nobody who was there to enjoy his execution could actually see the horror in his eyes. He was only five years younger than I was. He was healthy. A jury had recommended life in prison, but his judge had overruled that jury recommendation and sentenced him to death. Judges could do that in Alabama. Lindsey had been on death row for almost eight years. It was hard not to do the math—every inmate did the math when someone was executed—comparing how long the person killed had been there compared to how long you had been there. I learned that they gave you an execution date around a month before you were executed. A month to feel terror. A month to beg and plead for your life. I didn't want to know. I didn't want to spend my last month on this earth crying and begging for my life. I didn't want to count down to my death. It was hard not to know when the Death Squad would come for you, but I think it was even harder for the guys who knew.

Michael Lindsey had no last words. On Thursday night when they took him to the death chamber, I could hear him crying. We all could. He had no visitors in the days and hours before his death. He was completely alone. Shortly before midnight, when we knew he was being strapped into that chair, we began to make some noise. Up and down the row, men began banging on the bars and doors of their cells. I heard some men yell, "Murderers!" to the guards. We made a noise like I had never heard before. Some men screamed. Others called out Michael's name. Others just roared and growled like feral animals. I made a fist, and I slammed it against the door of my cell as loud and as long as I could—until my hand was red and raw. The noise was intense, and you could hear guys yelling from general population as well. I didn't know Michael Lindsey, but I wanted him to know he wasn't alone. I wanted him to know that I saw him and knew him and his life meant something and so did his death. We yelled until the lights stopped flickering and the generator that powered the electric chair turned off. I banged on the bars until the smell of Michael Lindsey's death reached me, and then I got in my bunk and I pulled the blanket over my head and I wept. I cried for a man who had to die alone, and I cried for whoever was next to die. I didn't want to see any more deaths. I didn't want to look at the guards tomorrow and wonder which one of them had done what to Michael as they brought me my food. I didn't want to live next to the death chamber, but there was nowhere to go. I would stay silent until I was set free. I started to think about what must have driven Lindsey to steal Christmas presents, and I thought about my own family. We didn't have many Christmas presents, but I never felt like I was missing anything. Christmas had always been about love and celebrating the birth of Christ and family and good food and laughter. As crowded as our home was, it was fun and freedom, and I wanted nothing more than to be a kid again living in Praco and playing ball and roaming the hills and woods with Lester. I wanted open space. I wanted the smell of fresh-cut grass. I wanted to know that somewhere, somehow, there was a place where the sun shined and death didn't come for you at midnight and put a bag over your head.

I closed my eyes and tried to sleep, but all I heard was Michael Lindsey begging somebody, anybody, to save him.

A few weeks after Lindsey was killed, another inmate, Dunkins, was given an execution date. I listened to the talk on the row. Dunkins was also twenty-eight. Everyone knew he was a bit "slow," and nobody thought he should be put to death. Alabama was making up for lost time, because another guy also got an execution date. Dunkins was going to be in July of '89, and Richardson in August. It seemed like they were planning on executing one man per month now, and the row was tense and quiet. Right after Lindsey was killed, the heat had started up, and it seemed to get worse every day. No air circulated on the row, so it felt like sitting in a sauna all day and all night. My fingers were wet and puckered like when you sit in water too long; that's how humid it was. I wanted to swim in cool water, and I was just imagining sitting in a cool stream when a guard came to my cell and opened the door.

"468!"

I just looked at him.

"468 . . . You got mail."

I didn't respond. I wasn't a number, and I wasn't going to speak to him.

"Still not speaking? You not dumb. I saw you last visit, talking and carrying on with your people."

I just looked down.

"You want this mail? It's a legal letter," he said. "You want it, you'd better say so."

I looked at the envelope in his hand. I could see *Law Offices of Sheldon Perhacs* stamped on it. This could be the answer I had been waiting on from the Alabama Supreme Court. My freedom! I could feel the hope rise up in me. Maybe they had caught the guy who did it, or maybe they were going to give me a new trial and a better expert, or maybe they had found out that I couldn't have been in two places at once, or maybe Reggie admitted to lying. I could feel the hope well up in me so big it surprised me. I smiled at the guard. I didn't mean to, but it just happened.

"Well, that's something, then. At least you're not just scowling at the ground. You got to learn to cooperate around here, and things will get easier," he said. "You'd best be getting a better attitude if you want more privileges."

I didn't want more privileges. I wanted out. I wanted to get away from people who fed you one day and killed you the next. I had to get away from the smell of death and the heat of being in a small box twenty-three hours a day. I was going to go crazy if I didn't get out of here.

I took a deep breath and held out my hand. He and I both knew he had to give me legal mail, and he wasn't allowed to read it first, either.

"Here you go." He handed me the letter. "And take a shower tonight. You stink."

I kept my head down until he went back out and closed my door. He could have just slipped the mail through the slot, but he wanted to mess with me. I sat down on the edge of the bed and held the letter up in front of my face. My hands were shaking.

June 19, 1989

Mr. Anthony Ray Hinton, #Z468
Holman Unit #37
Atmore, Alabama 36506
RE: Your appeal to the Alabama Supreme Court

Dear Anthony:

Although I have not received the opinion as of yet, my office received a phone call from the clerk of the Supreme Court on Friday afternoon. The clerk reported to our office that our appeal to obtain new trials was denied. Because the entire Supreme Court heard the appeal argument, we must now make a decision to act and to act quickly. I still believe in this appeal, and I think that the trials that you obtained were not fair. There remains another appeal that you can take. We can petition to the U.S. Supreme Court for a review. Rule 20 of the Supreme Court rules requires that a Petition for Writ of Certiorari to review the judgment of the Alabama Supreme Court be filed within 60 days after the entry of judgment. I may be able to obtain an extension for an additional 30 days for good cause. This means that an immediate decision must be made and immediate action needs to be taken.

The appointment of me as your attorney of record does not continue from this point forward. In order for you to petition the U.S. Supreme Court for a review, you will have to hire an attorney. There is no requirement that you hire me, and there is no requirement that the federal government appoint an attorney to represent you. I will be more than happy to handle the appeal of your case from this point to the U.S. Supreme Court, but my fee to do that would be $15,000.00. The conditions for the payment of the fee are difficult; it would be my requirement that the entire fee be paid immediately in order for me to begin the appellate process. Please contact your family instantly and contact me immediately with your decision about what it is you would like to do.

Sincerely,
Sheldon Perhacs

I don't think I moved for the next twenty-four hours. They came for me to take a shower, but I wouldn't respond or get up off the bed, and eventually, they gave up and moved on to the next guy. Once again, it came down to money. Was Perhacs shaking me down? Shaking down my family? Hell, I was on death row for supposedly killing people so I could steal some money—where did he think I had $15,000 hiding? I called his office and spoke to his secretary. "Can't your mom mortgage her house?" she asked. "That's what he's thinking will have to happen."

"Tell him thanks for everything," I said.

"That's it, then?" she asked.

"That's it. If he won't go on without money, then we're done. I don't have money. My family don't have money. I'm not going to let my mom mortgage her house."

I heard her sigh and say she would give Perhacs the message, and he'd get a message to the prison or come to see me to talk about it.

I knew I wouldn't see him again.

When my mom and Lester came at the end of that week to visit, I pulled Lester aside so we could talk for a minute away from our moms.

"Listen," I said. "Listen quick. Perhacs is done. My appeal is done. No matter what Perhacs says if he calls you, don't let him get to my mother. He wants her to mortgage her house, and that's just him still trying to shake us down for money. It's over."

Lester shook his head. "It can't be over. There's got to be something—"

"Listen," I interrupted him. "When they give me a date, that's it. I don't want you watching or anyone watching me die. You bring them for a visit, and then you take them to a hotel nearby to spend the night."

I could see Lester shaking his head, but there wasn't much time to talk privately, and he needed to hear this.

"When I'm gone—it will be a little after midnight, but don't wake her up; wait until morning—then you tell her, 'He's gone and he said he loves you.' "

Lester put his hands up over his face. "I can't tell her that you're gone. I can't."

"You're going to have to, and I'm sorry about that. I am." I took a deep breath. "You remind her of what she's always said: 'There's a time to live and a time to die.' You remind her. You keep saying it to her. You tell her that I love her, and that I wasn't scared, and that all of us is going to have to leave this world at some point and it was just my time. You tell her that when her time comes, I'm going to have some of her favorite food waiting, and I'll have a nice place for her to stay, and I'll be waiting."

Lester was crying and wiping at his eyes.

"You going to have to bring her own words back on her, over and over again. That's the only thing that will help her. Do you understand? You tell her what she's always said. You tell her God makes no mistakes. Everything happens for a reason. And you play that back to her over and over no matter how she be crying and carrying on. Tell her, God come got what was his, and there's a time to live and a time to die. That's what she taught me. That's what she's got to remember."

"Why do I have to do it? Can't your sisters or one of your brothers?" Lester's face had a pain in it I had never seen before, and my heart broke that I was the cause.

"You're my brother, Lester. You're the best, closest family I have. Do you see anyone else here on visiting day? Do you see a line of my sisters and brothers waiting to see me? You're the only one to do this for me, and she'll listen to you. She'll need you more than ever. Promise me you'll look after her. Promise me you'll comfort her. It's going to break her heart, but you tell her God needed me and brought me home. Tell her that we all have a season for living and a season for dying. Tell her that. Tell her it was just my time and you tell her I died with joy in my heart and I wasn't afraid, and I had God by my side."

I grabbed Lester's arm. "You lie to her, Lester. You lie to her until she's at peace, you understand?"

"I'm not going to let them kill you."

"Just promise me."

"We're going to find a way to get you out of here. I'm going to find someone else to help you. Someone besides Perhacs."

"You just keep him from Mama's house, you understand?"

Lester nodded, but he had a stubborn look about him that I recognized from when we were kids.

"There's a time for living and a time for dying," I said. "It's true."

"It ain't true today."

"It's true today, Lester. It's always true in this place."

They killed Horace Dunkins on July 14. I banged against the bars and the lights flickered and then we stopped. And then ten minutes later, the generator went back on and the lights flickered again. Human error, they called it. He had to be electrocuted twice over nineteen minutes because the guards hooked up the cables wrong. Herbert Richardson was executed a month later. He was a Vietnam veteran, a man who had served our country, and now our country saw fit to end his life. He asked to be blindfolded before he was brought in so he couldn't see the death chamber, or the people watching him, or anything. We banged on the bars for Dunkins and for Richardson, just so they both knew they weren't alone.

I found out after the execution that Richardson wasn't alone. A young attorney named Bryan Stevenson had sat with him all day and stayed with him through the end, even as he tried to get the execution stayed. I heard the other inmates talking about it. I wondered again who this guy was and what it must be like for him to have to watch his clients die.

I spent my days waiting to hear when they would come to give me my death date and my nights reliving every moment of my trial. I played things I could have said. Witnesses Perhacs could have called. Why didn't he bring up my family to tell the jury why I shouldn't be killed? Why not bring up Lester? The people from church? My neighbors? I thought about McGregor, but some of my hate had dulled to a kind of listless apathy. He was the devil, but who was I to do anything about the devil? My Bible had been under my bed for almost three years. I hadn't spoken to anyone. I hadn't gotten to know the guards or any other inmates except for what I overheard. I was completely alone. Even the miserable Perhacs was gone. I was going to die an innocent man, and nobody would know but me, Lester, and my mom.

"Hinton!" The guard yelled my name and startled me up out of the bed.

I heard the door open. Was this it? Were they giving me a death date? Taking me to the holding cell? Was it my time to be killed?

I clenched my fists. I wasn't going to willingly walk to my death. I was innocent. I didn't deserve to be electrocuted. No one did. No one deserved to die like this. We were all children of God. I wanted to reach my hand under the bed and pull out my Bible. Why had I left God? Why had I turned my back on his comfort? I needed him now. I was going to have my head shaved and a bag thrown over my face, and I wasn't going to be able to look anyone in the eyes so they could see that I faced my death an innocent man.

I stood up. It was time to fight. I would grab his gun. I would make a run for it. I wanted to die a free man. I wanted to die on my terms. My head was racing, and my heart was pounding. Adrenaline shot through my veins. I had to make my move. It was time. I couldn't be led like a lamb to slaughter. I couldn't. This was not God's will for me. This was not why I was born into this life. This was wrong, and I was going to fight my death to the end. I wanted to go home. I needed to go home. I just wanted to go home.

"Hinton! Legal visit!" The guard stood staring at me, his hand on his gun. What had he seen in my face? I had been seconds away from lunging at him.

I followed him up to the visiting area. There were no other inmates in the room. A solitary white woman, about my age, with short brown hair, sat at one of the tables.

She stood up and gave me a huge smile. Then she held out her hand for me to shake.

I just stared at her.

"Mr. Hinton, I'm Santha Sonenberg from Washington, D.C. I'm your new attorney."

I shook her hand, but I must have still looked a little skeptical or confused.

She cocked her head to the side and gave me another smile.

"Mr. Hinton, please sit down."

I sat.

"I'm going to file your writ of certiorari petition in the U.S. Supreme Court."

"I don't have any money."

She looked at me sharply. "I'm not asking you for money. No one expects you to pay any money."

"But my attorney wanted $15,000 to file this writ thing. He wanted my mom to mortgage her house. That's not going to happen. I will die first."

Santha inhaled and exhaled loudly. "Okay. Let's take it one step at a time. There's no money involved. I will file the petition, and honestly, it's not likely that the U.S. Supreme Court is going to do anything; they typically don't. The certiorari petition is basically asking the Supreme Court to review the lower court's ruling. They don't grant a review all that often. But the actual petition asking them to review is not a big deal to prepare. We're going to handle it in the time frame needed. Then we're going to investigate and do what's called a Rule 32 petition back in the circuit court in Jefferson County."

I kept staring at her. I didn't understand much of what she was saying, but she was here. She was going to investigate. She was going to file some new stuff.

"I want you to know I'm innocent. I didn't kill anyone. I hope you can believe me."

"I believe you." She took a deep breath.

"In my transcripts, you'll see that Perhacs got a phone call from someone who claimed he was the real killer. My mom got a call too. You have to find a way to trace that number. Nobody found him. He gave a fake name. We need to find him. You need to find him."

Santha nodded like she knew all about it. "We're going to investigate everything. But first I'm going to ask you a lot of questions—about your life, your family, what it was like growing up, the trial, your relationships, everything that matters. I'm going to review the trial transcript and Perhacs's records. I'm going to look at all the evidence, and we're going to see what we can do, okay? I want you to stay strong. Are you doing okay here?"

"Can they put me to death while you are investigating and we're appealing?" I held my breath.

"No, Mr. Hinton. They can't put you to death while your case is in the courts."

I put my head down on the table and took a few breaths. When I lifted my head back up, I knew I had tears in my eyes, but Santha didn't say anything about that.

"I'm going to need your help. We're going to have to work together on this. Do I have your permission to represent you?" She was staring at me intently. "Mr. Hinton, are you going to be okay?"

I smiled at her. "Yes, you have my permission, but call me Ray."

"Okay, Ray. Let's get to work."

"Just one more thing," I asked. "How did you become my attorney? Did Lester call you?"

She shook her head. "I'm sorry, I don't know who Lester is."

"How are you here?" I asked. "How did you know about me?"

Santha Sonenberg smiled at me. "Bryan Stevenson sent me. He knows about everyone."

| 11 |

WAITING TO DIE

I have no ill feeling and hold nothing against anyone.

—HERBERT RICHARDSON, LAST WORDS

The U.S. Supreme Court denied my petition on November 13, 1989. There was no opinion.

Four days later, Arthur Julius was executed.

I banged on the bars of my cell with the others until about ten minutes after midnight, and then the guards came through and angrily told us to quiet down. "He heard you," one of them said. "Everyone heard you."

Arthur Julius was convicted of raping and murdering his cousin. He had been out on a prison pass when the rape and murder happened. I didn't know what he had done when he was alive—what had been so beyond repair inside his heart that he thought it was okay to rape and to murder. I didn't know him or if he had done it or not, but I assumed he had. I was under no illusion that everyone on death row was innocent, but I also knew that not everyone was guilty. I didn't think that I was the only one who had been unjustly sent to his death by a bunch of white men, some of them wearing robes.

I knew Santha was working on my case, but I still wasn't speaking to anyone, and even though I didn't think they were going to come for me in the night and strap me to that yellow chair, I still had fear and anxiety that never went away. Apart from my visits with Lester and the moms, my time was spent lying on my bunk staring at the ceiling. It was like a black cloud had settled over me and I could find no energy to eat, talk, or even clean my cell. What was the point? I didn't want to make a home out of hell. I didn't want to make it okay that they had put me here. I couldn't stop seeing McGregor's face or hearing his words. He had called me Mr. Sneak. Mr. Robber. Mr.

Executioner. I thought about the year and a half I'd spent in jail before my trial. Every preliminary hearing before the judge during that year and a half, McGregor had just sat in that courtroom glaring at me while his cocounsel handled business. Why me? Why had he decided I was so evil he had to make it his personal mission to bend and twist the truth in ways that defied logic and common sense? I wanted to ask him. Why me? Or could it have been any black man? Every second of my arrest and my trial ran like a loop in my head. I couldn't control it. I couldn't stop it. I worried that I would go crazy before my next appeal even got started. McGregor was everything he accused me of being. He was the executioner. He was the liar and the sneak and the robber, because he had robbed me of my life. His exact words to the jury played over and over in my head. "Look at the evidence, take the time to," he had said to them, "and I'm going to ask you to find the truth. Find the truth in this case. Look at the evidence. Remember the testimony. You find the truth, and you do justice."

Those sentences played in an endless loop, like a song that just keeps starting over from the beginning. There was something in those words that seemed important to me, but lying awake in the middle of the night, with the unholy sounds of men who were as good as dead bouncing off the walls—I didn't know what it meant. McGregor deserved to die, not me. He was the guilty one. He was the murderer. He should be the one who felt afraid every time he walked to the shower, or went outside with killers, or smelled the burning flesh of dying men. He should be condemned. He was not innocent.

It had to be well after midnight when I heard the first sob. There were always men yelling and moaning and crying—every single night. But it had been strangely quiet for about twenty minutes, so when I heard the noise, it jolted me. I had gotten used to tuning out the endless sounds of pain on death row. It was just background noise and not any of my business.

But then I heard that first sob.

It was a sound low and guttural, almost more growl than cry. Then a guard walked past my cell door. I could see the silhouette of his legs from the light in the corridor. There was another sob and a catch, like someone was trying to hold it in. The sound was close to me. It had to be the guy next to me or one cell over. I couldn't tell. The sobbing got a bit louder, and I tried to tune it out, go back to McGregor and Reggie and Perhacs and Judge Garrett. They should have tried harder to find the guy who called Perhacs to say he was the killer. It was all too much work to investigate the real killer, so let's just make it so this guy did it, and we can say good night to these cases and the victims' families will feel better. Who was that guy who called in? Was he really the killer or just some weirdo who wanted to get into the action on a trial that was in all the papers? He had called my mom also, and Perhacs's home and office. It seemed like a lot of effort for a guy who wasn't serious. I'll bet he was surprised when no one seemed to care that they had the wrong guy. I'll bet he felt bad for me. I thought of him coming to the prison or going to the media—to confess and take my place on death row. He would want to save his soul. I started playing out the whole scenario in my head—the guy finding God and needing to confess and repent—maybe he would call McGregor next time or the judge . . .

"Oh my God . . . please help me. I can't take it. I just can't take it anymore."

I snapped out of my imaginings and listened to the man crying. He didn't say anything else, but the sobbing was deeper. Heavier. Did he really believe God was going to help him? There was no God in this place. There was no choice but to take it until you couldn't take it anymore or they killed you. God may sit high, but he wasn't looking low. He didn't see us here. There was no light in this dark place, so there was no God and no help and no hope.

I said all this in my head, but I couldn't drown out the sound of his crying. I tried going back to McGregor, but the man's crying was so low and deep it seemed to pound inside my chest like when someone has the bass turned way up on their stereo. It wasn't my problem. It was every man for themselves on the row, and I didn't trust anyone. I would never trust anyone again. People lied. People sold you for money. People didn't care about the truth, so I didn't care about people. The only people for me were the ones who showed up every week to visit.

I sat up out of bed and began pacing the few feet I had room to walk around in in my cage. It was steps from my toilet to my cell door.

One.

Two.

Three.

Four.

Five.

I counted them out in my head and then turned around and counted them again as I walked to the back of my cell. Then turned around again. Eventually, he would stop crying and I would go back to my bed, but I couldn't lie there while he sobbed like an animal who had his foot caught in a trap.

"God help me. Oh God. I can't take it. I can't, I can't, I can't . . ." The man was crying and moaning, and I could do nothing but count and walk and turn and count and walk and turn. Over and over again.

One.

Two.

Three.

Four.

Five.

I thought about my mom. I had called her earlier that day, and we had gotten to talk for a few minutes. She was cooking up a big dinner for Lester when I called. They were having a celebration dinner.

"What are you celebrating?" I had asked.

"Lester's getting married."

"Mama, you're crazy." I had laughed at her. If Lester was getting married, he would have told me himself. I mean unless he'd just met the girl since last week when he was here for a visit. Nobody had said anything.

"It's true," she'd said. "He's getting married to Sylvia—you know, that good girl from church whose husband died in a fire."

"Mama, you got to stop gossiping. You don't know what you're talking about." I'd laughed. It couldn't be true. Lester would have told me.

"Boy, I know what I'm talking about. Lester and Phoebe and Sylvia are coming over here tonight to have dinner. You think I'm fool enough to make a celebration dinner when there's no celebration? You're crazy." She'd laughed, and I'd changed the subject to our next visit.

"Now you try to sneak me some pie up in here. Bring some extra for the guards. Try to bribe them with some peach pie." She'd just laughed every time I'd said that. My mom would no sooner break the law than she would grow two heads. "Now, I'm going to hang up because these collect calls are expensive. I'll see you Friday. I love you."

"I love you too, baby."

I had hung up the phone and put Lester getting married out of my mind. But now, with nothing to do but pace and listen to the sorrow of another man, I had to admit it hurt. It hurt that he didn't tell me himself, but I understood why he didn't mention it. I understood why he wouldn't want to talk to me about dating and falling in love and getting married while I was stuck on death row. What really hurt was the stabbing sensation I felt at the idea that I might die before I got the chance to date again, or fall in love, or get married. I thought about my Sylvia, who I'd had to leave behind. And now Lester had a Sylvia. Lester's life was moving forward. That's what a life was meant to do. Things were supposed to change. Life was not supposed to be exactly the same every day—breakfast at 3:00, lunch at 10:00, dinner at 2:00. You weren't supposed to spend every single day in a small box doing exactly the same thing as you did the day before and that you would do tomorrow. I knew why Lester didn't tell me he was getting married—he didn't want me to think about what I was missing.

He didn't want me to hurt any more than I was already hurting.

No one can understand what freedom means until they don't have it. It's like being wrapped in a straightjacket all day every day. You can't make a choice about how to live. Oh, what I wouldn't give to have a choice to make—any choice. *I think I'll go for a walk rather than go to bed right now. I think I'll have chicken for dinner. I think I'd like to take a drive and just see where I end up.* I didn't begrudge Lester his life and his choices. I was happy for him. I wanted nothing more than for him to be happy. I would be sorry to miss the wedding and sad not to be able to stand next to him and be his best man. I had to get out of this place. I thought about the children I would never have if I didn't get off death row. I wanted a son. I wanted to play baseball with a son someday. And basketball. I wanted to take him to Auburn games so he knew there was only one team in Alabama that mattered. I wanted to show him the woods, and the river, and the quiet beauty of a night spent in the country. I wanted to show him how to fish and teach him how to drive. I wanted to show him that anything was possible in this world if you only had faith.

My breath caught, and I stopped pacing.

Faith. How could I teach anyone about faith when I didn't have it?

"Oh God. Help me, God . . ." The crying was intermittent now, and I realized I was holding my breath when it stopped and waiting for it to start again. I didn't know which was worse—the crying or the silence. Men killed themselves all the time in this prison. I went back to pacing. This wasn't any of my business.

One.

Two.

Three.

Four.

Five.

I was happy for Lester, but I would wait for him to tell me about his getting married. I didn't want to make him feel bad for making me feel bad. That's what real friendship was all about. Or any relationship, for that matter. You wanted the other person's happiness as much as, or more, than your own. Lester deserved love. Hell, everyone deserved love.

The man started crying again, and I realized that I was crying too. I sat down on the edge of the bed, and I wept silently for a man I didn't even know, who was most likely a killer, but who also wept in the dark, all alone, in a cage, in Atmore, Alabama. You didn't have to be on death row to feel all alone, and I knew there were people all over the world, at this exact moment, sitting on the edge of their beds and crying. Most days it seemed like there was more sadness than sense in the world. I sat there for a few more minutes, listening to the other man crying.

Lester had choices, and I was glad he was making them. I thought again about all the choices I didn't have and about freedom, and then the man stopped crying and there was a silence that was louder than any noise I'd ever heard. What if this man killed himself tonight and I did nothing? Wouldn't that be a choice?

I was on death row not by my own choice, but I had made the choice to spend the last three years thinking about killing McGregor and thinking about killing myself. Despair was a choice. Hatred was a choice. Anger was a choice. I still had choices, and that knowledge rocked me. I may not have had as many as Lester had, but I still had some choices. I could choose to give up or to hang on. Hope was a choice. Faith was a choice. And more than anything else, love was a choice. Compassion was a choice.

"Hey!" I walked up to my cell door and yelled toward the crying man. "Are you all right over there?"

There was nothing but silence. Maybe I was too late.

"Hey, you okay?" I asked again.

"No," he finally answered.

"Is something wrong? Do you need me to call for an officer or something?"

"No, he just left."

"Okay, then."

I stood at the bars. I didn't know what to say or what to do. It was weird to hear my own voice on the row. I only spoke during visits. I wondered if the man was as surprised as I was to hear me speak. I guess he didn't want to talk about it. I started to walk back to my bed, but then I thought about what he had been saying when he was sobbing. *Please help me. I can't take it anymore.*

I walked back up to the door. "Hey, man. Whatever it is, it's going to be all right. It's going to be okay."

I waited. It had to be another five minutes before he spoke.

"I just . . . I just got word . . . that my mom died."

I could hear him trying to hold back the tears as he talked.

I can't describe exactly what it is to have your heart break open, but in that moment, my heart broke wide open and I wasn't a convicted killer on death row; I was Anthony Ray Hinton from Praco. I was my mama's son.

"I'm sorry, man. I really am."

He didn't say anything back, and then I heard a guy yell from down below me, "Sorry for your loss." And then another from the left side of me yelled, "Sorry, man. Rest in peace." Nobody else was talking before that, but they had been listening too. How could you not hear him crying? I didn't have to think about people all around the world sitting on the edge of their beds and crying when there were almost two hundred men all around me who didn't sleep, just like me. Who were in fear just like me. Who wept just like all of us. Who felt alone and afraid and without hope.

I had a choice to reach out to these men or to stay in the dark alone. I walked over to my bed and got on my hands and knees. I reached my arm under the bed and felt around through the dust and dirt until the tips of my fingers brushed against my Bible. It had been under there for too long. This man had lost his mom, but I still had mine, and she wouldn't care for my Bible to be collecting filth. Even here, I could still be me. I walked back up to the cell door.

"Listen!" I yelled. "God may sit high, but he looks low. He's looking down here in the pit. He's sitting high, but he's looking low. You've got to believe it." I had to believe it too.

I heard an "Amen!" from somewhere on the row.

"It's a hard loss to bear. But your mom's looking down on you too."

"I know. Thanks."

I asked him to tell me about his mom and listened for the next two hours as he told story after story. His mom seemed a lot like my mom. Tough, but full of love.

He finished telling a story about her making a dress for his sister out of a tablecloth and two silk pillowcases just so she could go to a school dance in a new dress. "It was beautiful," he said. "My sister looked better than any other girl at that dance because my mom worked hard. She always found a way, man. She always found a way."

He started crying again, but softer than he had at the beginning of the night.

I wondered why it is that the cries of another human being—whether it's a baby or a woman in grief or a man in pain—can touch us in ways we don't expect. I wasn't expecting to have my heart break that night. I wasn't expecting to end three years of silence. It was a revelation to realize that I wasn't the only man on death row. I was born with the same gift from God we are all born with—the impulse to reach out and lessen the suffering of another human being. It was a gift, and we each had a choice whether to use this gift or not.

I didn't know his story or what he had done or anything about him that made him different from me—hell, I didn't know if he was black or white. But on the row, I realized, it didn't matter. When you are trying to survive, the superficial things don't matter anymore. When you are hanging at the end of your rope, does it really matter what color the hand is that reaches up to help you? What I knew was that he loved his mother just like I loved my mother. I could understand his pain.

"I'm sorry you lost your mom, but man, you got to look at this a different way. Now you have someone in heaven who's going to argue your case before God."

It was silent for a few moments, and then the most amazing thing happened. On a dark night, in what must surely be the most desolate and dehumanizing place on earth, a man laughed. A real laugh. And with that laughter, I realized that the State of Alabama could steal my future and my freedom, but they couldn't steal my soul or my humanity. And they most certainly couldn't steal my sense of humor. I missed my family. I missed Lester. But sometimes you have to make family where you find family, or you die in isolation. I wasn't ready to die. I wasn't going to make it that easy on them. I was going to find another way to do my time. Whatever time I had left.

Everything, I realized, is a choice.

And spending your days waiting to die is no way to live.

| 12 |

THE QUEEN OF ENGLAND

So that you will know exactly what my position is, I must inform you at this time that if Hinton's Rule 20 petition is not filed by the agreed-upon date, I will have no choice but to petition the Alabama Supreme Court for the setting of the execution date.

—KENNETH S. NUNNELLEY, ASSISTANT ATTORNEY GENERAL, MAY 1, 1990

Time runs differently in prison. Sometimes it passes as if in slow motion, when every hour feels like three hours, every day feels like a month, every month feels like a year, and every year feels like a decade. In regular population, time is something you count down until your release date. You cross off each day, happy to have gotten through it and thankful that you are one day closer to leaving—to freedom. On the row, it's different. The only date you would ever have to count down to is your execution date, and when you have that date, time speeds up. It runs as if someone has pressed fast-forward, and every day feels like an hour, every hour feels like a minute, and every minute feels like a second. In prison, time is a strange and fluid thing, but time on the row is even more warped.

Everyone knew there were only two ways to leave the row—on a gurney or set free by the law. I wasn't ready to leave on a gurney, so I started praying at night for my new attorney and for the truth to finally come out. I didn't pray for my release, because that wasn't enough. I wanted the truth to come out. I wanted people to know that I was innocent. I wanted McGregor to apologize. I wanted the jury to know they had gotten it wrong and for other juries to learn from their mistakes. The only way that could happen was if I was found innocent. I was also a bit suspicious. Growing up, I had heard too many stories of folks praying for things in a general way and having it turn out badly for them when it seemed like their prayers were answered in a literal way. I knew a guy in the county jail who used to pray every day to get to leave C block. Everybody knew he wasn't going to leave before his trial, but he said he was praying and he knew God was going to answer his prayers. The next day, he was caught smoking, and when they turned over his cell looking for his stash, the guards found a weapon he had made out of broken plastic off his meal tray. He did leave C block, but only to go into solitary confinement.

I said my prayers carefully. I prayed for Lester and our moms. I prayed for Lester's new wife, and I prayed for the members of our church, our neighbors, my brothers and sisters, and my nieces. I prayed for Sid Smotherman, and I prayed for the families of John Davidson and Thomas Vason. But mostly I prayed for the truth. *Truth* was a big, broad word, but I knew there was no gray area and no way to misinterpret my prayer. I prayed for God to reveal the truth—and whether that meant they proved me innocent or they caught the guy who really did it or Reggie confessed to lying, didn't matter. I knew that the truth would set me free. John 8:32: "Then you will know the truth, and the truth will set you free."

I also read Mark 11:24. "What things so ever you desire when you pray, believe that you receive them, and you shall have them." I read this over and over again, looking for a loophole. If it was true that God could do everything but fail, then the truth had to be known. The truth had to set me free. If I believed it, it would happen. It had to.

I had gotten a few letters from Santha Sonenberg, so I knew she was investigating my case. She and a woman named Laura had been calling my mom and my friends, looking into things. I spoke to Santha on the phone, and she apologized for not being able to come visit again but told me she was busy preparing my Rule 20 petition, which was a petition for relief from convictions and sentences of death. I wondered how she was going to be able to investigate things if she worked in Washington, D.C., but I didn't ask her. I was grateful she was keeping me from the electric chair. I had to pray and believe.

The assistant attorney general of Alabama, a guy named Kenneth S. Nunnelley, was now representing the State in my post-conviction appeal. Santha told me he gave her until August to file my petition, and she would be sending me a copy when she filed it. We were allowed to go to the law library once a week for an hour, and I had refused my time for the past three years, but now I went every week. We weren't allowed to bring any books back to our cells—all we were allowed were Bibles or other religious books—so for an hour every week, I would read about the law in Alabama. I learned what a capital conviction really was, and I read about aggravating and mitigating circumstances. I didn't know at the time of my trial that even though a jury said life in prison, a judge in Alabama could override the jury and still send you to the electric chair. It was called *judicial override,* and to me it just seemed like another way to put an innocent man to death.

I couldn't understand the point in having a jury if a judge could just go ahead and do whatever he wanted. How was that justice? I wondered. Why was Alabama so hell-bent on putting people to death one way or another? I got back to my cell after my law library trip. I could only read so much in an hour, and I had questions.

"Y'all heard of this judicial override business?" I yelled out.

"That's some bullshit right there."

I wasn't sure who the voice belonged to. I had just started talking to the guards, to the other inmates, so it felt a little like being the new kid at school.

Several other voices yelled out in agreement.

"It seems like it defeats the purpose of a jury if a judge can just do what he wants," I said. "As if the cards aren't stacked against you enough already."

"Preach it, brother!" another voice yelled out.

There was some laughter.

"I'm going to read up on it some more next week," I said. "Some of you should do the same."

A voice I hadn't heard earlier yelled out, "I'm here because of that judge overriding the jury. My jury said life."

"Me too," yelled another voice. "It's 'cause them judges got to get elected. That's all. They get more votes the more men they send to the death chair."

I stood at the front of my cell. It was weird to have a discussion when you couldn't see anybody and couldn't tell who was talking unless it was the guy on either side of you. I was beginning to distinguish guys from their voices. Their accents. You could tell who was a bit more educated and who wasn't, but that's about all you could tell.

"The police lied and said I took a dollar from the guy." It was the first voice again. "That's how I even got a capital case. I'm not saying what I did, or even if I did anything, but I'm just saying they lied and said I took one dollar. One dollar. That made it a capital case. And then when the jury said, 'Life,' the judge said, 'Nope . . . it's gonna be death.' "

I could hear his voice break a little, like he was choking up.

"What's your name, man?" I yelled.

He didn't answer for a few minutes, and the row got strangely quiet. Even though there were guys around him who had to know his name, it was his to tell or not to tell. You didn't speak for anyone on the row, and you didn't name names ever.

"My name's Ray," I said. "Anthony Ray Hinton, but folks call me Ray."

There was silence. I rested my left cheek up against the mesh wire of my door. I could wait. We had nothing to do here but wait. There was something in this guy's voice. He sounded alone.

"I'm from Praco," I said. "And proud to be the son of Buhlar Hinton, the best mother God ever sent down to this earth, who can make a pie like an angel and swat you like the devil if you try to eat it before she says so."

I heard a few guys laugh, but I didn't know if the guy whose name I was waiting on was one of them.

"My mom makes a pretty good pie herself," he finally said. "My name is Henry."

Henry didn't say his last name, and I didn't care to ask him. The guards called us by number or last name, rarely by our first name. I would no sooner ask him his last name than I would ask him what he was in for. Some things you never asked a guy. If someone wanted to tell you or talk about it, that was one thing. But you never asked. And really, what did it matter? We were all being careful. We were all protecting ourselves and reaching out at the same time. What else could you do?

"Nice to meet you, Henry. And I hope someday we can sit together in the shade on a beautiful Fourth of July, drinking sweet tea while our mothers compete to see who can make us the best pie. I don't know about your mom, but mine loves a good competition."

Henry laughed. "Well, that would be something to see, Ray. You have no idea. That would really be something."

"I'm sorry about your case, Henry," I said. "That doesn't sound right. It doesn't sound right at all. I'm going to do some more research next week on this judge override. You should do the same."

He didn't say anything back, so I dropped it.

"You know they don't like it when we educate ourselves," I yelled out. "The South still isn't happy we ever learned to read."

"Preach it, brother!"

"Is that you, Jesse?" I hollered back.

"Last time I checked, it was. I'm still here. You still here, Wallace?"

"I'm still here!"

And up and down the row it went, guys calling out to each other cell by cell. Sometimes they asked by name; other times they just asked in general. "You still here?" And a different voice would yell back, "I'm still here!"

And with each voice, it got funnier and funnier. I started laughing. Each man who yelled that he was still here made me laugh harder. Here we were in our cages. It shouldn't have been funny, but it was.

"We are all still here!" I yelled out one last time, and then I lay back on my bed. It was a good day when you could find a little bit of light.

I didn't hear from Henry again that day, but there was no need to push it. Maybe we would become friends, maybe not.

I thought about Wallace. He had been yelling and laughing, and everyone knew he had an execution date in less than two weeks. It made my stomach turn over a bit. Wallace and Jesse had started Project Hope—a kind of inmate advocacy group to fight the death penalty. I didn't see how it was really going to change anything, but I knew it helped to feel like you were doing something. I knew they had gotten permission to meet up as a small group, and I'm sure some guys just went to have another opportunity to get out of their cells. We were still only allowed less than an hour out of our cells every day. That and visiting day and law library was it. The warden only let a small group meet for Project Hope, and I hoped they didn't cause any trouble. If someone on the row caused trouble, it made a problem for all of us. The warden had no trouble locking us down all day or taking away our visits if anyone did anything. I was a nice guy to everyone, but I definitely wasn't going to let some fool stop my visits. Lester came every week, no matter what, and apart from those six hours with him and our moms, I had very few ways to keep myself occupied. I was reading my Bible again, but a man can't read only the Bible. It's like only having steak for dinner. You might love steak, but if you have it every day of the week, eventually you're going to get sick of it.

I read my Bible before Wallace was executed on July 13, 1990.

He wore a purple ribbon and a sign that said, "Execute justice, not people."

We banged on the bars for Wallace Norrell Thomas. Some banged on the bars to protest the death penalty. Others banged on the bars just to have something to do or as a way to let off steam. I banged on the bars so he would know that he mattered. That he was not alone. In the end, I think that's what we all want. To know we matter to someone, anyone. I knew I mattered to my mom and Lester and Phoebe, and that was more than a lot of these guys had. A lot of guys came here and died here without ever getting a visit. A lot of them never had a parent who loved them.

A few weeks after Wallace was killed, I got a letter from Santha, a handwritten note, which was unusual.

Mon 8/6/90

Mr. Hinton–

Apologies for the delay in getting this to you & for such an informal note. As I mentioned, I'm ½-way to finishing the Rule 20 petition. I met with Bryan Stevenson this morning and we have many ideas for your case.

I'm sorry not to have been able to visit you today. Please know that it's only because I want to do the best job I can on writing your petition.

Stay strong & stay in touch! I'll be sending you a copy of the petition next week.

Best Wishes,

Santha

I read the letter over and over again. She had written her home number in the bottom-right corner of the letter in red ink. I appreciated that, and I looked forward to getting the petition, not only so I knew my appeal was moving forward but also so I could have something else to read. Anything to occupy my mind.

I couldn't understand why we weren't allowed to have books. I thought about Wallace and his group. What if I started a group? What could my group be about? What would help the guys not feel so alone? What could help us all escape this place for a bit?

I thought back to being in the coal mines. I would give anything to be working in that coal mine again. I had hated it at the time, but I thought about how I had escaped the misery of it. I had traveled in my mind.

I closed my eyes and thought about where I would go if I were off death row.

I imagined myself walking out the front door of the prison. There was a plane waiting for me; it was parked right in the parking lot between the two fences. A private jet. It was white, and inside, it had soft leather seats the color of butter. I sat down, and immediately, a beautiful flight attendant appeared. She had dark skin and red lips and a smile so big I thought I would die right then and there.

"Mr. Hinton, can I get you something to drink? Champagne, perhaps?"

"Yes, thank you."

The pilot's voice came over the loudspeaker. "Please fasten your seat belts. We'll be taking off shortly. Flying time is approximately eight hours. Mr. Hinton, there is a bed in the back of the plane for you to sleep on during the flight."

I looked at the flight attendant.

"Where are we going?"

"We are flying to London. The Queen of England is waiting to meet you."

"Of course. Thank you." I waited until we were in the air, and then I walked to the back of the plane. There was a beautiful king-size bed with a velvet comforter and the blanket my mom had made me when I was a baby. There were dozens of soft pillows all over the bed, and when I climbed into the sheets, they smelled like freshly mowed lawns and magnolia blossoms.

The plane landed, and I stepped off to a waiting limousine. Buckingham Palace guards stood beside the car, and one saluted me and held open the door as I climbed in.

My suit was cream colored, and my tie a deep royal blue. When my car arrived at the palace, a whole regiment of guards—complete with the tall, furry black hats—stood at attention. I was brought through a large hallway, and two servants stood outside a grand ballroom. They bowed to me and opened up the double doors. I walked inside, and there she was. The Queen of England. She was wearing a blue dress that perfectly matched my tie, and a crown made of gold and rubies.

"Mr. Hinton." The Queen held out her hand, and I bowed deeply and kissed the back of it.

"Your Majesty."

"Please join me for tea, Mr. Hinton. It is an honor to meet you."

"The honor is all mine, and please, call me Ray."

The Queen laughed, and more servants came in with tiny sandwiches and cakes and tarts, and they served us tea that smelled like milk and honey and home.

"What can I do to help you, Mr. Hinton, Ray?" the Queen asked. "You don't deserve to be on death row. You must let me help you."

"Being here with you is help enough," I answered.

"Well, you must come see me anytime you can. We must put our heads together and find a way to get you home. Everyone needs to go home."

"We'll find a way," I said. "I know I will get back home. I know it. I am praying and I am believing, and it has to happen."

"Of course you will," she said. "Now, let me show you the castle, and the gardens, and all the secret rooms we have in the palace."

I followed the Queen of England around for hours and hours. We played croquet and had more tea, and she showed me where all the former kings had slept, and we talked about how hard it was to rule a country and how responsible she felt for everyone.

It felt great to be treated with respect. To be called *Mr. Hinton* instead of just *Hinton.*

"Hinton. Hinton!"

The voice came out of nowhere, and I could tell it startled the Queen as much as it did me. I tried to ignore it, but it only got louder, and I could see the palace guards rush in and surround the Queen as if she were under attack.

"I have to go, Your Majesty, but I will come back," I said.

"Hinton, look alive! Hinton, look alive!"

I blinked until my eyes seemed to focus, and then I saw the guard yelling at me. I sat up in my bed.

"You going to take your visit or what?"

I was confused. Visiting day wasn't until Friday, and it was only Wednesday.

"What are you talking about? Is my lawyer here?"

"No, you have a regular family visit. You want it or not? You've been acting strange for days."

"Of course I want it. Give me a minute to get dressed, please."

"You got exactly one minute."

I pulled out my dress whites. I kept one of my two sets of prison clothes just for visits, and between visits, I kept them folded and under my mattress so the creases in the pant legs would set in real sharp. I felt disoriented. If the guards wanted to give me an extra visit in the week, I wasn't going to complain.

I walked onto the visiting yard and smiled when I saw Lester, both of our moms, and Sylvia, Lester's new wife.

"How did you get an extra visit?" I asked. I was happy to see them but still confused.

"What are you going on about?" Lester laughed.

"This is our regular visit, baby. What's wrong with you?" My mom looked me up and down and furrowed her brows.

I sat down and looked at the four of them.

"What day is it?" I asked.

"It's Friday. Are you sick?"

I looked around. The other inmates were coming out for visits too. It was morning. It was Friday. It had just been Wednesday, and now it was Friday. I had completely skipped over Thursday.

"I'm starving. Did you guys bring in some money for the vending machines?"

Lester looked at me and then stood up. He started to walk over to the vending machines but stopped a few feet away and turned back toward me. "Where you been, man?"

"You wouldn't believe me if I told you," I said.

He shrugged and smiled at me.

I wasn't sure exactly what had happened.

There were only two ways to leave death row.

But I had just found another way. A third way. I felt better than I had in years. I jumped up to hug my mom, and even though the guards yelled at me to sit down, I held on to her. And then I started to laugh.

Time was a funny and strange and fluid thing, and I was going to bend it and shape it so that it wasn't my enemy. Someday I was going to walk out of here, but until then, I was going to use my mind to travel the world. I had so many places to go, and people to see, and things to learn.

"You sure you're okay?" My mom still looked worried.

"I'm sure," I said.

"Well, when are you coming home, baby? When are they going to let you out of here?" She always asked this question, and usually, it made me sad, but not today.

"Soon, Mama," I said. "I'm going to be coming home real soon."

After my visit, the guard walked me back to my cell. I changed back into my regular whites and carefully folded my dress whites and put them under the mattress.

And then I sat on the edge of my bed and closed my eyes.

My mom had planted some new flowers in front of her house. They were purple and white and pink, and I ran my fingers across them gently. I walked around the side of the house. The lawn needed cutting. I opened the door of the shed and pulled the mower out. I would take care of this for her and then go inside and have some tea and let her gossip about all the goings-on at church and around town.

"Is that you, baby?" She poked her head out the screen door.

"It's me, Mama. It's me." She smiled and clapped her hands together. "I told you I would be home soon. I told you."

| 13 |

NO MONSTERS

Mr. Hinton was denied effective assistance of counsel at the guilt/innocence penalty and appellate phases of his case in violation of his rights under the laws and Constitution of Alabama and the Sixth, Eighth, and Fourteenth Amendments of the United States Constitution.

—SANTHA SONENBERG, 1990 PETITION FOR RELIEF

Santha filed my petition the day before the deadline. In it, she listed thirty-one reasons why I should be granted a new trial—prosecutor misconduct and racial discrimination, ineffective assistance of counsel, and not being allowed to hire a real expert, to name just a few. I read the list over and over again, and I felt hope. I let some of the other guys read it. They passed it from cell to cell.

1. Newly discovered evidence.
2. Denied effective assistance of counsel at the guilt/innocence penalty and appellate phases of his case in violation of his rights under the laws and Constitution of Alabama and the Sixth, Eighth, and Fourteenth Amendments of the United States Constitution.
3. The trial court erroneously consolidated two separate capital indictments.
4. The trial court erroneously precluded Mr. Hinton from presenting evidence, at both the guilt/innocence and penalty phases of his trial, that he successfully passed a polygraph examination in which he denied involvement in the charged capital offenses.
5. Confiscation of records that supported Mr. Hinton's alibi defense to the uncharged offense which was the State's critical

link between Mr. Hinton and the two charged capital offenses violated his rights and rendered the verdicts and sentences in these cases unconstitutional.

6. The trial court erroneously permitted introduction of Mr. Hinton's oral statements to the police.
7. The publicity surrounding the charged and uncharged offenses made it impossible for Mr. Hinton to receive a fair trial in Jefferson County and thus his rights to a fair trial by an impartial jury under the Fifth, Sixth, Eighth, and Fourteenth Amendments to the United States Constitution were violated.
8. The prosecutor's misconduct and arguments at the guilt/innocence phase were improper and violated Mr. Hinton's rights.
9. The failure to fully transcribe trial court proceedings deprived Mr. Hinton of full appeal and statutorily mandated review of his capital sentence and conviction.
10. Mr. Hinton was deprived of a fair trial and a fair sentencing by the prosecutor's use of peremptory challenges in a racially discriminatory manner.
11. Mr. Hinton was deprived of an impartial jury through improper juror exclusion in violation of the Sixth, Eighth, and Fourteenth Amendments to the United States Constitution.
12. Mr. Hinton was deprived of an impartial jury through improper juror inclusion in violation of the Fifth, Sixth, and Fourteenth Amendments to the United States Constitution.
13. Mr. Hinton's rights to a fair trial by an impartial jury were violated by the trial court's restrictions on the voir dire examination of the prospective jurors and the trial court's interference in the jury selection process.
14. Mr. Hinton's rights to a fair trial and a fair sentencing were abrogated by his convictions and death sentences being based upon insufficient and unreliable evidence of his guilt in the charged offenses.
15. Mr. Hinton's right to present a defense was abrogated by the court's failure to grant trial counsel's request for extraordinary expenses to hire a ballistics expert to counter the two ballistics experts who testified for the State.

16. The seizure of the gun from Mr. Hinton's mother's home was invalid and thus its introduction into evidence, and any testimony based upon its seizure or regarding the gun was improper.
17. The trial court's failure to instruct the jury on lesser included offenses violated Mr. Hinton's rights and deprived him of a fair trial and rendered his convictions and sentences of death invalid.
18. Mr. Hinton's right to a fair trial was abrogated by admission of evidence regarding the Smotherman incident without which there was no evidence to support Mr. Hinton's convictions for capital murder.
19. Mr. Hinton's rights to a fair trial and a fair sentencing were violated by the admission of Reginald Payne White's testimony.
20. The State's introduction of prejudicial and highly inflammatory photographs and other documentary evidence at Mr. Hinton's trial violated his rights.
21. The prosecutor's misconduct and arguments at Mr. Hinton's sentencing hearing were improper and deprived him of a fundamentally fair hearing and due process.
22. The participation of the decedents' family members in Mr. Hinton's prosecution was highly improper and denied Mr. Hinton a fair trial, a fair sentencing, and due process.
23. The statutory presumption that any aggravating circumstance proven during the guilt/innocence phase is considered proven beyond a reasonable doubt for purposes of the penalty phase is unconstitutional and thus Mr. Hinton's death sentence has violated due process under the prohibition against cruel and unusual punishment.
24. Mr. Hinton's right to a public trial was denied when his mother and sister were asked to leave the courtroom.
25. Evidence of simulated trips between Ensley, where Mr. Hinton was working, and the location of the Smotherman incident was improperly admitted at his trial.
26. Evidence rebutting Mr. Hinton's alibi defense was improperly admitted before any evidence supporting his defense had been introduced.
27. Evidence of out-of-court identifications was improperly admitted at Mr. Hinton's trial.

28. Mr. Hinton's rights to a fair trial and a fair sentencing were abrogated by the way in which his trial and sentencing were conducted.
29. Expert witnesses were improperly permitted to testify based upon evidence that was not admitted at the trial.
30. The trial court improperly heard testimony from its own bailiffs at Mr. Hinton's sentencing proceeding in violation of his rights to a fair sentencing.
31. Alabama's death penalty is arbitrarily and discriminatorily applied in violation of Eighth and Fourteenth Amendments.

Soon everyone was talking about my case. I didn't know what some of the things on the list meant, but I used my time in the law library to research. I had studied the amendments to the Constitution in high school but definitely needed a refresher course. It was great just to have something new to read, something new to talk about. Henry seemed particularly interested in my case.

"It sounds good, Ray," Henry said, "like you should be let go. You have a solid case. You really are innocent."

I laughed. "I know everyone says it, but I really am innocent. And I'm really going to walk out of here someday. You just wait."

I didn't tell Henry that I left the row every day. I didn't tell anyone. I could be there for meals and when the guards needed me to do something, but the minute my mind wasn't occupied by the routine of the row, I left. My jet plane was always waiting, and it got easier and easier for me to travel in my mind. Sometimes Henry would ask me what I had been doing when he was calling out to me, and I would say, "I was in Spain, Henry, but I'm back now. What do you need?" I think people thought I was losing it a bit, but escaping in my mind gave me a sort of giddy sense of freedom. I could tune out the moaning and the roaches and the smell of death and the food that had no taste and the endless worry about who would be next to burn up in that chair. Every time an hour could pass without me being aware of every slow second of that hour was a gift. Every day was like the one before it and the one after it. And there were so many days when nothing at all happened. Nothing. Just silence or moaning or guys yelling nothing at each other. We each did our time in our own way. One guy would just draw spirals on a piece of paper—all day, every day. Spirals within spirals within spirals so that you never saw where anything ended and anything began. That's how it was. Some guys just spent the time between meals trying not to go crazy—they would hum, or rock themselves, or moan in a way that almost sounded like chanting. Humans were not meant to be locked in a cage, and a man couldn't survive in a box. It was cruel. A lot of guys had mental illness or were born slow; others would rip off your face with their bare hands if they were given the chance. We weren't a collection of innocent victims. Many of the guys I laughed with had raped women and murdered children and sliced innocent people up for the fun of it or because they were high on drugs or desperate for money and never thought beyond the next moment. The outside world called them monsters. They called all of us monsters. But I didn't know any monsters on the row. I knew guys named Larry and Henry and Victor and Jesse. I knew Vernon and Willie and Jimmy. Not monsters. Guys with names who didn't have mothers who loved them or anyone who had ever shown them a kindness that was even close to love. Guys who were born broken or had been broken by life. Guys who had been abused as children and had their minds and their hearts warped by cruelty and violence and isolation long before they ever stood in front of a judge and a jury.

I was there with these guys part of the time, but the rest of the time, I left them. I left them all. I watched college football games in my mind, and I learned to fly a helicopter. I had a boat and a Cadillac and more women than I knew what to do with. I would eat at the finest restaurants, wear the nicest clothes, and visit the most beautiful and wondrous places in the world. Traveling in my mind was like reading a good book and being transported to a completely different world, and a part of me felt a little guilty that I could escape this way when so many guys were suffering.

The State responded to my petition and basically denied everything we had claimed, saying that all my claims were "procedurally barred" because an issue was either already raised during my trial or in Perhacs's direct appeal or it could have been raised on my direct appeal but wasn't. It didn't make any sense to me. It didn't seem to matter that I was innocent, that people lied, that there were real issues with my trial—the State didn't want to admit that anything was wrong, and unless you knew it was wrong or should have known it was wrong or could have known it was wrong but didn't, you couldn't argue it. Henry explained it to me. "If your attorney could have raised something during your trial and first appeal but didn't, it's barred by the State. If it was raised at trial or in your first appeal, and you were still convicted and denied, it's also barred by the State."

"But doesn't that cover everything?" I asked. "I mean everything that you would appeal on?"

"Pretty much."

It didn't seem fair or right that the odds were stacked against me—against all of us. If you couldn't afford to get an attorney at your trial or appeal, it seemed like you would never be able to prove you were innocent. A hearing was set for April 23, 1991, but then at the beginning of the month I got a note from Santha that my hearing was being postponed. She sent me a copy of the official notice she filed with the court withdrawing as my attorney. She couldn't represent me anymore because of a new job in D.C., but she said that another attorney would be taking over. Bryan Stevenson's office would send someone. She told me that they were going to amend my petition and change the hearing date and that it was now called a Rule 32 hearing because Alabama changed the rules of appellate law, but not to worry.

Not to worry.

I tried not to take it too hard. I called Lester and asked him to check in with the resource center in Montgomery. "Try to get hold of this Bryan Stevenson and see if he knows anything about a new attorney," I asked. "Tell him I'm innocent and that I was supposed to have a hearing on my petition."

Lester always took care of things for me. He still drove to Holman every week, even though he had been turned away a few times because the prison was on lockdown or there weren't enough guards at work that day.

Ever since I had passed around my petition, guys were sharing their appeals as well. We started to have lively legal debates on our side of the row, but it was hard to yell to each other and know exactly who was talking and to who. "Listen to this!" I yelled out my cell as I read aloud from the petition. "The kind of justice a criminal defendant has cannot depend on how much money he has."

The guys debated this up and down the row all day.

Money determined everything, and none of us had any money.

I was showering next to a guy named Jimmy that night when he said, "Hays has money. If anyone's going to get out of this place, it's Hays."

"Who's Hays?" I asked.

"Henry. Henry Hays. The KKK guy. You know the KKK has money. He will get out."

I walked back to my shower in shock. I knew who Henry Hays was. Everybody in Alabama knew that he and a couple of other white guys had lynched a black boy named Michael Donald in Mobile in 1981. It was the last lynching. The kid had been a teenager, nineteen years old, and the KKK was mad that a black guy on trial might get away with killing a white policeman. I thought it had been a mistrial, but I couldn't remember. Henry Hays's father was rumored to be the head of the KKK or something. That poor Donald boy had been randomly picked up and beaten and stabbed and then hung from a tree like a piece of meat for his mother to find. She had sued the Klan or taken some other legal action. I couldn't remember exactly, but I remembered being sickened by the murder. Michael Donald hadn't been much younger than I was—five or six years—and the story had reminded me of the bombs growing up and the kids who had the dogs let loose on them and the girls who had been murdered in the church. The news about the lynching had angered me.

I'd had no idea that my friend Henry was actually Henry Hays.

I went back to my cell that night and stared at the ceiling. I was Henry's friend. He knew I was black. I wanted to talk to him. I wanted to understand.

"Henry!" I yelled.

"What you want, Ray?"

"I just figured out who you are. I didn't know." There was no answer right away, and I wondered what Henry was thinking.

"Everything my mom and dad taught me was a lie, Ray. Everything they taught me against blacks, it was a lie."

I didn't know exactly what to say back to him. "You know, just about everything I believe about people, I learned from my mom."

"So you know what I mean," he said.

"Yeah. I do. I guess I was just lucky that my mom taught me to love people, no matter what. She taught me to forgive."

"You was lucky, Ray. You was really lucky."

"She taught me to have compassion for everybody, Henry, and I have compassion for you. I'm sorry your mama and your daddy didn't teach you the same. I really am."

"Me too."

We didn't say much after that, but the row was pretty quiet that night. We weren't monsters; we were guys trying to survive the best we could. Sometimes you need to make family where you find it, and I knew that to survive I had to make a family of these men and they had to make a family of me. It didn't matter who was black and who was white—all that kind of fell away when you lived a few feet away from an electric chair. Right now, we had more in common than not. We all faced execution. We all were scrambling to survive.

Not monsters.

Not the worst thing we had ever done.

We were so much more than what we had been reduced to—so much more than could be contained in one small cage.

On the next visiting day, Henry had a visit too. I sat with Lester and Sylvia, and we were laughing about something when I heard Henry call my name.

"Ray! Ray, come here for a second." He gestured me over. He sat with an older couple; I assumed they were his parents.

I glanced toward the guard, but he wasn't paying me any mind, so I walked over to Henry's table.

"Ray, I want you to meet my father, Bennie. Dad, this is Ray Hinton. My friend."

I held out my hand to Henry's father. He just looked at me and then down at the table. He didn't say hello, and he wouldn't shake my hand.

"He's my friend. My best friend." Henry's voice shook a little bit.

His mom smiled at me faintly, and then the guard yelled to me to go sit down.

"Nice to meet you both," I said, and I walked back to my table.

"What was that all about?" asked Lester.

"That was about some progress, my friend, some crazy progress on death row."

I imagined it took a lot for Henry to stand up to his dad. To tell him that this large black man was his best friend. We never talked about the fact that his father wouldn't shake my hand. We just kept on living next to each other and surviving as best we could.

My new attorney came to see me a few months later. His name was Alan Black. He was from Boston. I had always been a Yankees fan.

"I'm going to ask Bryan Stevenson for some money to hire someone to test the bullets again. We need a new expert. We need to prove there's no way your mother's gun was used to kill those men."

I nodded. I had thought about this before. Payne was crucified on the stand, and even though he had told the truth, no one believed him. No one would ever believe him when he couldn't even operate the machinery or find the light on the microscope.

"I need you to get the best of the best," I said.

Alan Black nodded and kind of laughed nervously. He didn't look me in the eye, so while he wasn't who I would pick as my attorney, I was grateful he was there.

"I'll see what I can do," he said. "I think I know a guy out of Jersey. I'll talk to Bryan."

"Okay, you do that. It might be good if you find someone from the South, though. Judges around here don't really like guys from out of town." I didn't want to tell him what to do; that hadn't worked out so well with Perhacs.

I went back to my cell after the visit, and Henry asked me how it went.

"Well, Henry, it's like this. I can get over the fact that you used to be in the KKK, but I'm not sure I'm going to be able to get over the fact that my life is now in the hands of a Red Sox fan."

Henry and some of the other guys started laughing.

I smiled. As long as I was making them laugh, we were all still alive.

I was tired of talking through the bars, though. I was tired of standing with my mouth pressed against dirty mesh wire every time I wanted to talk to another human.

I thought about Wallace and his Project Hope. I thought about passing my list of thirty-one reasons up and down the row.

"Henry!" I yelled.

"Yeah?"

"I'm thinking about starting a book club."

"A what?"

"A book club. I'm going to see if we can meet in the library once a month and have ourselves a book club. You in?"

He paused a moment. "I'm in," he said.

"I want in!" yelled a guy named Larry.

"Me too!"

"Who's that?" I asked.

"It's Victor. I want in. What are we going to read, though? Wouldn't your book club just be a Bible study?"

"No, I'm going to get some real books in here. I'm going to talk to the warden, and we're going to get some real books," I said. "And we're going to have ourselves a little club."

I closed my eyes. I could leave the row in my mind, and now I was going to show these guys that they could leave too. I remember being in school and reading a book about California and getting so lost in it, I swear I could smell the salt water of the Pacific Ocean.

I just needed to get some books.

Then we could all leave this place together.

| 14 |

LOVE IS A FOREIGN LANGUAGE

In preparation of the case, counsel has determined that the requested fees and costs would significantly aid in the preparation for the Rule 32 hearing and to assist him in determining whether there have been violations of the petitioner's constitutional rights.

—ALAN BLACK, EX PARTE MOTION FOR FEES AND COSTS

The first thing Alan Black did was ask Judge Garrett for money for experts to investigate my case. Judge Garrett granted the motions, and I wondered why he would give money now in my appeal when he wouldn't give the money in my actual trial. If I'd had money, Perhacs could have found someone better than Payne. If I'd had money, they could have had an expert prove I couldn't have driven from work to Quincy's that fast. If I'd had money, I could have gotten an attorney who felt like he was paid for his time. If I'd had money, I probably wouldn't have been arrested in the first place.

It always seemed to come down to the money.

I received a copy of all my legal filings in the mail, and it was the only mail the guards couldn't open or mess with. Any letter you wrote had to remain unsealed so the prison staff could read it before it was mailed. Any letter that came in was also read by the prison staff. Every phone call was recorded. I couldn't understand why they had to read the letters that went out, but it became clear that they didn't want you to complain about how you were being treated. They didn't want someone to call in the attorneys. Holman was always short staffed, and the row was no different. We were like lab rats being closely monitored for any potential signs of revolt. It was easier for them to keep us in our cages where we couldn't get into trouble rather than let us out. Summers were the worst. They didn't allow any fans in our cells because they could be broken apart to use as weapons, but with the tight wire mesh covering our doors, there was zero ventilation or flow of air. It was over 100 degrees outside during the summer months, and in our cells, it had to be 110 or 120. It was like being in a sauna, and some days it felt like you were actually slow roasting. It's hard to talk, much less fight, when it is so hot you can barely move or take a breath. Much like the staff reading our mail and recording our conversations, the heat was a way to keep control, but the heat made some guys crazy. And even more violent. I knew that all the warden wanted was to keep the peace, especially on death row, where it was assumed that we had nothing to lose and would kill if given the chance. But he was going about it all wrong, and it was having the opposite effect.

"Hinton, lunch!" The officer who yelled looked just as hot as I was, and I wondered if he wouldn't also like some cool air blowing through the row.

"Hey, I need to ask you something," I said.

"What's that, Hinton?" He sounded annoyed and tired.

"I need to borrow your truck."

"What?"

"I need to borrow your truck. Just for a little bit. I'll bring it back with a full tank of gas, don't you worry about that."

"What the hell are you talking about?"

"I know this cool little swimming hole. It's hidden back in some trees outside of Jefferson County. There's an old, unmarked dirt road that leads to it, so not a lot of people know about it. You have to walk a bit through the woods. It's shady, and the water is so clear you can see right to the bottom. I think it's fed by an underground spring or something. The water is so clear and so cool you can drink it. I'm going to need to borrow your truck, and I'll bring it back later tonight, I promise. I just need to have myself a float in that spring water. Cool myself down, you know?"

He just stared at me, like I had finally lost it.

"Maybe we should go together? Get out of here and cool off? Otherwise, I just need your keys and you can keep working, and I'll be back before shift change. I heard you talking about your new truck, and I promise I'll take good care of it."

He started laughing and shaking his head. "I don't think so, Hinton, but here's your lunch."

And just like that, he was smiling at me.

"I need to talk to the warden about something," I said, smiling back at him. "Can you get him a message or let the captain know?"

"I'll bring you some paper, and you write it down and I'll get it to him."

"Thanks."

He shook his head at me, but he was still smiling as he moved on down the row delivering lunch.

"You making friends with the guards, Ray?" I heard the scorn in Walter Hill's voice. Hill had killed another inmate while in prison before Holman and was now on the row for a triple murder, so he was one of the guys who the warden thought had nothing to lose. He was angry all the time. I couldn't blame him for that. I also wasn't going to judge him. I didn't know his story. Whatever he had done was between him and God.

"Hey, Walter!" I yelled. "You know what my sweet mama always says to me?"

Walter didn't answer the question. "They're not your friends, Ray. They trying to kill us, and I don't like nobody who gets cozy with the guards. You know what I'm saying?"

I knew what he was saying. In general population, if you seemed like you were friendly to the guards, you were considered a snitch. Snitches didn't do well in Holman. You could get your throat cut if anyone suggested you were a snitch. I didn't know who Walter had killed in general population or why, but it didn't matter, and I wasn't going to let him or anyone intimidate me.

I raised my voice so they would hear me on the other side of the row. "My mama always told me that you get more flies with honey than with vinegar."

"I heard that before," said Victor. "I heard that too."

"Just because you pour out some honey doesn't mean you're a fly. You hear me, Walter? It's how you catch the flies. It's how we got an extra fifteen minutes on the yard. You use the vinegar. I'm going to use the honey."

I left it at that. I knew the guards were doing a job. Just like I hadn't dreamed of going into the coal mines and had hated every minute of it, I imagined most of them hadn't grown up dreaming of someday working on death row. We were all getting through this life the best we could, and our lives had intersected right here on death row, but it was up to us to figure out what happened next. It was hell on the row—every minute of every day—but in this hell, it could always get worse. It could also get a little better. I was going to do my part to make it that way. My mama had taught me about getting flies with honey, and she had also taught me that you had to work within the system. You couldn't grow up black in the South and not know how to work within the system. It was the same here—some people held all the power, and there were all kinds of ways you could fight back. I didn't believe violence was ever a way to get what you wanted. It didn't work in the real world, and it definitely didn't work on the row. Hill was a perfect example of that, but he didn't see it.

If I wanted the guards to cooperate, I had to cooperate. It was a tradeoff. I knew others, like Hill, would take my cooperation the wrong way, but it was about survival. Not just for me but for all of us. I had people who loved me and came to visit every week. I had money on my books from Lester. I had grown up with unconditional love. I had faith and a God and a Bible that promised me I would get out of here someday. I was better off than a lot of the guys next to me. We were all facing death, but I was facing it with love all around me. I tried to focus on that more than the fact that my life had been stolen from me. I didn't know who else was innocent. Maybe every other guy sitting in his rat cage was innocent. Who knew? Maybe every other guy in his rat cage had killed. It didn't matter. We were slowly roasting to death, and making it worse for ourselves was not a way to get payback. It only hurt us more. I was going to do what I could with what I had. A little bit of kindness was amplified on death row, because it was so unexpected. You can scream out in a crowd of voices also screaming out, and no one hears you—but when you yell into the silence, your voice sounds louder. I was going to be that kind voice screaming out on the row, and I was going to make it better for everyone—even for Hill. We were all the same here. We were all discarded like garbage and deemed unworthy to have a life.

I was going to prove them wrong.

Charlie Jones looked every bit like you'd imagine a Southern redneck warden to look like, straight down to his cowboy boots with spurs and a face that was white and fleshy and soft. He had a tough job—keeping a handle on things at the most violent prison in the country. Every day, he was responsible for his staff and an inmate population that would riot if given the chance. I knew this going into my conversation with him.

"I hear you're a talker, Hinton. And I hear that the guys listen to you. I still don't know why you didn't want to talk on camera when Geraldo was here."

Geraldo Rivera had spent a night on death row, brought in cameras, and pretended to be one of us. Worn whites and slept overnight in a cell, but it was all a joke. A pretend game where he was able to leave the next day. He didn't and couldn't know what it was like to be locked in a cage when you were innocent. He was playing a game that he knew nothing about, and he only did it for his own ego. We saw the show. He made sure he had his shirt off, but you could see when they handed him his tray of food they had another tray over it to keep out the dirt and the dust and rat hairs and the cockroach pieces. We didn't get our food served to us with a cover on it—and that small difference said it all.

"Well, I would have if you had sent me to New York to film the show. Why, I could have flown on an airplane for the first time and had some of those little peanuts I hear are so good. I was ready to be on the show if it meant I could have some of those peanuts."

He laughed. "Now what's this I hear about a club of some kind?'

"I want to start a book club. I was thinking we could meet once a month in the library. But we need to be able to read something other than the Bible. Not everyone cares for the Bible like we do. You know what I mean?"

"Yeah, and it's a damn shame," he said.

"So my best friend, Lester, said he would mail a few books here, and we could read them and then have ourselves a discussion."

The warden looked down, and I could see he was considering my proposal.

"Look," I said. "These guys need something to focus on besides what the guards are doing and not doing for them. Besides the heat. Besides the fact that our food tastes like dirt. You know? It's a way to keep the peace. A book club will help things stay more peaceful."

He nodded.

"You can't have guys spending twenty-three hours a day thinking about death. It makes them crazy. And when people go crazy, who knows what they'll do." It may have been a bit much, but it was the truth. I wanted him to believe that if we had books on the row, it would keep the inmates quiet. But really I knew that it would set them free. If the guys had books, they could travel the world. They would get smarter and freer. There was a reason back in the slave days the plantation owners didn't want their slaves to learn to read. Charlie Jones probably had family who once owned my family, but I wasn't going to bring that up. I wasn't going to show him anything but how a book club would keep the peace.

"Let me think on it, Hinton. You make a good point, but let me talk to my officers. They're the ones who are there. I don't want any trouble from death row. You understand what I'm saying? I let you have some extra time out on the yard, and that's been all right. But if I have any trouble from the row, we'll just keep you guys in for the full twenty-four, you understand? Take away them visits if anything gets to be a problem. I got a lot of guys in here who need to be managed."

"Yes, sir," I said. "I appreciate you taking the time to consider it. I do think it will help your men have an easier time doing their jobs, sir. Thank you for considering my proposal."

I think the manners puzzled Charlie Jones. He wasn't used to it. I watched him cock his head at me more than once. Like he couldn't quite figure out if I was joking or serious.

"They listen to you, Hinton. You keep things peaceful on the row, and I'll see what I can do. I can't have a bunch of you in the library at once. I don't have the staff for that. Four guys, maybe six. I'll think about it."

"Thank you."

"And we don't have a budget to be buying books. You'd have to have them mailed to us, and we'd inspect them first. No more than two books at a time. I can't see what it would hurt to let some other books on the row."

"That's a good idea, sir."

"Anything else, Hinton? I think we understand each other here. Anything else going on I need to know about?" And here it was: just like that, he wanted me to be an informer, but I wasn't playing that game.

"Well, about Geraldo, sir. Some of the guys noticed he got a tray turned upside down on top of his food tray to keep the dirt out. You know, as a lid on his food. And some of the guys thought this was a great idea. Was that your idea when Geraldo was here?" I paused then, and he nodded and smiled. "It was a great idea. I think it would go a long way if we could use that great idea for all of us, get lids on our food to keep the dust out. You know how dusty it is in here."

"All right, then, I don't see why not. I'll let the kitchen know."

"Thank you, sir."

I smiled all the way back to my cell. And when the captain of the guard let me know that book club was approved for six guys, I told Lester on visiting day.

"Can you send in a couple of books to the prison? Send them to the attention of the warden."

"What you up to now?" asked Lester.

"I'm starting a book club."

"A what?"

"You know, a book club. We're going to read books and then meet once a month as a club to talk about it."

Lester's new wife, Sylvia, had come with him to visit. Her nickname was Sia.

"What you laughing at, Sia?" I asked. "You never heard of a book club before?"

"I've heard of it, but I think it's funny that you guys are going to sit around having a book club. What books are you going to read?"

"I'm not sure. What do you think?"

Lester kind of shrugged. He wasn't a big reader, but Sia looked serious all of a sudden.

"I know," she said. "You guys need to read James Baldwin, Harper Lee, Maya Angelou. I just read *I Know Why the Caged Bird Sings*; you guys need to read that one. And *To Kill a Mockingbird*, and *Go Tell It on the Mountain*."

Sia was getting excited about the idea. "Okay," I said, "you send us the books. I'll pay you guys back when I get out of here, I promise. Just send me two books, care of Charlie Jones. We'll have to read and pass them around to share. You send them in whatever order you think we should read them first. Maybe we could talk about them when you visit, and you could help me think of how to talk about them in book club. How about that?"

Sia nodded. "Let's start with James Baldwin."

"James Baldwin it is. He's going to take these guys right out of death row!"

"What do you mean?" Lester looked at me, puzzled.

"Not everyone has my imagination. All day, every day, guys are drowning in fear and death. Imagine knowing the day you're going to die. How could you think about anything else? These guys have to find a way to think about life."

At that moment, there was yelling across the yard. Guards rushed over to another visiting table. I saw Henry jump up and then get pulled back by a guard. Sirens went off, and that meant we had to lie facedown on the ground.

"Don't worry. It's okay," I said to Lester and Sia, who looked scared. I was glad my mom hadn't felt well enough to make the drive. This would have scared her. I turned my head and looked over to Henry. He had been having a visit too, but I could see his dad was on the ground and the guards were around him. I wondered what had happened. I met Henry's eyes, and I could tell he was scared.

"Visit's over! All inmates return to cells."

I could hear ambulance sirens in the distance. I wondered if someone had stabbed Henry's father. I turned back to wave goodbye to Lester and Sia, but they were being taken out and didn't see me. Henry lined up behind me for count.

"What happened?"

"My dad was going off about his trial that's coming up, and then he just fell over. I think it's his heart. He turned completely white, almost blue."

I could hear Henry's voice shake. His father was an asshole—a racist, murdering asshole—but he was still his dad.

"I'm sorry, man. I really am. I hope he's okay."

"You know they declared a mistrial, because of his heart, before."

"Yeah," I said. The trial of Bennie Hays had been in the papers, and everyone knew about it, even though Henry never talked about it.

"I'm sorry, Henry. I really am."

"Thanks, Ray. Thanks for everything."

Henry hung his head and didn't talk anymore. The next day, Saturday, his father died. The guard came to give Henry the news. I said a prayer then for Bennie Hays. I prayed that in death he would know more than he did in life. Someone had taught Bennie Hays to hate, and Bennie Hays had taught his son Henry to hate. And now Henry was learning that hate didn't get him anywhere.

In Alabama, when someone dies, you bring food to the family. All day long, friends and neighbors show up bringing casseroles, pies, or some homemade grits. It's the way you show love and support. By the end of the first day of grieving, the family's fridge and table and counters are covered with food. Food is love and life and comfort and one small way to show others you are there wanting to nourish and nurture them in their grief.

As soon as the guard left Henry's cell, I passed some coffee out of my cell to Henry. The guys next to me reached out and took it from me and passed it down to the guy next to him. Up and down the row, all day long, men who might just as soon kill each other as look at each other on the streets passed their precious food items to Henry's cell—candy bars and soup and coffee and small pieces of chocolate and even fruit. Anyone who had something of value ordered from commissary or left over from a meal passed it one to the other until it reached Henry. Nobody took it for himself. Nobody interrupted the chain of comfort as it wound its way up and down and around the row until it reached Henry.

We all knew grief.

We all knew sorrow.

We all knew what it was like to be alone.

And we all were beginning to learn that you can make a family out of anyone.

Even the guards, perhaps caught up in their own humanity or because Henry's dad had collapsed under their watch, helped pass the food to Henry.

In a twisted way, they were also a part of this big, strange family on death row. They were the ones charged with our care every day—obligated to help us when we were sick yet also the ones who walked us to our deaths, strapped us into the chair, and then turned their backs as the warden flipped the switch to end our lives.

In the end, we were all just trying to find our way.

| 15 |

GO TELL IT ON THE MOUNTAIN

This burden was heavier than the heaviest mountain and he carried it in his heart.

—JAMES BALDWIN, *GO TELL IT ON THE MOUNTAIN*

The books were a big deal. Nobody had books on death row. They had never been allowed, and it was like someone had brought in contraband. Only six guys were allowed to join me in book club, but every guy on the row was now allowed to have two books besides the Bible in his cell. Some didn't care, but others made calls out to family and friends to let them know they could send in a book or two. It had to be a brand-new book and be sent directly from a bookstore to the prison. It was like a whole new world opened up, and guys started talking about what books they liked. Some guys didn't know how to read, others were real slow, almost childlike, and had never been to school beyond a few grades. Those guys didn't know why they were on death row, and I wondered about a world that would just as soon execute a guy as treat him in a hospital or admit he wasn't mentally capable of knowing right from wrong.

The very first book club meeting consisted of Jesse Morrison, Victor Kennedy, Larry Heath, Brian Baldwin, Ed Horsley, Henry, and myself. We were allowed to meet in the law library, but we each had to sit at a different table. We couldn't get up. In order to talk to everyone at once, you had to kind of swivel around in your seat so no one felt left out. If someone wanted to read something out of the book, we had to toss the book to each other and hope that the guy caught it or it landed in reach of someone because we weren't allowed to lift our butts up off the seats. The guards seemed nervous when they walked us to the library. We weren't planning a riot or an escape; we were five black guys and two white guys talking about a James Baldwin book. Perfectly normal. Nothing to see here.

When the books arrived, one of the guards had brought them to my cell and handed them to me. Two brand-new copies of James Baldwin's *Go Tell It on the Mountain*. I had read it in high school, but I read it again so I could pass it on to the next guy. All seven of us took about a week to read the book, so with two copies being passed, we were ready for book club in a month. That became the routine for each book. Some other guys had asked their families to send them the same book, so in our section of the row—with fourteen guys upstairs and fourteen guys downstairs—almost everybody seemed to be talking about the book.

Some people hated it because it talked so much about God, and others loved it for the same reason. A couple liked it because there were some sex scenes. For that month, it seemed like the row was transformed to another place. We were in New York City, in Harlem. Our parents had a complicated and sordid past, and no relationship was as it seemed to be on the surface. We were in church, waiting to be saved or feeling the glory of Jesus as it racked our body in convulsions. We were victims of violence. We were caught up in a strange family dynamic where we didn't know who our daddy was or why he hated us. We were John, the main character, turning fourteen and trying to figure out the world and make sense of what he was feeling. We were ourselves, but we were different, and the book occupied our days and our nights in a new way. We weren't discussing legal questions, playing pretend lawyers and trying to understand a system that didn't make sense half the time. We weren't the scum of the earth, the lowest of the low, the forgotten and abandoned men who were sitting in a dark corner of hell waiting for their turn to walk to the electric chair. We were transported, and just as I could travel the world and have tea with the Queen of England, I watched these men be transported in their minds for a small chunk of time. It was a vacation from the row—and everyone was a part of book club, even before the seven of us had our first official meeting.

When we finally did have our meeting, we sat at our respective tables and felt an awkwardness that wasn't there when we were yelling to each other through the bars of our cell. Larry and Henry, being the only white guys, looked especially uncomfortable. The guards had locked us into the library, so we were in there by ourselves. There could be no violating the rules, no getting in any fights, no foolishness whatsoever. It was strange after so many years to have a change in our routine. Every day, except for when they took you to shower, things happened at the same exact time. So when there was suddenly something new, especially for the guys like Baldwin and Heath and Horsley, who had been there over a decade, it was strange and they seemed on edge.

"So, what do you think?" I asked everyone.

"How do we do this exactly? What's the format?" Jesse Morrison was used to Project Hope, so he knew how to organize a group.

Everyone looked at me. "Let's just talk about whatever we read that we want to talk about. Whether we liked the book or not. What we liked about it, what we didn't. What left an impression. How does that sound?" I looked around at everyone, and they nodded. Henry looked serious. "You know what I liked?" I asked. "I liked this sentence: 'For the rebirth of the soul was perpetual; only rebirth every hour could stay the hand of Satan.' "

"What you like about it?" asked Larry.

"I like that it's about hope," I said. "It's like your soul can be reborn. No matter what you've done, you can be new again. It's a hopeful sentence."

"Yeah, but Satan is right there, pushing you every hour on the hour," said Victor. Victor was a quiet guy. He was sentenced to die for raping and killing an old woman. "When I drink, Satan takes over; that much I know."

We were quiet. Everyone knew he had been drunk the night he and Grayson had done what they did. Grayson was on the row too, but I never saw the two guys even acknowledge they knew each other. Baldwin and Horsley were both on the row for a crime they were accused of committing together. Horsley had told them he did it alone, Baldwin hadn't done it, but it didn't matter. Baldwin had been shocked with a cattle prod until he confessed. The jury had been all white. He and Horsley had both been tortured. Horsley tried to tell anyone who would listen that Baldwin wasn't there, but it didn't seem to matter. They were both sentenced to die. Just two more black men off the streets of Alabama.

Heath spoke like a preacher, so I expected him to have something to say about the church folk in Baldwin's book. He was strangely quiet, though.

"Everybody talking about being saved in this book," said Henry. "I've never been to a church where people falling on the ground getting saved."

I laughed. "Well, you never been to a black church, Henry. When we get out of here, I'm going to take you to a church where you will see the Holy Spirit come down and take over a person's body so much that it looks like that person is going to fly right up and out the window of that church!" I started laughing. "You are not going to believe how people carry on in a black church. The only problem is it's going to last all day and into the night, so you'd best be prepared to eat before you go and be ready to sit there until the Spirit moves you. You are going to be singing and praising the Lord like you've never praised the Lord before!"

Henry looked around the group. "I'm not sure they're going to want me in there—you know, not everyone is like you guys."

"Well, we will have to show them, won't we? We will have to show them how a man can change."

Henry smiled at me and kind of shook his head and shrugged a little. We all knew the row was different. Outside of here, the world was still different. Henry was a white man who'd lynched a black teenage boy. I was a guy who would blow a man's brains out for a few hundred dollars. Brian and Ed were the kind of guys who would kidnap and kill a sixteen-year-old girl. Larry had his pregnant wife murdered. Victor could rob and rape an eighty-six-year-old woman. Jesse would shoot a woman for five dollars, according to his case. I looked around at our unlikely group, locked in a library in Holman Prison. A few of us were innocent, a few were not. It didn't really matter.

"This is what I liked," said Baldwin. "The part where John's having to clean the house. Do you remember? Right in the beginning?" Baldwin unfolded a piece of paper he had brought with him. "I wrote it down while I was reading." He straightened out the paper and cleared his throat.

John hated sweeping this carpet, for dust rose, clogging his nose and sticking to his sweaty skin, and he felt that should he sweep it forever, the clouds of dust would not diminish, the rug would not be clean. It became in his imagination his impossible, lifelong task, his hard trial, like that of a man he had read about somewhere, whose curse it was to push a boulder up a steep hill, only to have the giant who guarded the hill roll the boulder down again—and so on, forever, throughout eternity; he was still out there, that hapless man, somewhere at the other end of the earth, pushing his boulder up the hill.

Everyone was quiet when Baldwin finished reading. He had read softly and carefully, like he had been practicing and didn't want to get it wrong.

"Are you like the guy pushing the boulder up the hill?" asked Victor.

"Yeah, pretty much." Baldwin cleared his throat. "Aren't we all pushing the boulder? Every day, all day, week after week, year after year, we push that boulder up, and then the giant just pushes it back down. And we're going to keep doing this until the giant crushes us to death with that boulder, or someone comes along at the top of the hill and gives us a hand. Someone tells the giant to make way, and we get to push our boulder up and over and then sit down and take a rest or something? Isn't that just how it is?"

A few guys laughed, but I nodded at Baldwin. Horsley just looked down. I had been pushing my boulder up the hill hoping that Perhacs, or Santha, or now Alan Black was going to move the giant out of the way. Or at least hold him back so I could get to the top. I knew what Baldwin meant. I knew how helpless he felt. I felt the same way.

"That's a good quote, Brian," I said. "That's something we can all relate to."

The others nodded.

Horsley raised his hand to speak, and we all laughed.

"What you want to say, Ed?" I asked.

"I like how you think the people are all a certain way, but then you find out their stories, their histories, and you see how they got to be that way. Yes, maybe the father is an ass, but he's had some loss, and it seems like the more you know of their story, the more you kind of forgive them for what they do. You know? It's kind of like that here, right? We all got a story that led to another story and led to some choices and big mistakes. All these characters make mistakes, you know? Nobody is living this life perfect."

Larry hung his head, but the other guys grunted in agreement. Then it was quiet, and I wondered who was thinking about their own mistakes. I had made mistakes, no doubt about it. Wouldn't we all do things over if we could if we knew now what we didn't know then? There wasn't a guy in this library who wouldn't have chosen differently if he could have.

"Who else read a passage that meant something to them?" I asked. I wasn't sure if this is how a book club was held in other places, but I didn't have a study guide or a printed list of questions from anywhere.

I had talked to Sia and Lester about it on my last visit, and Sia had said to just let people talk about what moved them. "Everybody feels something different when they read the same thing. You just have to see what made people feel something and then talk about that," she'd said. "Don't try to be the teacher; just talk about whatever the guys want to talk about." I had nodded. The point was to get them thinking about anything but the dark, grimy, hot hell of the row. It was a gift to spend time in your mind away from your own reality. I could take my private jet anywhere around the world. I spent my week between visits having dinner with the most beautiful women in the world. I had already won Wimbledon five times. I was just this week being recruited by the New York Yankees. I was busy in my cell, too busy to think about the giant at the top of the hill pushing my boulder down. That's all I wanted for these guys, an hour of freedom and escape. An hour away from the rats and the roaches and the smell of death and decay. We were all slowly dying from our own fear—our minds killing us quicker than the State of Alabama ever could. Men would do all kinds of crazy things rather than spend another night with their own thoughts. *Bring in the books,* I thought. *Let every man on the row have a week away, inside the world of a book.* I knew if the mind could open, the heart would follow. It had happened to Henry. Look at him sitting here in a locked room with five black men who had nothing to lose. He had been taught to hate us and fear us so much that he had thought it was in his rights to go find a teenage boy and beat and stab and lynch him just because of the color of his skin. I had no anger toward Henry. He had been taught to fear blacks. He had been trained to hate. Death row had been good for Henry. Death row had saved his soul. Death row had taught him that his hate was wrong.

"What about you, Ray?"

I looked around at the guys. "You know how he's walking in the city, I think on Fifth Avenue, and he knows it's not the place for him?"

"Where's that part at?" asked Victor.

"I don't remember exactly, but he's being taught that the whites don't like him, but he remembers a white teacher being nice to him when he's sick. He thinks someday that the white people will honor him. Respect him. Do you guys remember that?" I said.

Henry cleared his throat. "I remember that part because it was like the opposite of what I was taught, but just the same, you know?" He looked around a bit nervously. "I wrote it down too." Henry took out his own paper—a piece of inmate stationery with the lines printed on it as if we were too dumb to write straight. "Can I read it?" he asked.

Everybody nodded. "It reminded me of my dad. I thought of him, so I wrote it down."

"You go ahead and read it," I said. "Let's hear it."

Henry began:

> *This was not his father's opinion. His father said that all white people were wicked, and that God was going to bring them low. He said that white people were never to be trusted, and that they told nothing but lies, and that not one of them had ever loved a nigger. He, John, was a nigger, and he would find out, as soon as he got a little older, how evil white people could be. John had read about the things white people did to colored people: how, in the South, where his parents came from, white people cheated them of their wages, and burned them, and shot them—and did worse things, said his father, which the tongue could not endure to utter. He had read about colored men being burned in the electric chair for things they had not done; how in riots they were beaten with clubs, how they were tortured in prisons; how they were the last to be hired and the first to be fired. Niggers did not live on these streets where John now walked; it was forbidden; and yet he walked here, and no one raised a hand against him. But did he dare to enter this shop out of which a woman now casually walked, carrying a great round box? Or this apartment before which a white man stood, dressed in a brilliant uniform? John knew he did not dare, not today, and he heard his father's laugh: "No, nor tomorrow neither!" For him there was the back door, and the dark stairs, and the kitchen or the basement. This world was not for him. If he refused to believe, and wanted to break his neck trying, then he could try until the sun refused to shine; they would never let him enter. In John's mind then, the people and the avenue underwent a change, and he feared them and he knew that one day he could hate them if God did not change his heart.*

We were all quiet when Henry finished. We all knew why Henry had picked that passage. His family was KKK. And here was this kid's dad teaching him the same exact thing, only opposite.

"It's a shame," said Henry. "What fathers teach sons. It's a sin to hate, ain't that right, preacher man?" Henry looked over at Heath.

"That's right. It's a sin to hate, but God can forgive our sins. And the sins of our fathers."

"That was a good passage, Henry," said Victor, and both Horsley and Baldwin nodded. Everybody knew Henry had shame, and here we were, five black men in the South trying to comfort the white man who would forever be known for doing the last lynching of a black boy.

"I don't believe the world is not for him," I said. "Or for anyone. We are all God's children, and this world belongs to all of us. I know the sun will never refuse to shine. We may not see it, but I know it's there. I'm not going to have hate in my heart. I spent some dark years here with nothing but hate in my heart. I can't live like that."

"You are not a hater, Ray," said Jesse.

"My mama didn't raise me to hate. And I'm sorry for anyone who was taught to hate instead of love, to fight instead of help. I'm sorry for that and for anyone in this room who feels shame for what they were taught." I looked at Henry. "God knows what's in each man's heart. What someone did or didn't do is between a man and God and is none of anyone else's business."

Everyone nodded, and I could see the guard walking up to unlock the door. Book club had been a success. We had spent an hour talking about something that mattered.

"Someday, when I get out of here, you know what I'm going to do?" I asked.

"What you going to do, Ray?"

"I'm going to tell the world about how there was men in here that mattered. That cared about each other and the world. That were learning how to look at things differently."

"You're going to tell it on the mountain, Ray?" Jesse asked.

The other guys laughed.

"I'm going to tell it on every single mountain there is. I'm going to push that boulder right on up and over that giant, and I'm going to stand at the top of that hill, and on the top of every mountain I can find, and I'm going to tell it. I'm going to tell my story, and I'm going to tell your story. Hell, maybe I will even write a book and tell it like that."

"Everybody up. Back in the cell. This here is over right now." Two guards, one at the door, one in the library, rounded us up and walked us back over to our cells. I watched as Henry grabbed his paper where he had carefully copied down a whole page of James Baldwin's writing and folded it back up. Who would have thought those words would have mattered so much to him?

Larry Heath was the first member of book club to die. He didn't have a last meal for dinner, and when Charlie Jones asked him for any final words, he said, "If this is what it takes for there to be healing in their lives, so be it. Father, I ask for forgiveness for my sins."

On March 20, 1992, at a little after midnight, the guards put a black bag over his head, and the warden who had allowed him the privilege of reading a book and meeting with six other guys to talk about what that book meant to him turned the switch on and sent two thousand volts of electricity coursing through his body for a minute until he was dead.

At the next book club, we left his chair empty.

| 16 |

SHAKEDOWN

I love you.

—HENRY FRANCIS HAYS, FINAL WORDS

I married Halle Berry on a Sunday. It was a beautiful wedding, and she wore a slim white dress made up of the finest lace hand sewn in Paris by a hundred seamstresses. The train of her dress stretched out ten yards behind her and was covered in the smallest and finest pearls from the ocean. She looked up at me, her big brown eyes shiny with tears that threatened to spill over as I gazed at her beautiful face with a love so big it was impossible to explain.

We promised to love each other in sickness and in health, for better or for worse, for richer or for poorer, until death do us part, and my heart felt like it was going to burst open with happiness and joy. "Oh, Ray," she murmured, "I love you so much. I don't know what I would have done if I hadn't met you."

"Halle, my Halle," I said, gazing down at her smooth brown skin and full red lips. "I will never leave you. I promise. I will take care of you." The preacher pronounced us man and wife, and I smiled as Lester and my mama threw wedding rice at us as we ran to a white stretch limousine.

"Goodbye, everyone," I said. "We are traveling around the world, but we will be back in a year to see you all again."

"Goodbye, baby," my mama said as she wrapped her arms around me and squeezed me tight. "You bring me home a grandchild, you hear me? I want twin grandbabies. A boy and a girl."

"I'll see what I can do," I said, laughing and kissing her on the cheek.

Lester shook my hand and then patted me on the back. "You did it," he said. "You found the perfect woman for you. You are a lucky man, and Halle is a lucky woman."

I knew Lester was genuinely happy for me. We didn't compete with each other, and I knew he was glad I had finally found a love like he and Sia had found. Life was good. I picked up Halle, and I could feel her arms wrap around me, and then I slowly lowered my mouth until my lips were only an inch from her lips and she was pressing up against my body and I could feel her breath slowly blowing across my face . . .

"Hinton! Get your ass up, Hinton! Now!"

The door slammed open, and four guards rushed into my cell and grabbed my arms just as they were wrapping around Halle Berry's body. I felt myself pushed up against the wall, my head turned to the right so that my cheekbone pushed into the cold cement. One guard's hand was on my upper back, and they were outfitted in full riot gear with vests and weapons.

I didn't recognize these four guards. They started turning over my books and throwing my shorts and socks into the hallway outside my cell. Up went my mattress, and my perfect pressed whites that I had been working on creasing for the last few days were thrown to the ground and stepped on by a black boot. I watched as the pictures of my mama and of my nieces were thrown out into the hall as well.

"You don't like this, do you?" one of the guards asked.

I didn't answer.

"You got a television in here and everything. Seems like death row is pretty cushy here at Holman."

I waited to see if they were going to break my TV or throw it out in the hall, but they just looked under it and checked to see that there was nothing hidden behind the cord or that none of the electronics were loose.

"You got too many clothes in here. We're going to take half of them. You're not allowed to have so many shorts and socks. This isn't summer camp."

I watched them throw more clothes out into the hall.

"You don't like this, do you?" the guard asked again.

"No, I don't," I said.

"We might come back in five minutes and do this all again. We are here in your prison for twelve hours today, and your staff is over at Donaldson going through our prison. Fresh eyes see new things. Hell, we might do this every hour on the hour today, and what you gonna do about that?"

I could feel his elbow against my back, and he was pressing me harder into the wall.

"Why don't you just move in here if you want to do that? You can throw stuff around all day, then. I'll go out, and you just stay here and do what you need to do." I said it quietly, almost politely, and the three guards going through my stuff stopped for a second and turned to look at me.

One of them laughed. The other two shook their heads, and the one who had me up against the wall pressed in even harder.

"Strip search. Take it all off."

I looked down and shook my head. This was the worst of what they could do when they came to shake you down. Our regular guards rarely strip-searched us on the row—there had to be a good reason. A weapon found somewhere or a big drug bust in general population. Usually, they left us alone, and we kept the peace. All the warden cared about on the row was keeping the peace. We negotiated with him. Each tier side had a representative who met with the captain of the guards, and he told us what he needed and we asked for what we needed. Usually, we met somewhere in the middle. We didn't want trouble, and they were understaffed and didn't want trouble either.

But these were guards from another prison, and they liked coming here and flexing their muscle on death row. It made them feel big and powerful. I knew these guys. They were the guys in high school who were really short or bad at sports or who felt powerless and picked on, and now they had some small bit of power in their little worlds.

"Strip!"

I took off my whites and my socks, and I stood there naked. Two guards left, and two stayed behind.

"Stick out your tongue."

I opened my mouth and showed them I had nothing hidden under my tongue or in the cheeks of my mouth.

"Show us the soles of your feet."

I lifted up each foot and showed them the bottom.

"Spread your legs."

I spread my legs and kept a wide stance.

"Lift up your testicles."

I lifted up my testicles and let them drop back down. I wasn't hiding anything under my testicles. They knew it, and I knew it.

"Bend over and spread your cheeks."

I turned around and bent over in half. I grabbed my ass cheeks and spread them wide.

"Now cough."

I coughed, knowing that my anus was flaring open for them to see if I had anything hidden there. This was only done to humiliate me. *What kind of man enjoyed doing this to another man? What kind of joy did they get from going cell to cell and making a man bend over and show them his ass?*

They kept me bent over with my ass cheeks spread longer than they needed to. It was a game. I wasn't a man to them—I'm not even sure they thought of me as human.

"You can get dressed now. And clean this place up. We'll be here all shift. We might be back."

I kept my back to them as they walked out of my cell, and I pulled on my shorts slowly. Everything was a mess. My sheets were in the dirt on the floor. Their boots had stepped on my clean clothes and maybe even on my toothbrush, which lay in the corner next to the toilet.

I waited until they were off our tier, and I called out to Henry.

"Henry!" I said.

"Ray?"

"You okay?" I asked. "They throw your shit around too?"

"Not so bad," he said. "They just lifted up my mattress."

"I had to lift my testicles and my mattress," I said, and then I smiled as Henry laughed.

"I was just going off on my honeymoon with Halle Berry too. They interrupted that right at the good part."

"You been watching *Queen,* haven't you?"

"You bet I have, and she's my queen now."

A few of the other guys around us laughed.

"Nothing like a little shakedown on a Sunday!" someone yelled.

I sat back down on my bed and put my head in my hands. Tomorrow, our regular guards would come back and pretend to be shocked at what happened. They wouldn't mention that they had gone to one of the other prisons in Alabama and tore things up. This is how they kept themselves from being accountable. *He threw out your picture of your mama? You got to be kidding me!*

And that's how it worked with a shakedown. You never saw it coming, and no one was ever responsible.

Alan Black filed an amended Rule 32 petition in 1994. In May of 1997, Henry got his execution date. June 6. We tried to keep it positive.

"Hold your head up, Henry."

"You just never know what's going to happen."

"The governor could give you a stay."

"Stay positive."

Guys said these kinds of things to him in the yard, on the way to the shower. Compassion doesn't know what color you are, and I think Henry felt more love from the black men on death row than he ever did at a KKK meeting or from his own father and mother.

We had met a few more times in book club and had read *Your Blues Ain't Like Mine*, *To Kill a Mockingbird*, and *Uncle Tom's Cabin*. All the books talked about race in the South, and Henry at first had shied away from the subject, almost pretending not to know how unfairly blacks were treated until we called him out on it. He was ashamed of how he had been brought up and ashamed of the beliefs that had brought him to the row. "You never knew what a person could grow up to become," he'd say. "Why tell someone she can't be a nurse or a guy he can't be a doctor or a lawyer because they're black? That person could discover a cure for AIDS or for cancer. You just never know." I knew he was thinking of Michael Donald, the boy that he had killed. I knew he wondered what that boy might have grown up to become. Henry was the first white man to be put to death for killing a black in almost eighty-five years. His death meant something to people outside of the row. It was making a point about racism and justice and fairness like all the books we had been reading in book club, but to us, it was a family member being killed. There's no racism on death row.

The guards were extra nice to you the week before they killed you. Asking you how you were and what they could get you. You could have visitors anytime you wanted, without any paperwork or hoops to jump through. You got something cold to drink and food from the vending machine or made special for you in the kitchen.

Before Henry was moved to the death room to wait for his execution, we talked one last time.

"I'm sorry, Ray; I'm sorry for what I done."

"I know you are. God knows you are."

"I don't know if I ever told you this, but I have a brother named Ray. He's my brother too."

I could hear that Henry was crying, and my heart broke for him. In the end, none of it mattered. Who you were, what color your skin was, what you had done, whether you showed your victim compassion at the time of his death—none of it mattered. There was no past and no future on the row. We only had the moment we were in, and when you tried to survive moment to moment, there wasn't the luxury of judgment. Henry was my friend. It wasn't complicated. I would show him compassion, because that's how I was raised. That's how I could lay my head down at night in this hellhole and feel like I could make it through another day. A laugh here and there. A helping hand. Friendship. Compassion for another human who was suffering. I would keep my humanity. I wouldn't let them take that from me, no matter what.

At a few minutes before midnight on June 5, I stood at the door of my cell. I took off my shoe, and I started banging on the bars and wire. I wanted Henry to hear me. I wanted him to know he wasn't alone. I knew when they shaved his head, and I heard when the generator kicked on. I banged louder, as did every guy up and down our tier and every tier. We banged on our bars for Henry Hays. Black. White. It didn't matter. I knew he was scared. I knew he was alone. I knew that he was afraid that hell waited on the other side of death row because of what he had done. We banged and we yelled and we hollered as loud as we could. For fifteen minutes, I screamed until my throat was raw and hoarse. I screamed so Henry would know that he meant something. I screamed so that whoever was there to watch the State of Alabama kill in their name knew that we were real men and that you couldn't hide us under a black hood and pretend we didn't feel pain. I screamed because I knew that innocent men had been strapped into that horrid yellow chair, their heads shaved like a bad dog, their dignity stripped away little by little, their worth as humans tied up with electric wires and thrown away like garbage. Innocent men had died in that chair. Guilty men had died in that chair. Strong men had wept like babies, and weak men had held steady as they met their deaths. I yelled for Henry so he would hear me and so he would know that he didn't have to meet his maker alone. And that whoever stared at him in that death chamber with cold eyes was no match against the heat of our cries. We screamed in protest and we screamed in unity and we screamed because there are times when screaming is all there is left to do.

You can't watch a man die—see how one day he is there and the next he is gone—and not think about your own death. Alan Black hadn't been back to see me, but I had received legal papers when he amended my petition again. When I received word he was coming for a visit, I was hoping it was good news.

He had been working on my case for over seven years. I was grateful to him.

"Ray, I got good news," he said.

"What's that?" I asked.

"I'm working on a deal. I think I've got the State to the point where they will consider life without parole. I'm pretty sure we can get you off death row."

He actually smiled at me when he said that. Like I should clap him on the back and be happy for that.

"But I don't want life without parole. I'm innocent. I can't get life without parole. That's like admitting I did something that I didn't do." I was shaking my head at him. I had really thought he believed in me, that he knew I was innocent.

"It's a way to save your life, Ray. It's a great solution."

I stared at him for a good five minutes.

"No," I said quietly.

"What?" he asked. "No, what?"

"I'm not going to agree to that. If I get life without parole, I have no way of walking free. I can't prove my innocence if I agree to life without parole. I'm not going to spend my life in prison."

"Ray, they're going to kill you. They're not going to let you go free. They don't care if you're innocent. They don't have any reason to rule in your favor. The judge has given money for experts now because they don't allow you to appeal for anything you could have appealed on before. They are denying everything we're claiming. Life without parole is a good option."

"What about them experts? What about the bullets?"

Alan Black just stared at me like I was an idiot.

"I need money," he said. "I need $10,000."

"I don't have any money." I couldn't believe we were back to this again. "You do know that I'm in here for robbing people. Why do you lawyers seem to think I have money? Ask Bryan Stevenson if you need money. He's the one who sent you. I don't have any money, and neither does my mama. She's been sick. Don't go bothering her for money."

"You need to ask at your church for the money. With $10,000, I can get you life without parole. Your church needs to collect the money. They're nice people; they're going to do that to save your life. Nobody wants to see you die, Ray. Not your mama, not me, not Bryan Stevenson, not your friends and your family, and not your church. Nobody wants that for you." He was pleading his case.

I got up and stood over him. It wasn't just about the money. It was about my innocence.

"I want to thank you for your time and for your help, but I won't be needing your services anymore."

His mouth fell open, and he laughed a little. "What are you talking about, Ray?"

"I won't be needing your services any longer. You're not my attorney. I'm firing you."

"You're firing me?"

"Yes, I'm firing you. Thank you for everything up until now, but I'd rather die for the truth than live a lie. I'm not agreeing to life without parole. I'll rot and die in here before I agree to that. But thank you for working so hard."

I waved to the guard and walked out of the visiting area. I didn't look back at Alan Black, so I don't know if he still sat there with his mouth hanging open or if he had gotten up to try to follow me. I didn't care. He didn't believe in me, and I didn't believe in him.

I would bend over when the guards made me do it. I had no choice.

But I wasn't going to let anybody else shake me down.

I wasn't ready to give up on my life. I was going to walk out of this place as an innocent man, or I was going to die trying. Nothing more and nothing less.

| 17 |

GOD'S BEST LAWYER

We have a choice. We can embrace our humanness, which means embracing our broken natures and the compassion that remains our best hope for healing. Or we can deny our brokenness, forswear compassion, and, as a result, deny our humanity.

—BRYAN STEVENSON, *JUST MERCY*

After firing Alan Black, I felt alone again—alone in a way I hadn't felt since my conviction. What did I do now? Where did I turn? There was a bad joke that ran up and down the row, with guys repeating it all the time:

"What does capital punishment mean?"

"It means a guy without capital gets punished."

It wasn't funny, but it was true. It felt even truer now that I officially didn't have an attorney working on my appeal. I wondered how soon it would be before the courts found out I wasn't represented. I feared getting an execution date more than anything else. I asked one of the guards as he was making rounds if he could get me a phone number.

"What number you need?" he asked.

"I need to talk to your wife. She is sending you to work with some suspicious-looking lunch meat, and I want to ask her why she's trying to kill you. I'm trying to save your life."

He laughed.

"Who you trying to call? I have the yellow pages in the office."

"I would appreciate it if you could get me the number and the address for the Equal Justice Initiative in Montgomery."

He cocked his head to the side and stared at me for a moment. "You trying to get ahold of Bryan Stevenson?"

I nodded.

The guard smiled at me. "I hope that works out for you, Ray, I do. You're not like the other guys in here."

"We're all the same in here."

"Not in my opinion. I have his number; I'll bring it to you later on." He walked on, and I sat down on my bed to write a letter.

Hello, Mr. Stevenson,

My name is Anthony Ray Hinton, and I'm on Alabama death row. I would like to thank you for the lawyer from Boston; as you most likely know by now, it didn't work out. I know you're probably wanting to send a new lawyer, but I would like for you to be my lawyer. Please read my transcript, and if you can find one thing that points to my guilt, then don't worry about being my lawyer. I will take the punishment that Alabama is seeking. I don't have any money to pay you for your time, but if you would come see me, I can pay you for your gas. I am an innocent man. I would never kill anyone. I hope to hear from you soon. May the God who made us all, continue to bless us all.

Sincerely,
Ray Hinton, Z468

When the guard brought me the address and phone number later that night, I put the letter in an envelope and carefully wrote out the address. I left it unsealed and wrote *Legal Correspondence* on the front. The guards would still read it. They read everything.

The next day when it was time to go on the yard, I went to use the phone instead. I called Equal Justice Initiative—or EJI as it was called for short—collect. A woman answered, and I waited while the recording told her it was an inmate calling collect from Holman Prison. She accepted the charges.

"I'd like to speak to Bryan Stevenson," I said. "This is Anthony Ray Hinton from down at Holman, death row."

She had the kind of voice where you could hear a smile in it. "Why, nice to meet you, Mr. Hinton. Please hold and I will get Mr. Stevenson on the line."

Some generic hold music started playing, and I wondered how much it cost EJI to put collect calls on hold. I waited a few minutes, and then a man's voice came on the line.

"This is Bryan Stevenson." He sounded rushed and hurried.

"Hello, Mr. Stevenson. This is Anthony Ray Hinton from Holman. Death row."

"Hello?" he said, but it sounded like more of a question.

"I wanted to thank you for sending Alan Black, but I wanted to let you know that I had to fire him."

There was silence on the other end. It stretched out for what felt like minutes.

"You fired him?"

"Yes, sir. I had to fire him. He asked me for $10,000. He wanted me to get my church to get him money. I don't have that kind of money."

"I'm so sorry, Mr. Hinton. Let me call him and talk to him."

"I sent you a letter; I need you to read that letter. I don't want Alan Black to be my attorney. He was trying to get me life without parole. I can't do that. Do you understand? Will you read my letter?" I knew I only had a little bit of time before the phone cut off, so I was rushing my words.

"Let me talk to him, and I will get word to you. We'll figure this out. We'll figure out something," he said. His voice sounded sincere, but I had been down this road with attorneys before.

"Just promise me you'll read my letter and consider it."

"Of course. I promise."

Months later, I received word that I had a legal visit. I walked slowly to the visiting area, and seated at a table was a black man, bald, who looked a bit younger than I was. He was dressed in a suit and tie. I walked up to him, and he stood and gave me a wide smile.

"Mr. Hinton, I'm Bryan Stevenson." He held out his hand to shake mine, and when I lifted my arm to extend my own hand, it almost felt like I was moving in slow motion.

"Mr. Stevenson, it's nice to meet you," I said.

He grasped my hand in his, and we shook hands, and in that moment, I felt a strength and a compassion and a hope so big it seemed to shoot out of his hand and into mine. It was almost like an electric shock, and I gave him my best strong handshake back.

I sat down at the table and I looked into his eyes, and it felt like I could take a deep breath for the first time in over twelve years. There are some people you meet and you know they are going to change your life forever. Meeting Bryan was like that. I looked at his face and I saw compassion and kindness. He looked smart. He also looked tired. There were lines around his eyes and a sort of sadness hidden in the creases.

"How are you?" I asked.

"Well, I'm fine, thank you. How are you, Mr. Hinton? Everything going okay for you here? Any problems?"

"You can call me Ray," I said.

"All right, then. You can call me Bryan."

"Thank you for coming to see me. It means a lot to me. I know you do a lot for the guys around here."

He nodded.

"I talked to Alan Black. I'm sorry about that."

"Are you going to be my attorney?" I asked. "Is that why you're here?"

"Right now, I'm just here to meet you and get to know you. Just talk for a bit. I'd like to hear about your case and your trial and your family."

He smiled at me, and I felt that same hope bloom in my heart. I knew he was sent by God.

"You know, when I was convicted, I told that courtroom that someday God was going to open my case again."

"Did you?"

"Yes, I did. But I didn't know it was going to take so long. I've been here almost twelve years. I can't even believe I've been here so long. It's been hell. I can't even tell you the kind of hell it's been."

Bryan looked into my eyes, and I saw that he knew. He understood. He had been to executions here. He had lost people too.

"But today is a good day. Because today, God sent me his best lawyer. Today is the day that God opened up my case."

Bryan laughed. And then he got quiet and said, "Tell me what happened."

"I'm innocent. I've never been violent in my life." I took a deep breath and continued. I needed this man. I needed this lawyer on my side. I knew it stronger than I had ever known anything. I needed him to believe me. I needed him to believe I was innocent. "I made some mistakes. I drove off in a car that didn't belong to me. I wrote some checks, but I wrote them in my own name. I've made some mistakes. Sometimes I think God's punishing me for those mistakes, and other times I think God's got another plan for me, and that's why I'm here. I have a mother that loves me. She loves me more than any human deserves to be loved. Unconditionally. Do you know what that's like? Unconditional love. Not many guys here know that kind of love. A lot of them grew up without any kind of love at all. That hurts a man. It breaks him. It breaks him in ways that no person should be broken. You know what I mean?"

"I do." Bryan looked sad, but he was nodding at me.

"I was at work. I didn't try to rob and kill anyone. I was at work where a guard had to clock me in and clock me out. They told me it didn't matter that it wasn't me. They told me that a white man was going to say that I did it and that's all it would take. I was going to be guilty because I was going to have a white jury and a white judge and a white prosecutor. My defense attorney wasn't paid nothing. He couldn't get money for an expert. They took my mom's gun and said it was the gun that killed those men. My mom's gun hadn't been fired in twenty-five years. My expert only had one eye. I cried when he got off the stand. I knew they were going to find me guilty, but I didn't do it. I dated some sisters and people lied and I've never hurt anyone in my life. A man called during the trial and said he was the one, but my attorney was mad he woke him up. That guy knew things. I didn't know anything. I'd never hurt anyone. I didn't do it. I'm innocent and they have me in here and I can't get out. I'm suffocating in here. They're killing people. They're killing people right next to me. I have to smell my friends as they burn. Do you understand? I have to breathe in their death and it never leaves and they smile at you but someday they're going to come for me too and I am innocent. I need to get home to my mom. She's not feeling good. She doesn't come to visit anymore, and she needs me at home. I need to go back home. I'm innocent. I can't get out of here, and I'm innocent."

It all came out in a rush, and Bryan just sat there and listened to every word. I didn't feel any doubt coming off him. He looked me in the eye the whole time. He asked me questions about my mom and about other family. I told him about Lester and how for twelve years he had come to see me every visiting day. Never missed a day. That was true friendship, and I told him that I wished everyone had a best friend like Lester. He asked me about my trial and who had testified at my sentencing. He seemed surprised that Perhacs hadn't put Lester or my mom or anybody from church on the stand when I was sentenced. He asked me some questions about work and had me walk him through clocking in the night of the Smotherman incident.

We talked for over two hours. I felt comfortable with him. I asked him if he was an Auburn fan and told him that Alan Black was a Red Sox fan and I should have known then it would never work out between us. I told him that after he got me out of here, we could go to a Yankees game.

He laughed. I asked him about his work. Did he have any family? I told him funny stories about the guards, and I told him about book club and how the warden was shutting us down because some of the other guys were saying it wasn't fair that we got to go out to book club and that either everyone goes or no one goes.

I told him we needed some fans on death row, that it was too hot in the summer to even breathe right. He listened to everything I said. He didn't seem in a rush to finish. He didn't interrupt me. He just listened. It was a powerful thing to be listened to like that.

"I have an idea about my case," I said.

"What is it?" he asked. He leaned toward me, like he was really interested.

"Well, I don't know if you're an attorney who doesn't like it if your client has ideas—" I didn't want to offend him or put him off.

"Ray," he interrupted me. "I want to hear every idea you have. We are a team. Along with my staff at EJI, we're going to do everything we can. I want to know what you're thinking every step of the way. I'm going to review your transcript closely. Any idea you have is important to me. No matter what it is."

I smiled at him. This is what I wanted to hear. "I want you to get a ballistics expert."

"Yes, we're going to do that; I think Alan got someone."

"I need you to get the best ballistics expert there is. The judges here are so biased. It can't be a woman. It can't be someone from up North. It has to be a man, preferably a white, Southern man. He needs to believe in the death penalty. He needs to be the best of the best, the guy who taught the State's guys. He needs to have every reason in the world to want to see me die if I'm guilty, but he has to be honest. As long as he's an honest, racist, Southern, white expert, I'll be okay."

Bryan laughed. "I can see your point. That's a good idea. We'll look into it. I know someone from the FBI. I think we want to get more than one expert, but let me review your file. Let me see the reports from the State's experts. Let me see what your expert said and did. I need to get up to speed on everything, and then I'll come back to see you. Okay?"

We shook hands again, and our eyes locked as we said goodbye. He didn't promise me then he was going to get me out of there, but I saw it in his eyes. I saw the promise that he would make later. It was a promise I would hold on to through a lot of dark nights.

The guard walked me back to my cell, and as soon as the door shut behind me, I dropped to my knees. I folded my hands and bowed my head. *Thank you, God. Thank you for sending Bryan Stevenson. I trust things to happen in your time, so I'm not going to ask you why you didn't send him earlier. Please, God, watch over Bryan Stevenson. Take care of him, because he's doing your work. God, bless the men on death row. Bless my mom, and please put hope in her heart that her baby's coming home. I'm going to tell her you sent your best lawyer to me. God, please keep her in good health. Please, God, let the truth come out. Thank you, God. I know you've sent your best lawyer, and I know you've reopened my case.*

I finished my prayer just as the first sob broke loose from my chest. I spent the next two hours on my knees sobbing like a baby.

Some nights are just made for crying.

| 18 |

TESTING THE BULLETS

Standing alone, the evidence in this case was simply insufficient to prove Mr. Hinton's guilt.

—BRYAN STEVENSON, OPPOSITION TO STATE'S PROPOSED ORDER, 2002

My mom wanted to cook for Bryan Stevenson. It's the way she showed love, and after I told her about him, all she wanted to do was show her love.

"He's going to be coming to talk to you," I told her.

"Well, what does he like to eat?" she asked. "I want to make him something special. You find out what his favorite meal is, and I'll fix it right up. I'd like to give him some money also."

"No, Mama. You can't give him money. He won't take it. Please don't try to give him money."

"Well, what does he say? When are you going to come home, baby? I'm ready for you to come home now."

My breath always hitched when she said that. She hadn't been out to see me in a long time. The drive was just too difficult for her. I knew she was sick, in the way you know things about the people you love, but neither she nor Lester wanted to tell me anything. They didn't want me to worry, and it just seemed easier to pretend things were different from how they were. I couldn't be home to take care of her, and the pain of that fact was too much to face. I was a prisoner. It shouldn't have been so hard for an innocent man to get out of prison, but it was. There is a point in a struggle where you have to surrender. You have to stop trying to swim upstream, stop fighting the current. I hadn't given up the idea of walking out of prison, but I couldn't fight it every single day and survive. You try your best to get home, and then at some point, you decide to make a home where you are. I had to make a home of Holman to survive. I had to block out my real home and block out the outside world. It didn't matter anymore what other people did at 10:00 A.M. every day. For me, in my home, 10:00 A.M. was lunchtime. I had to accept that. I had to face the fact that in my home, men cried and screamed and moaned every day, all day. In my home, the rats and the roaches were free to come and go as they pleased, while I was not. In my home, people could come in at any time and turn my home upside down, and I had to take it. I had to say, "Yes, sir," and "Thank you, sir," in order to live. In my home, death was always at my door. It circled my house, watching and waiting and always present. I survived in my home mostly week to week—between visits with Lester, but sometimes it was minute to minute and hour to hour. In my home, I always knew when my family would die. In the real world, I didn't know that death stalked the ones I loved as well. I couldn't face that reality. I couldn't live in the real world—only in the world of my imagination and the world that existed in my cell.

"It's going to take some time, Mama. He has to undo what the other lawyers did. It's like he's starting over. But he promised me he was going to get me out of here. He knows I'm innocent, Mama; he believes me. He's proven it."

"Of course you're innocent. No child of mine would ever hurt someone. I didn't like how that other attorney used your name. He didn't do right by you. I don't think he believed in you."

She was talking about McGregor. It was hard to hear how confused she got at times. Lester told me she was fine, just got tired easily and it pained her to sit in a car for seven hours in one day, which I understood. His mom still came to visit, but only every few months or so. They were getting older. We were all getting older.

After Bryan had come to visit, I received a letter from him.

November 1, 1998

Anthony Ray Hinton, Z-468
Holman State Prison
Holman, 3700
Atmore, Alabama 36503

Dear Ray:

We have reviewed the trial transcript of your case and prepared a case summary. We are now organizing the investigation. I am sending you a copy of the trial summary and would like you to review it. I will want to talk to you again about some of the evidence presented against you at trial, and it may be useful for you to refresh your recollection by reviewing the trial summary.

I hope you are well. We are starting to make some progress in identifying areas where there may be a basis for moving your case in the right direction. I will be down to see you in the next couple of weeks. Hang in there.

Sincerely,

Bryan Stevenson

Bryan did come to see me a few weeks later, and a few weeks after that, and on a regular basis. We got to know each other, and for parts of the visit he was my attorney, and for other parts he was my friend. Sometimes we would go an hour or more not talking about my case—not the ballistics or McGregor or Reggie White or anything to do with my innocence. Instead, we would talk about the weather in Alabama, the college football season, food we liked and food we hated. Some days, I could see he was tired, and I wondered about the wear on a person when so many lives depend on what you do each day. He carried a big burden, and it wasn't just mine. He spoke of justice and of mercy and of a system that was so broken it locked up children and the mentally ill and the innocent. "No one is beyond redemption," he would say. No one is undeserving of their own life or their own potential to change. He had such compassion for victims and for perpetrators, and an intolerance and even anger for those in power who abused that power. Bryan Stevenson was not happy with McGregor, and he wasn't happy with Perhacs either. I learned he had a team of young lawyers, straight-A students from the best law schools in the country, working for him and volunteering to fight the good fight. "If those straight-A students can't get it done," I used to say, "you might want to bring in some of those C students. Those middle-of-the-class students sometimes know how to work the system. They have some hustle to them."

I liked making him laugh. He wore his work and his passion for his work on his face, but sometimes you could see it fall away and we were just two guys shooting the shit. Talking about football and politics and good barbecue and guys we knew who could act the fool. I wasn't condemned, and he wasn't a lawyer. We were just Ray and Bryan, more alike than different. We both knew my life was in his hands—but that's a burden we had to set aside now and then. It was always there for us to pick up again, but sometimes life is so damn heavy the only choice is to laugh at the ridiculousness of it all. It was a relief to know he truly believed in my innocence. There was no talk of life without parole. I was innocent, and he was going to yell and argue and fight until the State agreed to acknowledge it had made a mistake.

I hoped it would be soon.

I prayed it would be soon.

Hope can be a four-letter word in prison. It can tease a man by staying close but just out of reach. I had hope. I had lots of hope. But I was impatient at times. My life was passing me by quickly, and every year, I grieved for the year I lost. I was grateful to not be executed, but it was like existing in limbo—floating somewhere between life and death and never knowing where I was going to land.

The original case summary Bryan prepared was almost two hundred pages long. I liked that he wanted me to review it. I liked that he asked my opinion. I liked finally feeling that I had a voice in my own defense.

May 18, 1999

Anthony Ray Hinton, Z-468
Holman State Prison
Holman, 3700
Atmore, Alabama 36503

Dear Ray:

We have had a couple of useful days investigating your case. On Sunday, we spoke with Tom Dahl, who was your supervisor on the night of the Quincy's robbery. Dahl was very helpful and gave us additional information to support your alibi. We have also located two of the other Manpower employees who were working with you at Bruno's on the night of the crime. We are still looking for others. If you can think of anyone who you worked with on that night, please send me their name.

Earlier this month I met your mother in her home and we really enjoyed speaking with her. We were able to speak with Donna Baker, Wesley Mae Williams, and Rev. Calvin Parker from the church. We are tracking down a couple of other folks who would have been at the church that night.

I have spoken to Alan Black who understands that we will be filing an amended petition and formally entering our notice of appearance in your case next week. We will be up in Dora and Birmingham for three days next week investigating your case. I will give you an update at that time as to where we are. There is still a hearing scheduled for June 25, but I expect that will be postponed in a couple of weeks. I'm now thinking that the best time for a hearing for us will be sometime between August and October of this year.

Let me know if you need anything and hang in there. I'll be in touch with you soon.

Sincerely,

Bryan Stevenson

He always told me to "hang in there," and those words weren't throw-away words. They weren't just a way to end a letter or a phone call. We both knew a lot of guys on the row—eleven, to be exact, since I was there—who'd chosen not to hang in there. Giving up was always a temptation. Taking your own life sometimes seemed like a better choice than letting the State take it for you.

I wasn't going to take my own life, but I always appreciated Bryan's telling me to hang in there. It got me through another day. Another long night. I took comfort in his letters and his visits. He was working for me, and I prayed for him each and every night.

He found two good old boy experts from Texas and another from the FBI. They were the best of the best in the country. They usually only testified for the prosecutors in a case. They were white. They were honest. They had credentials that made Higgins and Yates look like hacks. They were unimpeachable, as Bryan liked to say.

"Ray, I have good news." Bryan's voice sounded excited. Like a little kid on Christmas.

"What's that?" I had gotten word from the guard that Bryan had wanted to talk to me and I should call him right away. He had an understanding with the guards that he could call them and they would give me a message to call him collect. Sometimes it seemed like the guards wanted to see me leave death row just as much as I did.

"I got the reports from Emanuel, Cooper, and Dillon. Their report says that none of the bullets from all three locations match your mother's gun. They also said that the recovered bullets and the test bullets do not match. We also found out that Higgins and Yates had worksheets that the State didn't turn over to your attorney. Their worksheets showed question marks and missing information. They didn't follow proper procedures, and they didn't record any land or groove information for any of the six bullets. We can prove this. We can prove that the only evidence against you is false. There's no way the bullets match your mother's gun."

I took a deep breath. Finally! "So what do we do now?" I asked. "When can I get out of here?" I was ready to pack it up right then and there. "Come pick me up, Bryan; I'm ready to go home!"

"Well, it's usual for experts to meet and review the tests together when they have conflicting results. It's a professional courtesy and part of their procedure according to their code of ethics. Emanuel, Cooper, and Dillon will have to meet with Higgins and Yates. It's a process, Ray, but we're on the right track. I'm going to make sure they understand there's a problem with your case. The ballistics are all they have; without that, they have no conviction. They said that in your trial. They conceded that fact."

"Thank you," I said. "Bryan, I can't tell you enough how grateful I am to you." I started to choke up.

"We're not home yet, Ray, but we're on our way."

"I'll be here," I said. "You just let me know when it's time to go home."

"I'll get you home, Ray. I promise you."

February 10, 2002

Anthony Ray Hinton, Z-468
Holman State Prison
Holman, 3700
Atmore, Alabama 36503-3700

Dear Ray:

I wanted to keep you posted on things. I've spoken with the chief deputy district attorney in Jefferson County and provided him with the attached memorandum. He has been appropriate in my conversations with him and knows that we are credible when we say there is a problem with a case. He is meeting with McGregor and I will be talking with him again this week. We are trying to see if they will join the motion to vacate your conviction and sentence pending before Judge Garrett. If Jefferson County concedes that mistaken ballistics evidence means that you are innocent, we would probably then agree to have the weapon tested by some government agency, perhaps the ATF or the FBI. Assuming those test results come back the right way, we would then ask for a declaration of innocence.

The odds are still not high that they will be agreeable to this, but our early conversations have gone well. You should keep praying about this because if we can work this thing by some consensus, I think you could be released sometime soon. It will be a longer process otherwise.

The hearing is scheduled for March 11–13. You are supposed to be moved to the Jefferson County jail on March 8. The attorney general's office is acting sort of crazy, not really dealing with the evidence and just arguing procedural issues.

I will be down to see you either the week of February 18 or the week of February 25. I have made contact with an excellent producer at *60 Minutes*. We are meeting in New York on Wednesday. If the State does not agree to a non-adversarial resolution, we will probably get them started right around the time of the hearing.

Anyway, things are going well for the case. Keep your head up, something may be soon to break. I'm enclosing some money to help you out. Let me know if you need anything else. I'll see you soon, my friend.

Sincerely,

Bryan Stevenson

I read the letter and the attached memo that Bryan sent with it. The memo began in bold type:

THE ANTHONY RAY HINTON CASE
Anthony Ray Hinton has been on Alabama's death row for 16 years for crimes he did not commit.

It went on to detail the newly discovered ballistics findings and my confirmed alibi of being at work at Bruno's; it listed the mistaken previous ballistics evidence; and it recounted how the police had pressured other employees at Food World to say they saw me there that night, and how they had refused and said they didn't see me there. Only Clark Hayes, the grocery clerk, said he saw me there, and he was pressured just like the others. It also brought up my polygraph. The polygraph nobody wanted to look at.

I held up the money order Bryan had sent with his letter. I was still amazed at how selfless Bryan was. Not only didn't he shake me down, he sent me cards and notes and money for my commissary purchases. The hearing was scheduled for March, and I went to bed thinking about that hearing. They would have to let me go, then. I was innocent. The FBI expert had even said so. The more Bryan uncovered, though, the more it seemed like this wasn't just an innocent mistake. To let me go, Alabama was going to have to admit they purposely sent me to death row. The police had coerced witnesses into saying I was at Food World. The detectives had given my name to Smotherman before he identified me from a photo that had my initials on it. I could feel the rage building again—the white-hot hate of anger at how much they had stolen of my life. Sixteen years. How much more could a man take? How did Reggie sleep at night, knowing he had sent me to my death because of two sisters from so long ago it hardly seemed like it could matter? Every day, I had to keep reminding myself that I still mattered.

Alabama had made a mistake.

I was innocent.

We could prove it.

I read Bryan's letter and the memo over and over again, and that night, I prayed harder than I had ever prayed before. The truth was shining a light so big that they couldn't ignore it. I prayed for Judge Garrett and for McGregor and for Higgins and Yates. I prayed for Perhacs. Bryan told me that Perhacs and McGregor were friends. He also told me that Bob McGregor had a history of racial bias and was twice found guilty of illegally discriminating against African Americans in jury selections, once in Mobile and another time in Jefferson County.

I hadn't known any of this, but I forgave Perhacs for not telling me he was friends with McGregor. I was young and stupid and so trusting of a system that was rigged against me from the start, so I also prayed I could forgive myself as well.

I prayed for Bryan's voice to be the voice of reason, and for fairness and justice. But I never forgot that Bryan was a black man like me. And he was up against the same ignorance I was up against. He was smarter than them all, though. And God was on his side.

That much I knew.

My mama had taught me well.

God had a plan, and God was always on the side of justice. God could do everything but fail. I had to believe. Sixteen long years. I was ready for God's justice. I was ready for mercy. My freedom was so close I could taste it and feel it, and sometimes at night, I would be back in my mama's yard on a hot day in July, cutting the grass and thinking about going to church. I would look around and realize this had all been a bad dream. I was only dreaming. I had not spent sixteen years of my life on death row. It was 1985, and I was twenty-nine years old and my whole life stretched out in front of me, full of sweet possibility. In my dream, I'd walk into the kitchen and I'd lay my head on my mama's shoulder, and she would pat my back like she always did when I had a bad dream.

It wasn't real.

I had my whole life in front of me, and my mama was there telling me everything was going to be okay. I was okay. There were no bad men trying to take me away.

It was only a nightmare.

It wasn't real.

How could any of it have been real?

| 19 |

EMPTY CHAIRS

Until I feared I would lose it, I never loved to read. One does not love breathing.

—HARPER LEE, *TO KILL A MOCKINGBIRD*

It took until June 2002 to finally have my Rule 32 hearing. In March, right before we were supposed to have the hearing, the State's Attorney General Office filed a writ of mandamus to force the lower court to dismiss my petition altogether. Basically, they didn't want the lower court to look at the evidence of my innocence. Their motion to dismiss said that they were not required to listen to or defend any of my innocence claims or look at the new ballistics tests because too much time had passed, or the evidence was cumulative rather than new. It was crazy. They said it was a waste of time. A stay was granted one day before my hearing, and the attorney general said in his brief that I should be blocked from establishing my innocence because it would "waste three days or two days of taxpayer money." They weren't even willing to hear me out. To look at the new evidence. To see what Perhacs had failed to show them in 1986. It hurt all over again. What kind of a world was it where an innocent man can lose sixteen years of his life and it's a waste of time to let him prove he's innocent? My sixteen years was less important than two or three days of the attorney general's time.

Bryan sent me a letter explaining everything and offering encouragement. He was always there to make sure my spirits never dropped too low at every legal twist and turn.

March 12, 2002

Anthony Ray Hinton, Z-468
Holman State Prison
Holman, 3700
Atmore, Alabama 36503

Dear Ray:

I just wanted to touch base with you after what seems like a very strange five days. I spoke with Judge Garrett on Monday morning to try and block your transfer to Birmingham and to confirm that we would not litigate this case piecemeal. The judge is very angry at the State. I think he is even more suspicious of their desperation to keep us from presenting this evidence than I had hoped. The State may have made a serious mistake in antagonizing the court this way. The State waited until the day before the hearing to file a stay motion, which is pretty bad form, if nothing else.

We will file a response to the State's papers in the next two weeks. The State is essentially arguing that our evidence will be the same as what was presented at trial and therefore we have no right to present it. We are saying that they can't know what the evidence is until we present it and if it's unpersuasive then they have nothing to fear. The appeal likely means that it will be May before we can schedule another hearing date.

We had a very good week last week and had organized a pretty compelling case. I'll talk to you about some recent developments, new witnesses we found, when I see you next at the prison. I will try to get down as soon as I can.

I know it's upsetting to have the hearing postponed like this. I was pretty furious all day on

Saturday. We had spent lots of money on nonrefundable plane tickets for witnesses, rented computer equipment for audiovisual presentations for the courtroom, and done a lot of stuff to prepare for this hearing. Most importantly, however, it's just wrong for you to spend more days and weeks on death row for something you did not do. However, our day will come. Don't be too discouraged, the race is not given to the quick but to the one who endures. I'm more hopeful than ever that we will prevail and you will go home.

Enclosed is the State's motion, our initial response, and the court's order. I'm trying to schedule a time to see you sometime in the next few weeks. Hang in there, my friend.

Sincerely,

Bryan Stevenson

I wasn't surprised that the State was doing its best to keep me locked away and quiet. It was what the court had done from the beginning. It was still a lynching. It was taking decades to get the noose wrapped just right. I also wasn't naïve. The State was unwilling to admit it had made a mistake. Alabama would rather stay wrong than admit that it had been wrong; rather accept injustice than admit that it had been unjust.

I knew that there were men before me and men after me who would abuse the system, who would be guilty but exhaust every claim to try to keep from getting killed. I didn't blame them. I couldn't blame them. Who wouldn't fight for their survival? For their right to live? And yes, the victims didn't have a chance to fight for their right to live. I understood that. What I didn't understand was how any killing could be justified. Man didn't have the right to take a life. The State didn't have the right to take a life either. They were killing us on behalf of the people, and I wondered what the people really believed. Yes, there were brutal, unremorseful, coldhearted, sociopathic, danger-to-society killers on death row. I knew this for a fact. I walked next to them on the yard. I showered with them. I talked to them. I knew some of them would kill me in a heartbeat if they could—not that they hated me, but killing was what they did. Some had the intellect of a child, and others had the intellect of a genius. But I still didn't believe any person or any institution had a right to take their life, no matter what they had done. *The people* was such a general term that I wondered what would happen if the prison asked the real people. "Jo Martin, we are going to kill Anthony Ray Hinton today, and we're going to do it in your name. We're going to say that we are killing you on behalf of Jo Martin. Is that okay?" Or Sarah Paulson, or Angela Ruiz, or Victor Wilson, or insert any name. *The people* were made up of real people, and so were the condemned men on the row. Life is brutal, tragic, unbearable, and inhumane at times. The pain one man can cause another is limitless, but I didn't see—I *couldn't* see—how creating more pain made anything better. When you took a life, it didn't bring back a life. It didn't undo what was done. It wasn't logical. We were just creating an endless chain of death and killing, every link connected to the next. It was barbaric. No baby is born a murderer. No toddler dreams of being on death row someday. Every killer on death row was taught to be a killer—by parents, by a system, by the brutality of another brutalized person—but no one was born a killer. My friend Henry wasn't born to hate. He was taught to hate, and to hate so much that killing was justified. No one was born to this one precious life to be locked in a cell and murdered. Not the innocent like me, but not the guilty either. Life was a gift given by God. I believed it should and could only be taken by God as well. Or whatever a man believed in. It didn't matter to me. But God never gave the guards, or the warden, or the judges, or the State of Alabama, or the federal government, or *the people* the right to take a life.

Nobody had that right.

I was afraid every single day on death row. And I also found a way to find joy every single day. I learned that fear and joy are both a choice. And every morning when I opened my eyes at 3:00 A.M. and saw the cement and the mesh wire and the sadness and filth of my tiny cell, I had a choice. Would I choose fear, or would I choose love? Would I choose a prison, or would I choose a home? It wasn't always easy. On the days that I chose a home, I could laugh with the guards, listen to the other guys, talk about our cases, talk about books and ideas and what we might do when we walked out of this hell. But on the days when I opened my eyes and felt nothing but terror, when every corner of that cell looked like a black-and-white horror film with an ax-wielding psycho killer just waiting to jump out at me and hack me to pieces, I would close my eyes again and I would leave.

I had to divorce Halle Berry for Sandra Bullock. I had seen the movie *Speed,* and I thought Sandra would be good to have in case I ever busted out of death row and needed a getaway driver. Halle didn't take it well, but I think it was for the best. Sandra and I were able to laugh together in a way that Halle and I just couldn't. Sandra had a passion for social justice. I watched her on my little television in the movie *A Time to Kill,* based on a John Grisham novel that I had read. I knew that if I had her by my side, she would fight for me. Demand justice. Not be afraid of the Alabama attorney general or Judge Garrett or McGregor. She would stand up to them all, and in my mind, she—along with Bryan—was my voice out in the world. Sandra and I settled into a beautiful home not far from my mama's house. Lester lived next door. We would all get together for barbecue, and while not many people knew this, Sandra Bullock could really sing. She could sing so well, birds used to gather round her to learn a thing or two. She would sing the saddest songs I had ever heard—in a voice that could crack a man's heart wide open. She used to look in my eyes and sing just for me. We loved each other, and I was grateful to be loved by a good woman. I was grateful she stayed by my side.

I never did have children—not with Halle or with Sandra. I couldn't bear the thought of being separated from them. There were times when I had to leave Sandra, leave my mom, leave my professional baseball career, and travel back to death row and be there for a while. I didn't want to do that to a child. I knew how hard it was for me to be apart from my mom, and I wouldn't wish that pain on anyone, especially not a child.

The guys on the row who had children bore a pain that was almost too much to witness. They ached and they cried and they missed all the things that other parents take for granted. And they also knew how much their children suffered—no child wanted to brag about his or her dad on death row. I knew there were women on death row, a couple of hours away at Tutwiler Prison. I couldn't imagine the guards putting a woman to death. Especially a woman with children. One of the guys on death row was a guy named George Sibley. He and his wife, Lynda, had both been sent to death row, and they had a nine-year-old son with them when they killed a police officer in 1993.

Lynda was executed before George. What must it be like for a man to be locked in a cell and have his wife about to be murdered and not be able to do a thing about it? I didn't spend a lot of time with George, but I knew his story. And through listening to him talk, I felt like I knew his wife. On May 10, 2002, they brought her to Holman. They walked her through the row. A woman on death row. She wore white like the rest of us. She held her head up and looked straight ahead. I don't know if she and George got to see each other. He never spoke of that day. When she was executed, we banged on the bars. We made some noise. For her. For George. For their son who was now eighteen years old. They shaved her head just like they shaved a man's head. They put a hood over her face and left her in the dark as they electrocuted her. I couldn't imagine the kind of pain George Sibley was in. I felt physically ill even trying to put myself in his shoes. How helpless does a man feel when his wife is being killed and he can do nothing to stop it?

I knew he wished he had gone first.

The guards who strapped her to the chair and then put her dead body on a gurney would finish those tasks and then hand George his breakfast a few hours later. They would smile and ask him how he was doing, but they would never be able to look him in the eye again.

How could they? How could they look any of us in the eye after they executed someone?

It was enough to make you insane.

Lynda was the last person to be electrocuted in Yellow Mama. After her execution, the prison began remodeling the death chamber and getting ready for a new way to kill us.

It was called lethal injection.

It was how they planned to kill the rest of us.

I walked into the Rule 32 hearing hopeful. Perhacs took the stand and admitted Payne as an expert had been a failure on his part. He told the court how he didn't have enough money to mount a defense or to pay for a qualified expert. The three new experts took the stand. They stated that there was no proof the bullets matched my mom's gun.

It was good to see Lester outside of the visiting yard. And my mom too. She looked frail and sick, and her hair was gone from places on her head. She looked at me and smiled, but it was a tired smile. I wanted to run to her and hold her in my arms, but I had to take a deep breath and be grateful to see her at all. Our phone calls were few and far between, and it was often too confusing for her to talk on the phone and understand who she was talking to. Phoebe, Lester's mom, sat at her side, and I soaked up her warm smile and reassuring nod. Perhacs barely acknowledged my presence in the hearing. He had talked to Bryan over the phone quite a bit, but when Bryan and another attorney went to meet with him in person prior to the hearing, he had taken one look at Bryan and said, "I didn't know you had a tan."

Apparently, Bryan had sounded white to Perhacs—however white sounded. I looked at Perhacs and could see how he had aged. My life had been in his hands, but he never valued my life. I was so young and stupid about the legal system to have believed he was fighting for me, that he actually cared that I was innocent. He knew, though. I could see it in his eyes the few times he glanced my way. I wondered if it ever kept him up at night. I wondered if he and McGregor ever talked about me. Probably not. I was just another black boy who wasn't going quietly—a pain in their side—but nothing to worry about.

McGregor wasn't at the hearing, but I didn't care one way or the other. My days of hating him were over. I didn't want to play that game. He knew what he had done. Most of all, I didn't want to go back to having hatred in my heart. I had forgiven McGregor. His sins were between him and God. I also forgave the rest of them. They were a shameful lot of sad men, and I prayed for their souls.

I was innocent, and the three ballistics experts could not be argued with. I closed my eyes and imagined Garrett banging his gavel and standing up to yell, "In light of these three independent ballistics experts and in the name of true justice, I hereby declare Mr. Hinton innocent and order for him to be released immediately!"

That didn't happen. In fact, I saw the judge yawn during their testimony.

There were three assistant attorneys general at the hearing: Houts, Hayden, and Deason. They had tried every which way to block the hearing from happening, but here we were, and they didn't seem too happy about it.

"What issues does the petitioner want to raise in the Rule 32 at this time?" asked Judge Garrett. I noticed he never once looked at me—it was like I didn't exist.

Bryan stood up. "Your Honor, we intend to present evidence relating essentially to the claim of factual innocence, claim of ineffective assistance of counsel, the Brady violation. And then there are legal claims, Your Honor, to which we don't believe we have to present any evidence. In our petition, we talk about prosecutorial misconduct with closing argument. The record speaks for itself on that issue."

I wondered what McGregor would've thought about that statement. Would Perhacs tell him?

"There are some legal issues, however," Bryan continued, "that we also think the new evidence relates to. For example, the consolidation issue is a legal claim. We don't really have facts that relate to that. However, if the evidence establishes that this weapon could not be matched to these crimes, it changes the legal analysis on consolidation. That's why that claim is included in the evidentiary portion of our presentation, but the facts actually go to the first claim."

Judge Garrett argued a bit with Bryan. Were we presenting the same evidence but on a different theory? We couldn't introduce evidence if it had already been considered by the courts. Bryan didn't back down.

"Our primary presentation is about the innocence claim and about the ineffectiveness of counsel claim and about claims flowing from due process violations relating to the withholding of exculpatory evidence. All those issues are cognizable in this Rule 32 process and cognizable by this court."

Score one for Bryan, I thought.

Bryan told Garrett he was going to present evidence from experts. I was amazed when Garrett played dumb about the evidence. They had been trying to get the court and the State to look at these new experts and their reports for years.

"Was there not evidence of both of those—by experts on both sides at trial?" Garrett looked at Bryan smugly.

"Well, Your Honor, I guess two things. We believe that the State was wrong, and we believe that Mr. Payne was not qualified to make the kind of examination that these experts are qualified to make."

"Well, that issue would be moot since that issue was raised in the trial of the case, wouldn't it?"

I sighed. Why wouldn't they just look at the evidence?

Bryan's voice got a bit louder. "No. We can present evidence that establishes that the State is wrong."

"What would be the nature of the testimony presented by your experts in this regard?"

Bryan stared at Garrett for a few seconds and then took a breath. *Give it to him, Bryan,* I thought.

"It will be basically that microscopic comparisons between the bullets recovered does not allow a determination that these bullets were fired from a single weapon. And as you recall, Your Honor, a single weapon was critical to the State's theory at trial. This court found Mr. Hinton guilty and sentenced him to death based on the belief that recovered bullets from all three of these crimes came from a single weapon. We believe that that belief is clearly inaccurate, that the evidence will make that clear. Secondly—"

Garrett interrupted him. "Well, isn't this just a differing of experts, one expert disagreeing with another expert? Of course we had that at the trial of the case."

"No, Your Honor. I don't believe that's what this is."

"Are these the ultimate experts in the whole wide universe that are going to testify to that?"

"Yes, sir. I believe they are."

"What if we come up with some different experts later on that are even more recognized as the ultimate experts? That's what we're getting into—a swearing contest between experts."

In that moment, I realized that the real killer could walk into this courtroom with pictures of himself committing the crime, and the judge wouldn't accept the evidence. The attorney general would just say, "That's an old story wrapped in a new cover."

"Your Honor, I don't think that's our case. We have been trying frankly for the last eight years to have the State reexamine this evidence. We don't believe that anybody from the Department of Forensic Sciences can now look at this evidence and come in here and tell you that these bullets were fired from one weapon or that they were fired from the weapon recovered from Mr. Hinton. We don't think they can do it. We think actually that they had an opportunity to do it and declined to do so. We have some information that they looked at in 1994 and concluded that they couldn't make a match any longer.

"This is not a battle of experts. We would welcome any expert the State could identify that the court appoints to look at this evidence and disagree with our findings. We have three experts from different places, because we want to make it clear that this is *not* a battle of experts. We think any competent, trained expert that looks at this evidence now is going to come to the same conclusion about how these bullets were not fired from a single weapon. They were not fired from the weapon recovered from Mr. Hinton. That's our evidence."

I watched amazed as Assistant Attorney General Houts argued with Bryan about Payne being a competent expert. At the time of my trial, they called him all sorts of names—*expert* wasn't one of them. Bryan argued that the new evidence established my innocence, and this made the evidence allowed in a Rule 32 proceeding.

Houts turned to the judge. "To the extent that Mr. Stevenson is attempting to make an actual innocence claim that is constitutional, the U.S. Supreme Court does not recognize actual innocence as a constitutional claim through which you can bring a habeas corpus action."

I knew a habeas corpus action was part of the federal appeals process that we would begin if I lost in all the state courts. I didn't want to think about that. Bryan had told me the federal appeals process was extremely narrow and difficult.

Bryan cleared his throat. "I feel some need, Your Honor, to just kind of be real clear about what we're saying here. And I can expect this court to do anything but hear me when I say this. But we believe this man is innocent, *innocent,* and that is why we think this evidence is so critical. And this is not like any standard Rule 32 case. It's not even like a standard death penalty case.

"The temptation that the Court of Criminal Appeals will have to face if they hear an argument from the State of Alabama that this evidence should have been precluded on appeal, in my judgment, is nothing like the temptation to ignore the possible execution of an innocent person. We believe this evidence is compelling. We believe it's compelling and will be compelling to this court. We believe it ought to be compelling to the State. But we think we ought to have the right to present it."

Judge Garrett was silent for a minute and then asked, "What makes this evidence so different from that evidence which was presented at trial except that it's by different persons?"

Bryan explained that it was rare to have three different experts separately find the same thing and even rarer that several people look at evidence, find the same thing, and that thing is not what was presented at trial. He also pointed out that no one from the State was prepared to prove a match now or say that they could find exactly what was found in 1985.

"Let me say this," began Judge Garrett. "Mr. Payne has been recognized or was recognized as an expert and testified both in civil and criminal courts all over the State."

"Well, he was characterized by the State at trial, Your Honor, as a charlatan, as someone who didn't know anything about this kind of testimony. He was mocked."

"Oh, well, I see that on experts quite often by either side."

"But you rarely see one, Your Honor, who's legally blind, who could not operate the machine, and who had never been qualified for this kind of examination and this kind of case. And that's the distinction."

Garrett didn't respond, so Bryan continued.

"What we have are experts or leaders in the association of firearms and tool mark examinations. Mr. Dillon was the head of the FBI in their unit for many years, its former past president for the Association of Firearm and Tool Mark Examiners. He's taught all over the country, consults with the FBI, consults with the ATF.

"Mr. Emanuel and Mr. Cooper work mostly for the prosecution. They've worked for the United States military, the State of Texas. They work for Dallas County prosecutors regularly. These experts have testified and examined over two thousand cases. They've been qualified over two hundred times. They're leaders in this field. And we've really spared no cost in getting the people we could identify as the best in the country, because we really wanted to make it clear to the court that this wasn't about a mere dispute but about a critical piece of factual evidence on which this conviction stands."

It should have been enough for Garrett. We had unimpeachable experts. Men who had every reason to find me guilty. Houts fought it the whole way. Garrett argued the State's side as well. But Bryan never faltered. I had never seen him like this. God's best lawyer was preaching the law at them like the law had never been preached at them before. I wished I'd had Bryan on my case in 1985. I would never have gone to death row. I probably would have never even gone to trial. It wasn't fair that justice could be so arbitrary and the truth so hard for the State to admit. How could Garrett sit there and say

Payne was a qualified expert? How could he in good conscience, when the State had argued the opposite?

Bryan didn't back down an inch.

"What we're saying, Your Honor, is that the State made a mistake. It's a 'made a mistake' case. And what I hear the State to be arguing is that it's too late. If they made a mistake, you can't do anything about it. We don't care about innocence, we don't care about your evidence, we don't care about the strength of your claim. It's too late. We're going to move on, and we're just going to have this case move toward execution. What I'm saying is that that's not what the law says, and it would be an unconscionable result. They made a mistake, and we think we can show that."

They argued back and forth until lunch. The State didn't think any of our claims should be allowed to be presented at this hearing. They just wanted Bryan to shut up and for me to go to the death chamber. Bryan persisted, and ultimately Garrett let the hearing happen, and we were allowed to present all our evidence and witnesses.

The State didn't defend the fact that Bryan found worksheets that Higgins and Yates and McGregor hadn't turned over to Perhacs that were full of question marks and hyphens and showed that they didn't know what markings were on the bullets, and they certainly didn't show the bullets from the victims matched the test bullets from my mom's gun. They didn't defend any of it. They didn't think that they needed to test the bullets or the gun again. In their mind, none of this was allowed because it was time barred or it didn't count as new evidence based on their obscure interpretation of the rules of appeal. I don't think proof of innocence should ever be disregarded. Who are we if we allow that? What part of our system is working if an innocent man can be killed and no one cares because of rules that were made to be able to kill him quickly? Like it was some kind of game. The clock was ticking. *Prove your innocence in five, four, three, two, one . . . too late now . . . off with your head.*

I was taken back to Holman after the hearing. Bryan was brilliant in court, but it was like he was talking to a wall. They wanted me dead. Guilty or innocent, they just wanted to kill me. I hadn't been able to say anything to my mom or Lester before I was taken away from the hearing. My mom had her head resting on Lester's shoulder and her eyes closed. She was safe. Lester would keep her safe. I knew Bryan would talk to them and offer encouraging words, just as he always offered them to me. I should have been excited, but I didn't have a lot of faith. Our evidence was compelling, but it was the same old cast of characters who had put me away to begin with, plus the assistant attorney general who thought I was nothing but a waste of time. I went back to my cell and ignored the questions of the guys asking how it went. Even the guards wanted to know and seemed hopeful that I might get released. Some nights, however, just called for silence and prayer. And on the row, we knew not to push. There were a lot of bad days and a lot of bad nights, and if someone didn't want to talk, you backed off. Survival was at stake, and we cared enough for each other to let each other survive in our own way.

I woke up to a bootleg book club discussion. The thought of book club made me sad. When I thought of it, all I could think of was those empty chairs in the library as they killed us off one by one. First Larry, then Horsley; Henry, then Brian, and finally Victor. Nothing but empty chairs with every execution. After they had closed us down, the books we had read, plus some new ones, circulated around the tiers. There was no meeting in the library, but guys would talk about the books, yelling from cell to cell. If you hadn't read the book, you just listened. If you had read the book, you could give ideas, offer opinions. And always questions got thrown to me, as if I were the book club teacher. I didn't know the answers, and I told the guys that. There was no right or wrong in book club. You just had your own thoughts and interpretations and beliefs and ideas. It was new for a lot of guys. Giving their honest opinion, and having that listened to and respected, was a new kind of drug that traveled around the row. Matters of the heart were discussed. Politics were discussed. Racism and poverty were discussed. Violence was discussed. And if you had already discussed the book, you let others have the discussion, let them have a chance to talk their way through the big ideas.

"Ray! You listening, Ray?" It was a guy named Jimmy Dill. Jimmy was a former drug addict who had been going to nursing school before he was convicted of robbing and killing a man for cocaine and a couple of hundred bucks. He had a broad forehead and brown eyes that were spread just a little too far apart on his face. It made him look a bit unsure of himself when he talked. Jimmy loved to eat, and all day long he would talk about his favorite foods. Okra. Biscuits. Fried chicken. It was enough to drive you crazy.

But Jimmy had a kindness about him that made it hard to imagine him shooting someone in the back of the head.

"What you need, Jimmy?" I asked.

"I want to read that book *To Kill a Mockingbird*. Do you have it?"

"I have it."

"Can you send it my way with the guards next time they come round?" he asked.

"I can."

"Okay. Johnson wants to read it too; we're going to talk about it after. I've heard it's good. I don't know if that white boy is gonna understand it, but we'll see what he has to say."

I heard a few of the guys laugh. This was how it worked, and the book or books would get passed around, and then one day, without any planning, someone would yell, "How about that Scout girl?" and the discussion would begin.

That summer was hot and slow. We were waiting for word back from Judge Garrett about my Rule 32 petition, but there was nothing but silence. I couldn't imagine it would take him more than the summer to rule. He was the judge in the original trial. He knew the case inside and out. Where I used to pray that the truth would come out, now I prayed that the truth would be heard. The truth was proven in that hearing. I was innocent. I had been set up. I had been thrown away. I needed Garrett to do the right thing. I needed him to do the honorable thing. I was ready to get out.

Lester's visit in August had to be the hottest day of the year. It felt like it was 120 degrees in the shade, and without air, I thought we were all going to melt into a puddle on the visiting yard. I tried to keep my visiting whites clean and fresh, but I was sweating so hard that I decided to cut the visit short just so he and Sia could get back to the air-conditioning in the car.

"Lester, before you go, one more thing," I said.

"What's that? What do you need?" Lester got me everything I needed even before I needed it. He made sure I never went without commissary or a television and radio or extra socks and shorts.

"I need my birth certificate."

"Your what?"

"I'm going to need my birth certificate for when I get out of here. I won't have any identification. I'm going to need some, and all I'm going to have to prove I am who I am is my birth certificate."

Lester was quiet for a minute or so. He looked down at the ground and then took a breath. "You are going to need that," he said. And then he gave me a big smile. "How should I go about getting it? I will mail it to you, but tell me where to find it."

"You know God can do everything but fail, right?"

"That's right."

"Well, God is going to have to release me or be proven a liar."

"How do you figure that?"

"'What things so ever you desire when you pray, believe that you receive them, and you shall have them.' Mark 11:24," I said.

Lester smiled. He knew this was my favorite, and I had talked about it a million times before. "What about it?"

"God can't fail. Therefore, this scripture has to be true, and I have to be set free or God is a liar because he would have failed."

"You're trying to trap God in some kind of loophole?" Lester laughed. "Man, you really should've been a lawyer."

"Maybe I will be. Maybe I will get out of here, go to law school, and start working with Bryan to start freeing all these innocent men up in here. Put an end to the death penalty once and for all. Maybe I will." I was forty-six years old, and we both knew I was too old to go to law school even if I walked out of there with Bryan. "Or maybe I will open up a restaurant. You know I can cook."

"Yeah, what are you going to call this restaurant of yours?"

"Behind Bars, or the Death Row Grill." I started laughing.

"That's just sick now; nobody wants to eat what they're grilling up on death row."

"People would eat my barbecue no matter where I was grilling it. Even the guards are having me cook them some meals in their break room. Gets me out of my cell, and I can work on my menu for when I walk out of here."

"Okay. I'll get you your birth certificate. I'll talk to your sister."

"Why don't you ask my mom? She might have it."

A shadow passed over Lester's face for a brief second. There was something there that I didn't want to look at or think about.

"Okay. I'll ask them both, and I'll get it."

I looked over at Sylvia, who was smiling as big as could be. "What are you smiling at?"

"You're going to walk out of here, Ray. We all know it. And it's going to be a happy day. A bright day. It's going to be soon. We'll get the birth certificate, and then you can come to our house and cook us some dinner."

"You'd better count on it," I said.

It was September 22, 2002, when the captain of the guards came to my cell.

"Ray, I got some news for you."

I stood and looked at him standing in my doorway, and I felt my heart begin to pound. It wasn't news of my release. I had seen enough death in there to know the way it showed on a man's face. He had death on his face, and even before he said it, the screaming began in my head.

"It's your mom, Ray. She died today. We just got word. I'm sorry. The other guards and I want to offer our condolences."

I didn't say a word. The screaming in my head was so loud I just wanted him to leave so I could put the pillow over my ears. I turned my back to him and walked a few feet to stand over my bed. I leaned over at the waist, my palms resting on the bed. I wondered if I was going to pass out. He cleared his throat, and then I heard his footsteps walk away.

I cried quietly at first. And then it was as if my body were possessed, because it started shaking so hard I couldn't even hold my hand in front of my face. Maybe I was having a seizure. I didn't care. I felt my stomach turn over, and I ran to the toilet, thinking I might throw up. I wanted my mama. She was dead. I couldn't understand what kind of world this was now. I was nothing. I was nobody. I was Buhlar Hinton's son, and Buhlar Hinton was dead. I started sobbing, the deepest cries I have ever felt. It was like my body was turning itself inside out. She had died and I wasn't there. I couldn't live with that. I couldn't even breathe with that thought. I wasn't there. I was here, and I didn't get to hold my mom as she passed. I would never get to hold her again. I couldn't tell her I loved her. I couldn't tell her goodbye.

When are they going to let you come home, baby?

I could hear her voice.

Soon, Mama. I'm going to be home soon.

I had lied to my mom. I hadn't come home. Not soon. Not ever. I had lied to her, and she had died without me to take care of her. I pushed my face into my pillow and let the tears fall until it was so wet I wondered if my tear ducts had split wide open. None of it mattered anymore. Bryan. The hearing. Whether I lived or I died. Getting out of here. What did it matter? My mama was dead. I was going home to her, and she had gone home first. It felt like a million razors were slicing through my chest. Maybe I could have a heart attack. I could drop dead and be with her in moments.

I'll be home soon, Mama. I promise.

I don't know how long I cried. When I lifted my head up, the lights were out. I knew word had gotten around the row, but I had ignored people trying to send me coffee and I had ignored their condolences. I just didn't care anymore. I wasn't going to recover from this one. I couldn't go somewhere in my mind and pretend my mother wasn't dead. Sandra Bullock wasn't real, and she wasn't there to comfort me. I was Ray Hinton. A condemned man on death row who couldn't convince anyone he was innocent.

I lay on my back for hours, and then I heard a deep voice say, "The only person who believed you were innocent is gone."

I nodded, and the voice continued.

"Why keep fighting? Why let them execute you? Take away their power. There's nothing to live for now. Let Bryan Stevenson save someone else. There's no use in staying here. They are never going to let you leave. You're just a poor, dumb nigger, and no one cares if you live or die. They're going to kill you one way or another."

On and on the voice went, and I listened to it. I listened to it until it took me to the darkest place I had ever been, darker than those first three years on the row. My mother was always the flicker of light in those years, but now there was nothing but darkness. Flatness. It was like all light ceased to exist. There was no hope. There was no love. My life was over, and I knew this in the quiet way you know some things to be true. I had failed. There was nothing left inside me to keep me going. I didn't want to live. I didn't deserve to live. I didn't have the strength to live. They had won, and I was okay with that. I was ready to go.

I took a deep breath. My face felt raw in the darkness. My eyes were swollen and gritty. I just had to figure out how to do it. I was too tired to smash my own head in. I didn't have anything sharp to cut my wrists. I would have to hang myself somehow. It would be morning soon, and then I would wrap the sheet around my neck and find some way to hang myself in my cell.

"Boy, I didn't raise no quitter!" I heard my mother's voice loud and sharp, and I automatically flinched because I knew that tone of voice always preceded a smack upside the head. I sat up in my bed.

"I didn't raise a quitter, and you're not going to quit."

I looked around my cell in the darkness. I didn't believe in ghosts, but I could hear my mama's voice as plain as the day is long.

"You're going to get out of here. You're going to keep fighting."

"I'm tired, Mama; I want to be with you," I whispered. "I want to hurt them like they've hurt us. They want to kill me, and I don't want to give them that chance."

"There's a time to live and a time to die. This is my time to die. No use crying about it. You knew I had cancer. You didn't want to talk about it, but you knew."

I started crying again. She was right.

"This isn't your time to die, son. It's not. You have work to do. You have to prove to them that my baby is no killer. You have to show them. You are a beacon. You are the light. Don't you listen to that fool devil telling you to give up. I didn't raise no child of mine to give up when things get tough. Your life isn't your life to take. It belongs to God. You have work to do. Hard work. I'm going to talk at you all night long if I have to and all day and all night again, and I will never stop until you know who you are. You were not born to die in this cell. God has a purpose for you. He has a purpose for all of us. I've served my purpose."

I cried softly as she talked.

"Now you wipe them tears, Ray, and you get up and you get in service to someone else. There's no time to be crying about yourself. There's no cause to be listening to the devil's voice in your head telling you that nothing matters. It all matters. You matter. You are my baby, and you matter more than anything in the world. When I'm done talking at you, I'm going to be talking at God. He's going to listen to me, if I have to talk to him for all eternity. He's going to get you out of there, or he's going to have a hard time of it, that's for sure."

"Okay, Mama. Okay," I whispered.

"Don't disappoint me, Ray. I taught you to believe in yourself even if no one else in the world believes in you. Do you believe in you? Do you?"

I nodded in the darkness.

"Well, then, the next time that devil tells you to wrap a bedsheet around your neck, you tell him to go to hell where he belongs."

I laughed softly. "Yes, Mama."

"I'm going to talk to God, and we're going to give Mr. Bryan Stevenson a little help from here. There's a time to live and a time to die, Ray."

"Yes, Mama."

"And it will never be your time to die in that place. Never."

"Yes, Mama."

"I'm not fooling this time, Ray. Don't make me come back here."

I fell asleep then, a deep, dreamless sleep, and when I woke up, it was long after breakfast, almost time for lunch.

The gifts started arriving immediately after I woke up. Coffee. Chocolate. Sweets of all kinds. Cards. Books. Death row was holding its own memorial in the only way it knew how. "She loved you a lot, Ray. I've never seen a mother love her son more."

"She's proud of you."

"Rest in peace, Ray."

"I'm sorry, Ray."

"My condolences, Ray."

All through the day and into the night, men shouted out their words of sympathy. Sorrow shared is sorrow lessened.

And then I heard Jimmy Dill. "Ray!" he yelled. "Can you help me with something?"

I took a deep breath. My mama told me to be in service to someone else.

"What do you need?"

"In the book, it says, 'They've done it before and they did it tonight and they'll do it again and when they do it—seems that only children weep.' What does that mean, exactly?"

I smiled. It seemed book club had started. "Well, Atticus says that after the verdict, right?"

"Yeah."

"I think it's because only the child cries when an innocent man is convicted.

All the adults just accept it. It's happened before, and it will happen again. What do you think?" I asked.

"I think that's right, Ray. I think that's right. But here's what I want to say. Just because they've done it before and they'll do it again doesn't mean you stop fighting, right? I don't think it's something people should ever get used to, do you?"

"I don't think people should get used to injustice," I said.

"You know what we have to do then, Ray, right? You know what we always have to do?"

"What's that?"

"You have to fight, Ray. You have to never stop fighting."

And if I didn't know better, I would have thought that the voice of my mother was coming out of a convicted killer on death row by the name of Jimmy Dill.

| 20 |

DISSENT

It's really bad that it's gone on this long without a final resolve on it, and I'll take part of the responsibility for that.

—JUDGE JAMES GARRETT, JANUARY 28, 2002

Phoebe, Lester's mom, came to visit me after my mom died, and even though it wasn't supposed to be allowed, the guards looked the other way as she put her arms around me and held me as I cried all over her shoulder. Lester kept clearing his throat and wiping at his eyes. My mom was also his mom, and he had taken care of her for almost twenty years. I had lost my mom, and Lester's mom had lost her best friend.

"I want you to know something, Ray," she said, patting me on the back like she used to do when I was a little boy. "One of us is always going to be here, until the very end. No matter what, one of us will always be here. Do you understand?"

I nodded and swallowed my tears. I was grateful to have them. How could I have survived this long without them?

"No matter what," she said again, and then she kissed me one last time on the top of my head.

When she passed away a couple of years later, Lester and I cried together and then had a good laugh about how God was really in trouble now. There was going to be no sleep or peace in heaven until those two women got their way and God set me free.

We had no word from Judge Garrett. Bryan wrote letter after letter, filed brief after brief, and still nothing. After a year, he decided that pressure from the public might be the only way to get the State to do the right thing, and he began contacting the media about my story.

November 19, 2003

Anthony Ray Hinton, Z-468
Holman State Prison
Holman, 3700
Atmore, Alabama 36503

Dear Ray:

How are you? I hope you're hanging in there. I wanted to update you on a couple of matters. Judge Garrett, as you know, has retired effective November 1. We heard that he would keep some cases and give others to different judges. While we can't get any definite indication, it appears as if he intends to keep your case. Following the debate I had with Pryor, I pressed him for what he was willing to do. He has indicated that they won't do anything but wait for Judge Garrett's ruling. While this is disappointing, it's not surprising.

Today, I've sent a letter to the chief deputy district attorney just so that we can represent to the press that these folks have had every opportunity to do the right thing. Our experts have similarly pressed the guy the State brought to your hearing from the Department of Forensic Sciences about doing something. No one appears to want to claim any responsibility, so we will have to put more pressure on them publicly.

I'm meeting with someone from *The New York Times* next week about an article, and I think we'll also work with someone from a national magazine. *60 Minutes* is supposed to call Pryor this week. I'm worried about them because they keep talking about the war with Iraq and are becoming somewhat vague on when they'll actually do something. Anyway, I'm supposed to talk with them again on Friday.

I'll be down to see you during the first week of December because we will likely need to facilitate some interviews between you and the *Times* reporter and the magazine reporter next month. I want to talk to you some about that before it begins.

Things have been typically busy here, but we're pressing on. I look forward to seeing you, my friend.

Sincerely,

Bryan A. Stevenson

Another nine months passed, and we still had no answer on my Rule 32 hearing. Bryan was frustrated, and I tried to imagine how he could hold up with so many lives depending on him. I kept telling him that if things didn't turn out the way we wanted, I knew he had done everything he could. Eventually, he went straight to the source.

September 23, 2004

Judge James Garrett
c/o Anne-Marie Adams, Clerk
Jefferson County Circuit Court
207 Criminal Justice Center
801 N. Richard Arrington, Jr. Blvd.
Birmingham, AL 35203

Dear Judge Garrett:

I'm writing to inquire about the status of the Anthony Ray Hinton case. As you know, Mr. Hinton is on Alabama's death row, although we maintain and have presented evidence that he is innocent and had nothing to do with these crimes. Over two years ago, we presented evidence in support of Mr. Hinton's claim of factual innocence. I know that since that time you have retired, which is why I'm writing to determine the status of this case and whether you are still reviewing the case. We filed a renewed motion for a judgment granting relief on February 23, 2004, and we have not been able to confirm from the clerk's office whether you received that pleading or our subsequent requests for a ruling.

While I appreciate that the length of time required in death penalty cases has been an issue for lots of people, we're especially concerned about this case because we believe that the evidence clearly supports Mr. Hinton's innocence and that he has now been wrongly held on Alabama's death row for nineteen years.

I would greatly appreciate it if you could inform the parties of the case status or determine what, if any, other arrangements have been made for a resolution of this case. I'm sorry to disturb you with a letter of this sort, but I genuinely believe that Mr. Hinton is innocent and this case represents a terrible mistake.

I appreciate your consideration of this matter and sincerely hope that all is well with you.

Respectfully,
Bryan A. Stevenson
Counsel for Anthony Ray Hinton

cc: James Houts, Assistant Attorney General
Jon Hayden, Assistant Attorney General
J. Scott Vowell, Presiding Judge

Time kept marching on, and then finally, after hearing nothing for two and a half years, Judge Garrett finally issued a ruling. Bryan sent me a letter at the end of January. I read it aloud to the other guys. A couple of the guards stood in the hallway listening as well.

January 28, 2005

Anthony Ray Hinton, Z-468
Holman State Prison
Holman, 3700
Atmore, Alabama 36503

Dear Ray:

We've looked at Garrett's ruling and determined that it is a verbatim, word-for-word replication of the State's proposed order. In effect, he waited two and one-half years and then just signed the State's proposed order that was filed on August 26, 2002. Garrett let all this time go by and then just signed the State's order. It's clear that he wasn't working on anything when he told the presiding judge he would get something out by the end of December. While it's not surprising, it builds another layer into the worst example of corrupt, unjust administration of the death penalty anywhere. We knew not to expect much from him in terms of relief, but he didn't have to unnecessarily take another two and a half years of your life for no good reason.

Garrett printed out the State's order and changed the margins; I guess he thought that made it look better. But it appears word for word to be the State's proposed order. I attach it even though I think we sent you the State's order a couple of years ago. You may recall that we filed a lengthy response challenging the State's proposed order, which I'm also resending in case you don't have that anymore.

We will file a motion objecting to Garrett signing the State's order just to preserve that issue for appeal. That will be filed next week. However, we won't wait for a ruling on that. After ten days, a motion is deemed denied, so we'll file the notice of appeal at that time and begin working on the appeal papers to file by the end of February.

We've called your family and Lester Bailey, and I'm sending stuff to our experts today, who I expect to be pretty outraged about this too. I'll look to talk with you on Monday afternoon. Hang in there.

Sincerely,
Bryan

P.S. Jerline got the package you sent and absolutely loves it! Thank you for doing that.

Bryan was livid, but at some point, I just had to realize that the State would lie, cheat, steal, and stall to keep from admitting they were wrong about me. Evidence didn't matter. Nothing seemed to matter. Bryan filed an appeal with the Alabama Court of Criminal Appeals. A hearing was scheduled, and Bryan had upped the ante involving Amnesty International, the local news, and the national news.

In August, they killed George Sibley. His last words were, "Everyone who is doing this to me is guilty of a murder." I banged on the bars for him and said a prayer for his son. I wondered what it was like for that boy to have both his parents executed. It was too much for any person to carry.

In November of 2005, right before the hearing—prisoners were not allowed to attend appeal hearings at this level—a series of articles ran in *The Birmingham News*. I did an interview by telephone. The series of articles were about the death penalty, for and against. Bryan wrote the piece against, and as I read the article to the other guys on the row, I was proud to call him not only my attorney, but my friend.

The Birmingham News
Sunday, 11/7/05

THE DEBATE OVER DEATH

AGAINST

State's justice system does not deserve to kill

by Bryan Stevenson

Last week, I spent two hours at Holman Correctional Facility with a condemned man who has been on Alabama's Death Row for nearly 20 years.

Anthony Ray Hinton is innocent. He has never committed a violent crime. Hinton is generous, thoughtful and tries very, very hard to be cheerful. He helps guards and prisoners, he's never had a disciplinary violation, and he sends handmade presents whenever he can save up enough money.

Although he has struggled for two decades to remain positive and hopeful, after you talk to him for a while you begin to see the profound sadness and unbearable grief emerge. He believes his wrongful conviction has contributed to his beloved mother's death. He's been tormented by more than 30 executions "just down the hall." He's been locked down in a tiny cell year after year after year. He cries a lot, and each day he struggles to control the pain and anguish of a continuing nightmare and an American tragedy.

Hinton was not sent to Death Row because he was in the wrong place at the wrong time. He was actually in the right place at the exact time of the crime, working as an unskilled laborer in a secure warehouse 15 miles away from where he was alleged to have shot someone. Hinton passed a polygraph test before trial, and he begged police to believe he is innocent. However, his life, freedom and rights were simply never taken seriously by anyone.

Hinton is on Death Row because he is poor. He is a victim of Alabama's grossly under-funded indigent defense system. His appointed lawyer, like 70 percent of those still on Alabama's Death Row, could by *law only be paid $1,000 for preparing his capital case for trial. Hinton was given $500 for an expert to prove that a gun police found in his mother's home was not the gun used to commit these crimes. With so little money, the only expert he could afford was legally blind in one eye and had no experience using the equipment necessary to test the evidence.*

Like most Death Row prisoners, Hinton was presumed guilty before trial. Without money, political power or celebrity, he was a nameless black man imperiled by a system of justice that is shockingly tolerant of error, a system that treats you better if you are rich and guilty than if you're poor and innocent.

Hinton is not the only innocent person who has been sent to Alabama's Death Row. In 1993, the state ultimately admitted that Walter McMillian spent six years on Death Row for a crime he did not commit. Gary Drinkard, Louis Griffin, Randal Padgett, Wesley Quick, James Cochran and Charles Bufford were all acquitted of capital murder after being wrongly convicted and sentenced to death. With 34 executions and seven exonerations since 1975, one innocent person has been identified on Alabama's Death Row for every five executions. It's an astonishing rate of error.

What most defines capital punishment in Alabama is error. Reviewing courts have concluded nearly 150 Alabama capital murder convictions and death sentences have been illegally and unconstitutionally imposed. Reversals outnumber executions almost 5 to 1. While some states have seriously examined their death penalty systems and pursued reforms, Alabama leaders have recklessly called only for speeding up the execution process.

The U.S. Supreme Court has ruled that executing the mentally retarded is unconstitutional, but the Alabama Legislature has refused to enact laws enforcing this limitation. The Supreme Court has called for greater deference to jury verdicts, but Alabama persists as the only state in the nation that allows elected trial judges to override jury verdicts of life imprisonment to death with no restrictions or standards. Since 1990, nearly 25 percent of all Alabama death sentences have been imposed after jurors concluded that life without parole was the appropriate sentence.

I have represented people on Alabama's Death Row for nearly 20 years. I know that not everyone on Death Row is innocent. I also know that Alabama's death penalty is not about guilt and innocence. Anthony Ray Hinton can painfully tell you a lot about that.

Alabama's death penalty is a lie. It is a perverse monument to inequality, to how some lives matter and others do not. It is a violent example of how we protect and value the rich and abandon and devalue the poor. It is a grim, disturbing shadow cast by the legacy of racial apartheid used to condemn the disfavored among us. It's the symbol elected officials hold up to strengthen their tough-on-crime reputations while distracting us from the causes of violence. The death penalty is an enemy of grace, redemption and all who value life and recognize that each person is more than their worst act.

With so much fear, anger and violence, it's easy to see the appeal of capital punishment. The pain of victims of violent crime is real.

However, the tragic number of innocent people wrongly condemned, the scores of illegal convictions and sentences, the unequal treatment of the poor and racial minorities have made capital punishment a question that is not about whether some people deserve to die for the crimes they've committed. Rather, the death penalty in Alabama is about whether state government, with its flawed, inaccurate, biased and error-plagued political system of justice, deserves to kill.

*It's time to acknowledge that it does not.**

I read the article again and again. Next to it in the paper was an opposing opinion piece—pro death penalty—by the attorney general, Troy King. His basic argument was an eye for an eye, and I understood that. I had grown up with that in church. Justice demanded a life for a life. Retribution. The perpetrator should not live while the victim has no choice. People on death row had earned their spots on death row, and justice cannot be consumed with protecting the rights of the guilty. But the system didn't know who was guilty. I wasn't blind. There is a moral difference between kidnapping and murdering a man, and imprisoning and executing a man. There is no moral equivalence, even when both things end in death. But death has never deterred death. And we can't be sure of guilt, save for an admission of guilt. A person could believe in the death penalty and still believe it should be ended, because men are fallible and the justice system is fallible.

---

* Bryan Stevenson, "The Debate of Death: Against," *The Birmingham News,* November 7, 2005.

Until we have a way of ensuring that innocent men are never executed—until we account for the racism in our courts, in our prisons, and in our sentencing—the death penalty should be abolished. Let Troy King spend a decade or two in prison under a sentence of death as an innocent man and see what kind of opinion he writes then. There was no humane way to execute any man. And regardless of any law, no one had the right to execute an innocent man. One line in particular in the pro article struck me: "To be sure, the death sentence must never be carried out in a way that allows the innocent to die." There was an irony there. If he believed that, why was he refusing to objectively look at the evidence of my innocence? Bryan's editorial was moving and impressive. Even the guards were reading pieces of it out loud. I didn't know what was going to happen in appeals court, but I did know that I still had God's best lawyer fighting for me.

On the day of the hearing, another article came out quoting both me and McGregor. He was still mad twenty years later that I'd stared him down in the courtroom, and he also threatened that if I was released, he'd be "standing right outside the gate with a .38 and it won't be an old one." I hoped that quote would help prove my case to the appeals court. Two decades later and he was still saying, on the record, he was going to get me one way or another. Bryan seemed hopeful after the oral arguments.

November 30, 2005

Anthony Ray Hinton, Z-468
Holman State Prison
Holman, 3700
Atmore, Alabama 36503

Dear Ray:

How are you, my friend? Last week, the State filed another pleading in your case following oral argument. It's amazing that they now want to discuss the evidence in your case after saying for so many years everything is barred and defaulted. In any event, they have filed a motion to supplement their brief because I stressed the fact that the gun evidence exonerates you so much at oral argument, I think they are worried about that. I attach a copy of what they sent. We filed a response to their pleading yesterday, which is also enclosed with this letter.

I think it's good that they now feel some need to address the merits of these issues. The letters to the newspaper following *The Birmingham News* articles have all been good. I'll get copies of them to you as soon as we have them collected.

I'm really hoping that you've had your last Thanksgiving on death row. It's always better to not get too optimistic when you are dealing with the Alabama justice system, but you deserve relief soon.

I'm going to try and get down before Christmas. The court issued a bunch of decisions in older cases last week, so we've been pretty busy. I hope you're doing okay. All the best, my friend.

Sincerely,

Bryan Stevenson

I tried not to get too hopeful as we were waiting for the Court of Criminal Appeals. I kept as busy as possible and was grateful the guards let me spend much of the day in their break room. I would cook for them and counsel them on everything from money problems to marriage issues. There was a certain irony to the fact that they came to me for advice when I had spent over two decades locked in a cell and cut off from the outside world. I also helped deliver meals to the guys on the row. It was a way to say hi to each of them, to look in their eyes and see if I saw signs that they were heading to the dark place we all knew too well.

I was in service to others. It was what my mom wanted, and it got me through each day of each month until my visit with Lester.

At the end of June 2006, I got word to call Bryan. He told me the Alabama Court of Criminal Appeals had denied my appeal. We were now going to appeal to the Alabama Supreme Court. I went back to my cell and told the other guys. Jimmy seemed especially upset. The newspaper articles had established my innocence in a way that was more real than what I had been saying all these years. My freedom was a cause that everyone on the row wanted to fight for. No one doubted my innocence, and after Bryan's article, I had told them all that when I got out, I was going to fight to end the death penalty. I had dreams where I spoke at colleges, in churches, around the country, and across the globe. I was going to be a voice like Bryan's. I was going to tell my story so that this never happened to anyone else.

First I had to be set free.

And we were now going to another court, one that I had appealed to back in 1989. It was like my case was bouncing around inside a state pinball machine. Circuit Court. Appeals Court. Supreme Court and back again. Over and over. I wasn't upset, though. I was ecstatic. The ruling in the Alabama Court of Criminal Appeals was 3–2. It was a ruling against me, but for the first time, two judges believed in my innocence.

Dissent was a beautiful thing.

And it was all I had.

| 21 |

THEY KILL YOU ON THURSDAYS

The degree of civilization in a society can be judged by entering its prisons.

—FYODOR DOSTOYEVSKY

We appealed to the Alabama Supreme Court, and they refused to rule until a determination was made as to whether Payne was a qualified expert. This took us back down the ladder through the Court of Criminal Appeals and then back to Jefferson County. Judge Garrett had retired completely now—and had let go of my case. I was hopeful that the new circuit court judge—Laura Petro—might be a bit more receptive to my case. It took until March of 2009 before Judge Petro ruled.

March 11, 2009

Anthony Ray Hinton, Z-468
Holman State Prison
Holman, 3700
Atmore, Alabama 36503

Dear Ray:

Well, unfortunately, Judge Petro did not help us. She wrote a very bizarre order which attempts to only address what she thinks Judge Garrett thought of Payne. She concludes that she thinks that Judge Garrett thought Payne was competent. We'll interpret this as Petro being unwilling to independently find Payne competent. Very disappointing. Call me. I'll be around all next week if you want to talk and we can discuss next steps. Because this order is so bizarre, it's a better order than if she did what the court actually ordered which is to make independent findings about Payne's competence. Anyway, I said I'd write unless there was good news so I wanted to get this in the mail to you right away. I'll speak with you soon.

Hang in there.

Sincerely,

Bryan Stevenson

It was getting harder to hang in there. Jimmy Dill was scheduled to be executed in a month. Since the day we had hoped I would spend my last Thanksgiving on the row, I had watched thirty-seven men be put to death. Two had been put to death already in 2009. I had watched ten men die since Garrett had denied my Rule 32 petition. The mood on the row was solemn. There were no more bootleg book club discussions. We were all just trying to survive, and the younger guys who came in were angry and agitated in a way I had never seen before. They had no interest in discussing literature. And it only became tenser between the guards and the men on the row when an execution date was set. They didn't practice turning on the generator, but they still practiced.

"We'd never kill you, Ray," one guard used to say to me. "I'm just doing my job."

"You volunteer for this, man. You volunteer to be on the Death Squad. I know it. You know it. All the guys know it."

"I'm just doing my job."

I knew that the guards would kill me if I got an execution date. They knew it too. There would be no way around it. I would imagine what would happen if they all just refused to kill. If they took a stand. How could they take us to the doctor, feed us, commiserate with us, and then lead us to our deaths? It messed with our minds after a while. These men were our family also. We were all in this dark, dank, tiny corner of the world acting out some perverse play where we laughed together six days of the week, but on Thursdays, they killed us.

My case went back to the Court of Criminal Appeals, and they bounced it back down to Judge Petro again because, as Bryan had said, she didn't rule on whether Payne was a qualified expert, only on what she thought Garrett had believed in 1986. In September 2010, she ruled that Payne was an expert because he "had acquired a knowledge of firearms identification beyond that of an ordinary witness." That was like the court saying I was qualified as a heart surgeon because I'd had once had an EKG. We bounced back up to the appeals court, who affirmed the lower court, and sent us back up to the Alabama Supreme Court. They punted my case back down, saying the wrong standard had been applied when the court determined Payne was a qualified expert.

It was enough to make a man dizzy.

Bryan never gave up, and I could see how hard this was on him. He carried the world on his shoulders, and there were visits where I could see the strain and the stress in his eyes. I wasn't his only case, and neither of us were getting any younger. I was tired, and I didn't pray any longer for the truth to be known. The truth was known. Alabama knew I was innocent, but they would never admit it. They wouldn't in 1986. They wouldn't in 2002. They wouldn't in 2005. And they weren't going to in 2013.

Bryan had an arrangement that he would get a message to the prison when he needed to talk to me. Because there had been so much press, when there were rulings on my case, they ended up on the local news. Court rulings came in around 2:00 P.M. The news ran at 5:00 P.M. Bryan didn't ever want me to find out about my case on the news first.

When I got the message to call him, I tried to keep my expectations low.

"They denied us, Ray. I'm sorry."

I held the phone away from my ear. I had been so sure that there would be a miracle. I was so sure that because two judges had finally taken my side, everything would be fixed. I was never going to get out of here. I was going to be strapped to that gurney and have a cocktail of drugs first paralyze me so I couldn't scream and then slowly and painfully kill me from the inside out. I was going to be put to sleep like a stray, rabid dog. My life mattered only that much—maybe even less. The dog would have comfort in his death, perhaps. I would miss this life. I would miss Bryan. I knew he had watched men he cared about die. I had watched the same. There are no words for how that scars you. There are no words for how every death kills a little piece of you off. Your soul dies a little, your mind cracks a bit, your heart pounds and bleeds as a piece of it tears off. A mind, and a heart, and a soul could only take so much.

I wiped at my tears and took a deep breath before I held the phone back up to my ear. Bryan was still talking. "Maybe I didn't do enough. I should have—"

My heart ached for this man, so I interrupted him.

"Mr. Stevenson, this is Ray Hinton's assistant, and he asked me to tell you to go on home now; it's Friday. He said you have yourself a nice dinner, drink a glass of wine, watch a movie . . . do whatever it takes to feel better, and he said that you should just forget about Ray Hinton for the weekend."

"Ray—" Bryan tried to interrupt me.

"This is Ray Hinton's assistant, and he said to tell you that if they let him go outside this weekend, he is going to shoot some basketball and relax and take some time away from all these legal matters. He said you should do the same, and he'll call you first thing Monday morning."

Bryan laughed softly.

"Ray also said you have his permission to enjoy your entire weekend. Enjoy the sunshine. Take a nice walk in the woods. Forget about Ray Hinton, because Ray Hinton is going to forget about Ray Hinton for a while."

"You tell him thank you for me." I could hear that Bryan's voice was lighter.

"You can tell him yourself when he calls you Monday morning."

I hung up the phone and went back to my cell. What lawyer needs a convict's permission to go out and enjoy his weekend? Bryan cared about me so much that it moved me in a way that was beyond words. I knew he was doing everything he could to save my life. He deserved to have a weekend free of the burden. I wanted Bryan to hold his face up toward the sunshine. He deserved some moments away from this place, away from the disappointment of the courts.

It was dark in my cell, darker than it should have been for 5:00 P.M. in April. I wondered if I would ever get a chance to turn my face to the sun as a free man. I wondered if there would come a time when the fight was over.

On Monday morning at 9:00 sharp, I yelled to the guards that I needed the telephone. I called Bryan's office collect. Ms. Lee answered and then put Bryan through right away.

"Ray, how are you doing this morning?" Bryan asked.

"I'm fine, Bryan. How was your weekend?"

"I had a great weekend, Ray, a really great weekend." I could tell by his voice that it was true. There wasn't much I had to give to Bryan, so I was happy I could give him the weekend. But the weekend was over.

"Well, it's 9:00 A.M., and I told you I would call, so now get back to work on my case!"

Bryan laughed. "I'm going to come see you. I have something I'd like to talk to you about in person."

"You have an idea about what to do next?"

"I do, Ray. I do."

"All right, then, I will see you as soon as they let you come."

We said our goodbyes, and I was happy to know that Bryan wasn't giving up yet. If he wasn't giving up, then I wasn't going to give up either.

I gave Lester the news the next time he visited. Sylvia wasn't with him. She'd had a difficult time with a female guard during her last visit, and she was taking a break from death row for that reason. I was livid when I heard. I would talk to the guards. They could mess with me all they wanted, but they weren't going to mess with the people I loved or with my visits.

Lester had gotten my birth certificate, and we talked a little bit about where I would go if I ever got out. My mom's house had been empty for ten years and would need a lot of repairs before it was habitable again. We had been talking about me walking out of there for twenty-seven years. Before long, I would be on death row for longer than I had been a free man. There was less energy in our imaginations about the future. We were both getting old. I looked at him, and for a second, my whole time on death row flashed before my eyes—but this time without him in it. He had never missed a visit since I had been arrested in 1985. It was 2013. The world had changed, but Lester's friendship had remained the same. I could feel tears forming in my eyes.

"What's wrong?"

"Remember those days when we used to walk home and jump in the ditch and hide?" I asked.

"Yeah, I remember."

"What were we afraid of, exactly?"

Lester didn't say anything. He just stared at me, and his eyes were sadder than I had ever seen them before.

"I'm getting tired," I said. "The court denied my rehearing. I don't think I have many more options. They don't seem to care about the new evidence. They don't seem in any hurry. They're going to either give me a date or bounce me around from court to court until I die. For the first time in a long time, I don't know if I'm going to walk out of here. I just don't know."

"You can't stop fighting."

"Why? Why can't I stop fighting?" I wasn't being funny. I just was tired. "I've lived a full life."

Lester gave a grunt like he didn't believe me.

"Lester, I've won Wimbledon five times. I've played third base for the Yankees and led the league in home runs for ten straight years. I've traveled the world. I've married the most beautiful women. I've loved and I've laughed and I've lost God and found God again and wondered for too many hours what the purpose is for me going to death row for something I didn't do. And sometimes I think there is no purpose—that this is just the life I was meant to live. I've made a home here and a family out of some of the most terrifying men you'd ever meet. And you know what I've learned? We're all the same. We're all guilty of something, and we're all innocent at the same time. And I'm sorry, but a man can go crazy trying to make it all fit into some plan. Maybe this is the plan. Maybe I was born to live most of my life in a five-by-seven so I could travel the world. I would have never won Wimbledon if I hadn't gone to death row. Do you see what I'm saying, Lester? Do you understand what I'm saying?"

Lester cleared his throat. "I remember walking home with you and jumping in that ditch and you saying to me that it's strange what a person could get used to. Do you remember that?"

I shook my head. I didn't remember that.

"Well, you said it. And you know why we were so afraid? Do you know why, Ray?"

"No. Why?"

"We were afraid because we couldn't see what was coming at us. So we hid in those ditches. We hid rather than face whatever might be in front of us."

I nodded.

"We're not kids anymore, Ray, and we're not afraid. We're not going to hide in a ditch together. We're going to face whatever happens. We're going to face it, and we're going to fight if we have to fight, and we're not going to ever get used to this. You were not born to die on death row. I know that for a fact."

Lester had never been a talker, but he had something to say this time.

"Okay," I said.

"We're still walking home, Ray. We're still just walking home together."

When I walked into the visiting area and saw Bryan waiting for me, he looked serious. More than serious, he looked determined in a way I hadn't seen before. We'd had so many denials, so many phone calls where he had to tell me they'd ruled against me, that sometimes we didn't even want to talk about my case. Sometimes we just laughed. At nothing in particular, and everything. Some days we were like two teenage girls who can't stop laughing even when their teacher yells at them. Some days it all seemed so crazy that I was still in here that we just had to laugh our heads off. It felt good to laugh like that. It kept us young, and it kept us sane.

Bryan smiled when I walked up. "How you doing, my friend?"

"I'm doing all right."

"Listen, I have an idea. I want you to really think about everything I'm about to say before you decide. We've got some strategic decisions to make. As we've discussed before, our next option is to apply for a petition of writ of habeas corpus in federal court. The options are limited. We have severe time restraints and very limited issues we can claim violated your federal rights. Federal habeas doesn't provide the same opportunity to prove your innocence, Ray. They can't look at an innocence claim. We are only going to be able to bring up the suppression of evidence with the worksheets and the ineffective assistance of counsel. If we lose in the U.S. District Court, then we would file an appeal with the U.S. Court of Appeals for the Eleventh Circuit. The State will file their briefs. It will be similar to the Rule 32, but with a more limited focus. The State is going to argue that the federal courts have to defer to the rulings made by state court judges in federal habeas. Do you understand what I'm saying?"

I nodded and motioned for him to go on.

"There's only one last opportunity for us to talk about your innocence, and that is if we go to the U.S. Supreme Court now. We can't claim innocence in the federal habeas, only how your federal rights were violated. The Supreme Court is not going to grant relief on the innocence claim alone, but I think we can present to them a narrative that might motivate them to do something. Your innocence will matter, Ray. It's the last time it will matter to a court."

I nodded again. I wanted my innocence to matter. I wanted it to matter forever.

"Listen, though. If they deny the cert, then nobody's going to ever listen to your innocence claim again. If we don't go to the Supreme Court now, we'll have another chance at the end of this federal habeas process, which could take years. You should know that. Be prepared for that. But when the Supreme Court reviews then, it will be only a review on the very restricted issues we bring in federal habeas. What I mean is, they're not going to look at your innocence. They're going to be very narrow in what they consider, and the chance for relief will be greatly reduced."

"And in federal habeas, I can get bounced through different courts again? Bounced back and forth, but just federal courts this time?"

"Pretty much. You know how the State's been with your appeal. That's not going to change. If anything, they're going to ramp up the opposition in federal habeas. I mean, we can go to the Supreme Court after for review, but we could be in litigation for years, and they rarely, I mean, it's going to be hard either way . . . and there's something else, Ray. If we take your case to the Supreme Court and we lose, things could speed up. It could make it harder for us to win in federal habeas and harder for us to stop them from killing you."

I interrupted Bryan.

"Do you have money for the vending machine? I'd like a drink."

"Sure, Ray. Sure." Bryan gave me some quarters, and I walked over and got a Coke out of the machine.

I sat back down and opened the soda. "A man needs a drink when he's making a big decision."

"Ray—"

I held up my hand to silence him and drank a long swig of the soda. For the first time in my life, I wished I had some hard liquor. I had never been a drinker, but I imagined that soda was full of scotch.

"Bryan, I'm innocent. I want the courts to admit I'm innocent. I want the world to know I'm innocent. I don't want life without parole. I want to walk out of here. I want to live the rest of my life a free man. I would rather die. If I can't prove my innocence, I would rather die."

"So what do you want to do, Ray? It could take another eight or nine months to file, and there's no guarantee and—"

"I want to go to the Supreme Court now, Bryan. I want them to know I'm innocent. I want them to hear my case now, when we can present everything. I don't want to spend another ten years in the courts. I don't think I can do it. I don't think I can be here until I'm seventy years old and still be fighting."

We were quiet for a while after that. I looked around the visiting area. I had spent so much time here over the last few decades. I had eaten a lot of key lime pie out of the vending machine. And I had come to respect and love this man who sat in front of me. He was tired too, and I was just one of many battles he was fighting. We both deserved a win.

It was time.

And if it wasn't, then I would take my Thursday. I would eat my last meal, and I would thank Lester for being the best friend a guy could ever have, and I would tell Bryan Stevenson that he couldn't save everyone and I knew he had done everything he could. I would have joy knowing that I lived as big a life as anyone ever could live in a five-by-seven cell.

And God have mercy on their souls, but I knew what my last words would be.

I am innocent.

| 22 |

JUSTICE FOR ALL

As there is no issue here worthy of certiorari, this court should deny review in this matter.

—LUTHER STRANGE, ALABAMA ATTORNEY GENERAL, TO THE SUPREME COURT OF THE UNITED STATES, NOVEMBER 2013

There are certain moments that stay with you. For most people, it's when they get married or give birth to their first child. For others, it's when they get their first job, or meet the woman or man of their dreams, or maybe it's something as simple as being acknowledged by someone or finally getting the nerve to do something they've always been afraid of.

I spent the six months it took for Bryan to file my petition with the U.S. Supreme Court reflecting on my moments—but only the good ones. I didn't want to review the bad moments. My mother's death. The arrest and conviction. The fifty-four human beings I had watched walk to their own executions. I knew all their names, and in July, the night before Andrew Lackey, a white man who had only been on the row for about five years, was taken to the death chamber, I said fifty-three of them aloud in my head. Some people count sheep. I counted the dead. *Wayne. Michael. Horace. Herbert. Arthur. Wallace. Larry. Neal. Willie. Varnall. Edward. Billy. Walter. Henry. Steven. Brian. Victor. David. Freddie. Robert. Pernell. Lynda. Anthony. Michael. Gary. Tommy. JB. David. Mario. Jerry. George. John. Larry. Aaron. Darrell. Luther. James. Danny. Jimmy. Willie. Jack. Max. Thomas. John. Michael. Holly. Philip. Leroy. William. Jason. Eddie. Derrick. Christopher.* I didn't want to add Andrew's name to the list. Not yet. Not when there was still hope. The man before Andrew had only been there four years. Like Andrew, Christopher didn't want to appeal. They were young guys, but both were not in their right minds. You could tell they were slower than most. I wasn't sure they really understood where they were or that they were choosing not to appeal their convictions. It was sad, and I felt older than my fifty-seven years. I banged on the bars for Christopher and for Andrew, just so they would know they weren't alone. I had made noise for a lot of men as they faced their own deaths.

I tried to keep my mind focused on the good moments. The moments before my arrest were warm summer nights playing baseball with Lester and the other kids in Praco. We were so blissfully unaware of how dangerous the world was. Even the bombings and protests in Birmingham had seemed far away from our sanctuary in Praco. I wished we had never left there. What if we had stayed in Praco and I had stayed in the mines? How would my life have turned out? What would have been my important moments? What if I had married my Sylvia when I had the chance? I would be a father, maybe even a grandfather by now. How many baseball games had I missed? How many walks in the woods? How many sunrises and sunsets could one man miss in his life and still have a life? I had lived in darkness for so long, I almost couldn't imagine what it would be like to be a free man under a shining sun. I thought about what it felt like to make a woman laugh. A simple moment when a woman reaches out and touches your arm. I remembered how good it felt to hold a woman in my arms and have her look into my eyes. Would I ever kiss a woman again? Even if I got out, who would want to kiss the man from death row? I tried to remember the moments I spent fishing with my mama or sitting next to her in church and praying. I remembered the food she used to make and the love that I could taste in every bite.

The good moments after coming to death row were harder. Doubled up laughing with Lester and Sylvia at visits. Telling them stories that kept them grinning and helped them to believe that life on death row wasn't as bad as it seemed. Sitting with Bryan talking about my case and also talking about football. Making him laugh. Seeing the strain leave his eyes for a half an hour. Helping another man get through a long, dark night on the row. Just voices in the darkness calling out to each other. We all did our time differently. I traveled in my mind. I had a whole, full life in my imagination, and so I didn't always ache for what I was missing. Some guys never spoke. Some guys never stopped being angry. Some guys prayed to God, and some nurtured a darkness that no man should ever carry. I tried to remember the moments on the row that would make my mama proud. I tried to focus on the moments that held light and laughter. It's what helped me get through. My case was winding down. I knew that. There was a clock counting down to the day I ran out of time—the day when I got my execution date and had to learn how to live with knowing the date and time of my death. I didn't want to know. I would rather it be a surprise than have to live out thirty or sixty days seeing the faces of the men practicing for my death.

It was hard not to spend time wishing for a different life, but I tried not to dwell on all the what-ifs. What if I had never driven off in that car? What if I had taken a job somewhere besides Bruno's? What if I hadn't been born poor? What if I'd had Bryan as my lawyer from the start? I was still fighting for my freedom, but it was with a quiet acceptance of what seemed inevitable. They were never going to admit they had put the wrong man on death row. I was never going to walk out of there.

Bryan filed our petition for a writ of certiorari in the U.S. Supreme Court in October 2013, and the State filed their response in November. We filed a response to their response a week after. There was no New Year's celebration on death row, and 2014 came in like a quiet thief in the night. What could we celebrate, really—another year of being alive or another year of being closer to death?

How did free men celebrate a new year?

I didn't know, and I couldn't remember.

It was near the end of February when I got word to call Bryan. How many of these phone calls had I made over the last fifteen years? And how many had ever been good news?

Bryan seemed breathless when he got on the line. And excited. I tried not to get my hopes up, but I felt my heart start to beat faster.

"Ray, I only have a few moments, but I need to tell you—"

"What is it, Bryan? Did Kim Kardashian call looking for me?" I had recently decided to divorce Sandra for Kim. It was a big drama that I was dealing with every night.

Bryan laughed.

"No, Ray. The U.S. Supreme Court ruled."

I took in a breath. I hoped they were going to grant review, let there be oral arguments. I knew Bryan could work his magic if he got in front of them. It was rare, I knew, but I had imagined it in my mind. Bryan pleading my innocence in front of the justices of the Supreme Court. Maybe even Obama. We had a black president, and nobody ever thought that would happen.

"Ray, it was a unanimous decision. They ruled on your case. They didn't say they would review; they reviewed and ruled. Here, let me read something to you."

"What do you mean, Bryan?" I asked. I couldn't understand what he was saying.

"Listen to this: *Anthony Ray Hinton, an inmate on Alabama's death row, asks us to decide whether the Alabama courts correctly applied Strickland to his case. We conclude that they did not and hold that Hinton's trial attorney rendered constitutionally deficient performance. We vacate the lower court's judgment and remand the case for reconsideration of whether the attorney's deficient performance was prejudicial.*"

I didn't say a word. I wanted to be sure I understood what Bryan was saying.

Bryan went on, "*The petition for certiorari and Hinton's motion for leave to proceed in forma pauperis are granted, the judgment of the Court of Criminal Appeals of Alabama is vacated, and the case is remanded for further proceedings not inconsistent with this opinion. It is so ordered.*"

"It is so ordered?"

"Ray, it is so ordered. By the United States Supreme Court. They didn't grant review; they ruled outright. In your favor. They overruled the appeals court. Ray, it was a unanimous decision."

I dropped the phone and sat down on the floor and wept like a baby. Nine Supreme Court Justices. Even Scalia. They believed me. Who was going to argue with them? Could Alabama?

It was a few moments before I picked up the phone and put it back to my ear. I didn't know if Bryan was still there.

"Bryan?"

"I'm here, Ray."

"Will you call Lester for me?"

"I will. Ray, we still have work ahead of us, and we have to go back through the state courts, but this is a win, Ray. A big win. They're going to have to issue you a new trial."

"When should I start packing?"

"Not yet, but hopefully soon. It's still going to take some time, and you still need to hang in there, but hopefully soon, my friend. Hopefully soon."

I went back to my cell, but I didn't tell anyone the news. I still had a ways to go, but for the first time in twenty-nine years, there was a flicker of light at the end of the tunnel. I didn't know how the appeals court was going to act now that the U.S. Supreme Court told them they had made an error. Because Perhacs hadn't asked for more money to hire a better expert, I was prejudiced by his performance. Payne had been a horrible expert. Perhacs hadn't tried. The United States Supreme Court was on my side.

Holy shit.

The Court of Criminal Appeals sent me back down to circuit court—back to Judge Petro—so that court could determine whether Perhacs would have hired a better expert if he had known there was money to do so, and whether that expert would have led to reasonable doubt about my guilt. The answer was yes. On September 24, 2014, the circuit court found that that I was prejudiced. Perhacs was ineffective, and my Rule 32 petition was granted. In December, my case was redocketed in Jefferson County. I was going back to where it all started. I stayed awake in my cell and rang in the new year alone but with joy—2015. It was my only New Year's celebration in thirty years on death row. I wasn't free yet, but I was going to have a new trial, with Bryan Stevenson as my attorney and three of the best ballistics experts in the country testifying on my behalf. In January, the judge ordered Holman to have me back in Jefferson County for a February 18 hearing at 9:00 A.M.

I was finally leaving death row.

Not on a gurney. Not in a body bag.

I gave away my television and my tennis shoes. I passed out my commissary food and my books and my extra clothes. It was a joyful time on my block of the row. When the guard came to walk me out, I yelled out to the twenty-eight guys on my tier.

"Can I have your attention for a minute?"

There were some hoots and hollers.

"I want you to know that I'm fixing to go. I'm leaving here. It took me thirty years to get to this moment. It may take thirty-one years for you. It may take thirty-two or thirty-three or thirty-five years, but you need to hold on. You need to hold on to your hope. If you have hope, you have everything."

The guys began to make a noise. They didn't bang on the bars like we did for executions; it was a joyful noise. It was a mixture of applause and laughter and chanting. "Hin-ton! Hin-ton! Hin-ton!"

I was taken back to high school and the basketball court and the time when I thought the crowd was chanting my name but they weren't. Life was a crazy, strange mix of tragedy and sorrow and triumph and joy.

I walked off the row with my head held high and my birth certificate in my hand.

Free at last.

Free at last.

Thank God Almighty, I'm free at last.

When I climbed into the van, I could see the cages I had walked in almost thirty years earlier. I could see the razor-wire fences and the dry, dusty yard. I never wanted to see this place again. I wasn't home yet, but I was one step closer.

| 23 |

THE SUN DOES SHINE

You can't threaten to kill someone every day year after year and not harm them, not traumatize them, not break them in ways that are really profound.

—BRYAN STEVENSON

I had just finished a meeting with one of Bryan's staff attorneys and said my goodbyes when he came running back into the room set aside for legal visits. "Ray, Ray, you have to call Bryan. You have to call him as soon as you get back to the phones."

I waited for the guard to take me back, wondering what it could be this time. I had been back in county jail for two months awaiting my new trial. A date hadn't been set yet. We had a few hearings, but we had gotten delayed because the district attorney's office couldn't find the gun or the bullets. He had accused Bryan of stealing them. It was incredible. Bryan Stevenson had supposedly stolen the most important evidence in my case. We had to pull the transcripts from the 2002 hearing with Judge Garrett to prove they had been admitted back into evidence then after being tested by my experts. Later, the clerk found a box in a court storage facility off-site that had a bag in it with the gun and the bullets from my case. We had been waiting for the prosecutors to run new ballistics tests. Lester was worried they were going to frame me again and send me back to the row, but I wasn't too worried. I had faith in Bryan. I had faith in the truth.

I got back to my cell block and went over the bank of phones on the wall. I called Bryan's phone collect. A young guy came up next to me.

"What's going on, Pops?"

I pointed to the phone and shook my head at the kid. He was supposedly a big gang member. They were all little thugs to me—little wannabe gangsters playing at a game they knew nothing about. I wanted to sit each one of them down and show them their future if they didn't choose a better way. Life was precious. Their freedom was precious. They each had the potential to be so much more than whatever had landed them in jail. I didn't want to end up on death row. I tried to tell them what it was like. They all called me Pops, because my hair and beard had patches of gray throughout. I had been twenty-nine years old the last time I was in County, not much older than most of these guys.

I listened as Bryan accepted the collect call.

"Hello, Mr. Stevenson!" I shouted at him. "I heard you wanted to talk to me, so here I am."

I smiled at a few of the guys who had looked my way when I yelled my greeting into the phone.

"Ray!" I could hear the excitement in Bryan's voice. "How are you doing?"

"I'm good. I was just meeting with Ben to talk about the case. He told me Yates said he didn't see what he saw thirty years ago. I couldn't believe it, Bryan. Yates changed his opinion about the bullets. He was honest. It's a miracle."

"Ray, I have to tell you something. Yes, it's great news about Yates, but there's something else."

"What is it?"

"Well, Ray, I'm up here in New York City, in a hotel. You know I'm speaking at a couple of colleges. I was driving here, and I got a call from Judge Petro."

"Yeah?"

"Ray, I had to have the guy pull over to the side of the road. She told me the district attorney had filed something electronically today. Without a word to anyone, they just filed a document electronically."

Bryan sounded breathless.

"What was it?" I asked him.

"Ray, you're going home. They dropped all the charges against you. You're going home, my friend. You're finally going home."

I crouched down and sat on my heels. I leaned my back up against the wall and closed my eyes. I couldn't speak. I couldn't think. I couldn't even breathe.

Home.

It had been so long since I'd heard those words.

Home. I was going home.

"Pops! Pops! You okay?" I opened my eyes, and the young thug was standing over me, concern on his face.

I smiled up at him and nodded.

"Bryan, this isn't no April Fools' joke, is it? You wouldn't do that to me, would you? It's April 1. That's not funny."

Bryan laughed.

"It's no joke, Ray. The judge wanted to release you Monday, but I told her it had to be Friday. You are going to be released Friday morning. I'll be there, Ray. I'm not sure how I'm going to get there, but I will be there Friday morning at 9:30 A.M., and you and I are going to walk out of that jail, Ray. You're going to be a free man."

I laughed. "I'll see you Friday, Bryan, and you'll bring me something to wear, won't you? I can't be walking out of this jail naked."

"We'll take care of it."

We were both quiet for another minute. There was so much to say that I couldn't find the words. How did I thank this man? He had been by my side for fifteen years and behind the scenes for longer than that. I had gone to death row, and Bryan Stevenson had come there to bring me home. There were no words. There was no way I could repay him.

"God bless you," I said.

"Thank you, Ray." He sounded as choked up as I was, and we said our goodbyes. I hung up the phone, sat on the floor, and cried like a baby in front of all those gangsters.

I was going home.

Bryan was there Friday morning, and he brought a nice black suit and a shirt that was the exact color of the Alabama sky. I changed out of my jail issue and walked over to Bryan.

"How do I look?" I asked.

"You look good, Ray. You look good." Bryan had a suit on also, and a tie.

"We both look mighty fine. Is Lester here?"

"Yes, he's waiting for you outside. He's going to take you out of here, take you to his house. We'll give you a few days at home, but then I'd like to have you come down to EJI. There's a whole lot of my staff that have been waiting to meet you."

I nodded at Bryan. I was excited and nervous and just a bit overwhelmed. After so many years imagining this day, it was hard to believe I was going to walk out a door of my own free will.

"Ray, there's a lot of people out there. There's a lot of cameras and press. This is big news. I'm sure you've seen it. They want you to say a few words. Whatever you want to say, and if you don't want to say anything, then you don't have to."

I felt a flash of fear, and then I thought about the guys on the row. They would be watching the news. They would be seeing my release. I didn't know what I was going to say, but I would say something when the time came.

"Are you ready?"

"I'm ready."

I signed some papers for the jail and then walked to the double glass doors. I could see the crowd. I could see the cameras. I reached my hand for the door and then looked back over my shoulder at Bryan.

"You ready?" he murmured.

"I've been ready for thirty years." I took a deep breath and walked out those doors with Bryan right behind me.

The crowd swarmed toward me. My sisters. My nieces. I could see Lester and Sia. I started hugging them all. My sisters were crying and praising God, and the cameras just kept pop, pop, popping at me. I reached out my hand to grab Lester's shoulder. He was in a pretty fancy suit himself.

It seemed like ten minutes before the crying and carrying on died down. Everyone got silent, waiting for me to speak. I looked around at all the faces. I was a free man. There was no one who could tell me what to do or not to do. I was free.

Free.

I closed my eyes, and I lifted my face to the sky. I said a prayer for my mama. I thanked God. I opened my eyes, and I looked at the cameras. There had been so much darkness for so long. So many dark days and dark nights. But no more. I had lived in a place where the sun refused to shine. Not anymore. Not ever again.

"The sun does shine," I said, and then I looked at both Lester and Bryan—

two men who had saved me—each in their own way. "The sun does shine," I said again.

And then the tears began to fall.

I climbed into Lester's car and buckled my seat belt. It was the first time I had been in the front seat of a vehicle in thirty years.

"Nice car," I said.

"It's old and tired. Like us." Lester laughed. "Where to?"

"I want to go to the cemetery. I want to see Mama's grave." He pulled out onto the street and drove toward the highway. Sia had gotten a ride home with friends, letting Lester and me have some time alone.

"Take a right in two hundred feet."

I jumped in my seat. It was a woman's voice, and I whipped my head around to look in the back seat. I didn't see anybody. I looked at the third row of seats in the way back, and I still didn't see anyone back there. Where was she?

"Turn right," the voice said again.

"Where is she?" I whispered to Lester.

"Where is who?"

"The white woman in the car telling you which way to go?"

Lester looked at me blankly for a second and then started to laugh. He laughed for at least two miles. "It's GPS—the car's navigation system. There's no white woman hiding in the car, Ray, I promise you."

I obviously had a lot to learn.

I looked at the gravestone with my mama's name. It made my heart hurt all over again.

"I'm home, Mama. I told you I'd be home. Your baby's come home."

Lester stood next to me in silence as I cried for the third time that day. It was weird to be outside. No guards. No fences. I felt a weird kind of anxiety I'd never felt before. Lester must have sensed my uneasiness because he put his hand on my shoulder and gave it a little squeeze. We made one more stop before home—this time at a local restaurant with a buffet. I couldn't believe all the different choices. I loaded my tray with barbecue and biscuits and fried okra and banana pudding. I waited for my sweet tea while Lester walked in front of me. He stopped and handed a card to the cashier, and she handed it back to him. Without looking back at me, he kept walking toward a table.

I froze.

I didn't have any money. I hadn't seen Lester give the woman any money. I started to panic, and then I saw Lester turn around to look for me. I met his eye and just stared at him while the cashier stared at me. He walked back to me and whispered, "What's wrong, Ray?"

"I . . . I . . . don't have any money to pay her," I whispered back.

"I already paid her, Ray. Don't worry about it."

I could feel my chest pounding. Lester hadn't given her any money. I had been watching. I didn't understand what he was doing.

"Lester, I didn't see you give her any cash. I was looking the whole time. I'm not going back to jail for stealing some okra!"

"I paid with a debit card, Ray, not cash. It's okay. We're all paid up. You don't need to worry."

I followed Lester to the table and sat down. I could feel a lot of eyes on me. I had been all over the news since Wednesday when my release was announced. I hoped that's why people were looking at me. I hadn't used a fork in thirty years, so I fumbled with it and tried not to worry. What if people were looking at me as the guy who got away with murder? What if they thought I really did it? What if they said something? What would I say? I could feel the panic beginning again.

"Ray," Lester said quietly. "It's okay, Ray. Everything's okay. We're going to eat and then go home. You're going to sleep in a real bed tonight. It's all going to be okay."

I nodded. I wanted to get out of there. It was strange to be around so many people, to have my back to people. It made me uneasy. I ate quickly, and when we got to Lester's house, I was happy to see Sia. She smiled at me, and I felt the anxiety leaving.

I was free. I was really free.

"Welcome home, Ray. Welcome home." She wrapped her arms around me, and I knew that before this day was done I was going to cry again.

We stayed up until close to 2:00 A.M. laughing and talking. We watched the late news and talked about how good I looked in my suit. When we finally said good night, I lay down in the guest room in the softest bed I think I had ever felt.

I knew on the row they would be just getting ready for breakfast. I could hear the sound of the guards walking up and down the tier. The clang of trays against each other. Men yelling good morning. The smell of sweat and grime. I could see and hear and smell it all.

It felt more familiar than the soft pillow under my head and sweet-smelling blankets that I had pulled up to my chin. It was all so strange, and I could feel the anxiety start again. I began to breathe heavy and fast. What was happening to me? I wondered if I should wake up Lester and have him take me to the hospital. Was this how it ended? The day I get my freedom, I have a heart attack? I tried to steady my breath, but it was like the walls were moving in and out and the room was spinning. I didn't like this. I got out of bed and ran into the bathroom. I locked the door behind me and sat on the floor with my head between my knees.

Immediately, my heart stopped pounding and my breathing slowed. I lifted my head and looked around. The bathroom was almost exactly the same size as my cell. I stretched out on the floor, my head resting on the bath mat.

I would sleep in here tonight.

This felt like home.

| 24 |

BANG ON THE BARS

Race, poverty, inadequate legal assistance, and prosecutorial indifference to innocence conspired to create a textbook example of injustice. I can't think of a case that more urgently dramatizes the need for reform than what has happened to Anthony Ray Hinton.

—BRYAN STEVENSON

The water is the brightest turquoise blue I have ever seen. The beaches are made up of soft white sand that feels like pillows under your bare feet. Lester is playing with a lemur, and I'm playing basketball with George Clooney. I'm playing basketball with George Clooney and I'm winning.

It's a good day.

I've had days like this before, when I was on the row, but I'm not traveling in my mind. I'm really playing basketball with George Clooney, and Lester is really playing with a lemur. Later, we will jump into Richard Branson's swimming pool with all our clothes on, and it will be the first time I have been in a swimming pool in thirty years. I will forget that there are things called cell phones now, and I will also forget to take mine out of my pocket before I jump into the deep end of the pool.

Sometimes I wonder if I'm still imagining things and I'm actually locked down in my cell—but have had a complete break with reality. I tell people I'm the only man to get MVP in the NBA, the MLB, and the NFL. They look at me and some of them say out loud what all of them are thinking: "You really lost it in there, didn't you?"

I've spent the year since my release telling my story to anyone who will listen. I was asked to come to Necker Island—Richard Branson's private island—and tell my story to a group of celebrities and others who are working hard to end the death penalty. I go where I'm asked to go—churches, colleges, small meeting rooms, private islands. I'm a curiosity—the man who survived death row—but I'm also a voice. I'm a voice for every man who still sits on the row. "I believe in justice," I tell crowds of people. "I'm not against punishment. But I don't believe in cruelty. I don't believe in useless punishment."

At a church not too far away from Birmingham, a man raises his hand after I'm done speaking and asks me what advice I would give to someone who found themselves in my position. "Pray," I say. "And when you're done praying, call Bryan Stevenson." People always laugh when I say that. They laugh when I tell them about my marriages to Halle and Sandra and Kim. But laughing puts people at ease in a way that helps them to listen. It was true on death row, and it's true outside of death row.

Lester bought a house about two hundred yards from my mama's house. I fixed up her house—not easy after it sat abandoned for over ten years—and now I live there by myself. I repaired the gazebo she loved so much. I still mow the grass the same as I did the day I was arrested. People ask me how I can stay in Alabama. Why wouldn't I leave? Alabama is my home. I love Alabama—the hot days in the summer and the thunderstorms in winter. I love the smell of the air and the green of the woods. Alabama has always been God's country to me, and it always will be. I love Alabama, but I don't love the State of Alabama. Since my release, not one prosecutor, or state attorney general, or anyone having anything to do with my conviction has apologized. I doubt they ever will.

I forgive them. I made a choice after those first difficult few weeks at Lester's when everything was new and strange and the world didn't seem to make sense to me. I chose to forgive. I chose to stay vigilant to any signs of anger or hate in my heart. They took thirty years of my life. If I couldn't forgive, if I couldn't feel joy, that would be like giving them the rest of my life.

The rest of my life is mine.

Alabama took thirty years.

That was enough.

It hasn't been easy to get used to life outside of death row. Computers and the internet and Skype and cell phones and text messaging and email. I had none of that. A whole world of technology happened while I was in my cell, and it's been difficult to catch up. And as much as I try to change it, my body and my mind still stick to the routine it learned on death row. I am up at 3:00 A.M. and ready for breakfast. Lunch is at 10:00. Dinner is at 2:00 P.M. I only sleep on one corner of my giant king-size bed. It's hard to create a new routine, but I try.

Freedom is a funny thing. I have my freedom, but in some ways, I am still locked down on the row. I know what day they are serving fish for dinner. I know when it's visiting day and at what point the guys are walking in the yard. My mind goes back there every single day, and I realize it was easier for my mind to leave the row when I was inside than it is now that I'm free.

The first time I felt rain on my skin, I wept. I hadn't felt the rain in thirty years. Now when it rains, I rush into it like a crazy man. Rain has a beauty I never knew until it was gone. I walk every morning—three miles, or four or five miles—as long as I want and as far as I want. I walk because I can walk. That also has a beauty I never saw before.

I carry scars that only Lester and Bryan really see. I document every day of my life. I get receipts. I purposely walk in front of security cameras. I don't like to stay home alone for too long without calling a few people to tell them what I'm doing. I always call someone and say good night. It's not that I'm lonely or that I'm afraid to be alone. In many ways, I prefer to be alone.

I create an alibi for every single day of my life.

I live in fear this could happen to me again.

I don't trust anyone but Lester and Bryan.

A few days a week, I go to Montgomery and work with Bryan and his staff at the Equal Justice Initiative. I travel around the country with Bryan or one of his staff and I tell my story. I'm sixty years old, and I don't have any retirement. I don't have the luxury of retiring, and I don't think I would want to if I could. Retire from what? I had my retirement in my thirties and forties and fifties. Now I'm ready to live. I wake up every morning grateful to be alive and grateful to be free. I'm a voice for the men still on the row. I'm a voice for justice. I'm the poster boy for all that is broken in our prison system.

I want to end the death penalty.

I want to make sure that what happened to me never happens to anyone else.

I want to buy Lester an Escalade to pay him back for all the miles he put on his cars—for never missing a visiting day in thirty years.

I want to meet Sandra Bullock.

There are so many things left to do in this world that I pray to God I will have time to do. I talk to my mom's picture every night and tell her that I'm home. I care for the place we called home, and I feel her presence every single day.

I sit in the gazebo she loved, every evening. When there is an execution at Holman scheduled, I bang my palm against the wood and murmur the words I said fifty-four times before. "Hang in there. Don't give up. Hold your head high. We're here. You're not alone. It's going to be okay." Fifty-four times I never knew the right thing to say.

I still don't know.

I have lived a life where I have known unconditional love. I learned on the row how rare that is. My mother loved me completely; so does Lester. Our friendship is rare and precious, and every time I'm invited somewhere to speak—like Necker Island or London—I bring Lester with me. It's the least I could do, and every once in a while, we look at each other and smile at the craziness of it all. We are two poor boys from the old coal mining town of Praco, and they just shut down Buckingham Palace to give us a private tour.

I got to see a Yankees game.

We went to Hawaii.

I've kept busy, and I've been blessed. But I would trade it all to get my thirty years back. I would trade all the days with George Clooney for just one more minute with my mother. Sorry, George. It's hard not to wonder what would have happened in my life—wonder who I would be—if they hadn't come for me. I try not to ask, "Why me?" That's a selfish question.

Why anyone?

Why do we judge some people less worthy of justice? Why does innocence have a price? McGregor passed away, and he wrote a book before he died. He mentions me in the book and says how evil I am. How clever a killer I was. How he *knew* just from looking at me that I was guilty. I forgive him. Someone taught him to be racist, just as someone taught Henry Hays. They are two sides of the same coin.

I forgive Reggie. I forgive Perhacs and I forgive Acker and I forgive Judge Garrett and every attorney general who fought to keep the truth from being revealed. I forgive the State of Alabama for being a bully. You have to stand up to bullies. I forgive because not to forgive would only hurt me.

I forgive because that's how my mother raised me.

I forgive because I have a God who forgives.

It's hard not to wrap your life in a story—a story that has a beginning, a middle, and an end. A story that has logic and purpose and a bigger reason for why things turned out the way they did. I look for purpose in losing thirty years of my life. I try to make meaning out of something so wrong and so senseless.

We all do.

We have to find ways to recover after bad things happen. We have to make every ending be a happy ending.

Every single one of us wants to matter. We want our lives and our stories and the choices we made or didn't make to matter.

Death row taught me that it all matters.

How we live matters.

Do we choose love or do we choose hate? Do we help or do we harm?

Because there's no way to know the exact second your life changes forever. You can only begin to know that moment by looking in the rearview mirror.

And trust me when I tell you that you never, ever see it coming.

| AFTERWORD |

PRAY FOR THEM BY NAME

If this court had not ordered that Anthony Ray Hinton receive further hearings in state court, he may well have been executed rather than exonerated.

—STEPHEN BREYER, U.S. SUPREME COURT JUSTICE

As of March 2017, these are the men and women who sit on death row in this country. Statistically, one out of every ten men on this list is innocent. Read through the names. Each has a family, a story, a series of choices and events that have led to a life spent in a cage. Read their names. Do you know who is wrongfully convicted? Do you know who is innocent? Read their names. My name was once on this list. Just another name in a long list of names. Another person deemed irredeemable. *The worst kind of cold-blooded killer that ever walked this earth.*

Only it wasn't true.

Read these names. Know their stories. Can we judge who deserves to live and who deserves to die? Do we have that right, and do we have that right when we know that we are often wrong? If one out of every ten planes crashed, we would stop all flights until we figured out what was broken. Our system is broken, and it's time we put a stop to the death penalty. As my good friend Bryan Stevenson says, the moral arc of the universe bends toward justice, but justice needs help. Justice only happens when good people take a stand against injustice. The moral arc of the universe needs people to support it as it bends. And yes, it also needs people to pick a side.

Read the names out loud.

After every tenth name, say, "Innocent."

Add your son's or your daughter's name to the list. Or your brother's or your mother's or your father's name to the list.

Add my name to the list.

Add your own.

The death penalty is broken, and you are either part of the Death Squad or you are banging on the bars.

Choose.

Seifullah Abdul-Salaam
Abuali Abdur'rahman
Daniel Acker
Stanley Adams
Michael Addison
Isaac Creed Agee
Shannon Agofsky
Nawaz Ahmed
Hasan Akbar
Rulford Aldridge
Bayan Aleksey
Guy S. Alexander
Billie Jerome Allen
David Allen
Guy Allen
Kerry Allen
Quincy Allen
Scott Allen
Timothy Allen
Juan Alvarez
Brenda Andrew
Terence Andrus
Antwan Anthony
William Todd Anthony
Anthony Apanovitch
Azibo Aquart
Arturo Aranda
Michael Archuleta
Douglas Armstrong
Lance Arrington
Randy L. Atkins
Quintez Martinez
Augustine
Perry Allen Austin
Rigoberto Avila, Jr.
Abdul H. Awkal
Carlos Ayestas
Hasson Bacote
John Scott Badgett
Orlando Baez
Juan Balderas
John Balentine
Terry Ball
Michael Eric Ballard
Tyrone Ballew
John M. Bane
George Banks
Stephen Barbee
Iziah Barden
Steven Barnes
William Barnes
Aquila Marcivicci Barnette
Jeffrey Lee Barrett
Kenneth Barrett
Anthony Bartee
Brandon Basham
Teddrick Batiste
John Battaglia
Anthony Battle
Richard Baumhammers
Richard R. Bays
Jathiyah Bayyinah
Richard Beasley
Tracy Beatty
Bryan Christopher Bell
Rickey Bell
William H. Bell
Anthony Belton
Miles Sterling Bench
Johnny Bennett
Rodney Berget
Brandon Bernard
G'dongalay Parlo Berry
Donald Bess
Norfolk Junior Best
Robert W. Bethel
Danny Paul Bible
James Bigby
Archie Billings
Jonathan Kyle Binney
Ralph Birdsong
Steven Vernon Bixby
Byron Black
Ricky Lee Blackwell, Sr.
Herbert Blakeney
Roger Blakeney
Andre Bland
Demond Bluntson
Scott Blystone
Robert Bolden
Arthur Jerome Bomar
Aquil Bond
Charles Bond
Melvin Bonnell
Shaun Michael Bosse
Alfred Bourgeois
Gregory Bowen
Nathan Bowie
William Bowie

Marion Bowman, Jr.
Terrance Bowman
Richard Boxley
David Braden
Michael Jerome Braxton
Alvin Avon Braziel, Jr.
Mark Breakiron
Brent Brewer
Robert Brewington
Allen Bridgers
Shawnfatee M. Bridges
Dustin Briggs
Grady Brinkley
James Broadnax
Joseph Bron
Antuan Bronshtein
Romell Broom
Arthur Brown
Fabion Brown
John W. Brown
Kenneth Brown
Lavar Brown
Meier Jason Brown
Micah Brown
Paul A. Brown
Michael Browning
Charles Brownlow
Eugene A. Broxton
Jason Brumwell
Quisi Bryan
James Nathaniel Bryant
Laquaille Bryant
Stephen C. Bryant
Duane Buck
George C. Buckner
Stephen Monroe Buckner
Carl W. Buntion
Raeford Lewis Burke
Junius Burno
Kevin Burns
William Joseph Burns
John Edward Burr
Arthur Burton
Jose Busanet
Edward Lee Busby, Jr.
Ronson Kyle Bush
Steven A. Butler
Tyrone Cade
Richard Cagle
James Calvert
Alva Campbell, Jr.
James A. Campbell
Robert J. Campbell
Terrance Campbell
Anibal Canales
Jermaine Cannon
Ivan Cantu
Ruben Cardenas
Kimberly Cargill
Carlos Caro
David Carpenter
Tony Carruthers
Cedric Carter
Douglas Carter
Sean Carter
Shan E. Carter
Tilon Carter
Linda Carty
Walter Caruthers
Omar Cash
August Cassano
Juan Castillo
Eric Cathey
Ronnie Cauthern
Steven Cepec
Tyrone Chalmers
Terry Ray Chamberlain
Frank Chambers
Jerry Chambers
Ronald Champney
Kosoul Chanthakoummane
Davel Chinn
David Chmiel
Troy James Clark
Sedrick Clayton
Jordan Clemons
Curtis Clinton
Billie W. Coble
James Allen Coddington
Benjamin Cole
Jaime Cole
Wade L. Cole
Timothy Coleman
Douglas Coley
Jesse Celeb Compton
Gary Cone
Michael Conforti
Jerry W. Connor
James T. Conway III
Derrick L. Cook
Robert Cook
Wesley Paul Coonce
Odell Corley
Raul Cortez
Luzenski Allen Cottrell
Donney Council
Bernard Cousar
David Lee Cox
Jermont Cox
Russell Cox
Daniel Crispell
Dayva Cross
Billy Jack Crutsinger
Obel Cruz-Garcia
Edgardo Cubas
Carlos Cuesta-Rodriguez
Daniel Cummings, Jr.
Paul Cummings
Rickey Cummings
Clinton Cunningham
Jeronique Cunningham
George Curry
Brandon Daniel
Henry Daniels
Johnny R. Daughtry
Tedor Davido III

Lemaricus Davidson
Erick Davila
Brian E. Davis
Cecil Davis
Edward E. Davis
Franklin Davis
Irving Alvin Davis
James Davis
Len Davis
Michael Andre Davis
Nicholas Davis
Phillip Davis
Roland T. Davis
Von Clark Davis
Jason Dean
Eugene Decastro
Jose Dejesus
James Anderson Dellinger
Reinaldo Dennes
James A. Dennis
Paul Devoe
Robert Diamond
Anthony James Dick
William Dickerson, Jr.
Archie Dixon
Jessie Dotson
Kevin Dowling
Marcus Druery
Troy Drumheller
John Drummond, Jr.
Steven Duffey
Jeffrey N. Duke
David Duncan
Joseph Duncan
Timothy Alan Dunlap
Harvey Y. Earvin
Keith East
Dale Wayne Eaton
Stephen Edmiston
Terry Edwards
John Eichinger
Scott Eizember
Gerald C. Eldridge
John Elliott
Terrence Rodricus Elliott
Clark Richard Elmore
Phillip L. Elmore
Areli Escobar
Joel Escobedo
Noah Espada
Gregory Esparza
Larry Estrada
Kamell Delshawn Evans
Henry Fahy
Nathaniel Fair
Richard Fairchild
Robert Faulkner
Angelo Fears
Leroy Fears
Donald Fell
Anthony James Fiebiger
Edward Fields
Sherman Lamont Fields
Cesar R. Fierro
Ron Finklea
Robert Fisher
Stanley Fitzpatrick
Andre Fletcher
Anthony Fletcher
Robert Flor
Charles Flores
Shawn Eric Ford, Jr.
Tony Ford
Linwood Forte
Kelly Foust
Elrico Fowler
Anthony Francois
Antonio Sanchez Franklin
Robert Fratta
James Frazier
Darrell Wayne Frederick
John Freeland
Ray Freeney
James Eugene Frey, Jr.
Danny Frogge
Clarence Fry, Jr.
Robert Ray Fry
Chadrick Fulks
Barney Fuller
Marvin Gabrion II
David Gainey
Tomas Gallo
Bryan S. Galvin
Joseph Gamboa
Larry James Gapen
Ryan Garcell
Edgar Baltazar Garcia
Fernando Garcia
Hector L. Garcia
Joseph Garcia
John Steven Gardner
Daniel T. Garner
Humberto Garza
Joe Franco Garza, Jr.
Bill Gates
Malcolm Geddie, Jr.
Jonathan Lee Gentry
Ronald Gibson
John Gillard
Richard Glossip
Milton Gobert
James Goff
Tilmon Golphin
Ignacio Gomez
Nelson Gongora
Michael Gonzales
Ramiro Gonzales
Mark Anthony Gonzalez
Clarence Goode
Christopher Goss
Bartholomew Granger
Donald Grant
John Marion Grant
Ricky Jovan Gray
Ronald Gray
Gary Green

Travis Green
Randolph M. Greer
Allen Eugene Gregory
Warren Gregory
William Gregory
Wendell Arden Grissom
Timmy Euvonne Grooms
Scott Group
Angel Guevara
Gilmar Guevara
Howard Guidry
Geronimo Gutierrez
Ruben Gutierrez
Randy Guzek
Daniel Gwynn
Randy Haag
Richard Hackett
Thomas Hager
Kenneth Hairston
Conan Wayne Hale
Delano Hale, Jr.
Billy Hall
Charles Michael Hall
Darrick U. Hall
Gabriel Paul Hall
Jon Hall
Justen Hall
Leroy Hall
Orlando Hall
Randy Halprin
Ronald James Hamilton, Jr.
Phillip Hancock
Gerald Hand
Patrick Ray Haney
James Hanna
Sheldon Hannibal
John G. Hanson
Alden Harden
Marlon Harmon
Garland Harper
Donnie Lee Harris, Jr.
Francis Bauer Harris
James Harris, Jr.
Jimmy Dean Harris
Roderick Harris
Timothy Hartford
Nidal Hasan
Jim E. Haseldon
Larry Hatten
Gary Haugen
Thomas Hawkins
Anthony Haynes
Michael James Hayward
Rowland Hedgepeth
Danny Hembree
James Lee Henderson
Jerome Henderson
Kennath Henderson
Warren K. Henness
Timothy Hennis
Fabian Hernandez
Fernando Hernandez
Charles Hicks
Danny Hill
Genesis Hill
Jerry Hill
Anthony Darrell Hines
George Hitcho, Jr.
Henry Hodges
Timothy Hoffner
Michael Hogan
Brittany Holberg
Norris Holder
Allen Richard Holman
Mitchell D. Holmes
Dave Taberone Honi
Dustin Honken
Cerron Thomas Hooks
Darien Houser
William Howard Housman
Gregory Lee Hover
Jamaal Howard
Samuel Howard
Gary Hughbanks
Marreece Hughes
Robert Hughes
John Hughey
Stephen Lynn Huguely
John Hummel
Calvin Hunter
Lamont Hunter
Jason Hurst
Percy Hutton
Terry Alvin Hyatt
Johnny Hyde
Ramiro Ibarra
Dustin Iggs
Jerry Buck Inman
Billy R. Irick
William Irvan
Ahmad Fawzi Issa
David Ivy
Andre Jackson
Christopher Jackson
Cleveland Jackson
Jeremiah Jackson
Kareem Jackson
Nathaniel Jackson
Richard Allen Jackson
Shelton Jackson
Daniel Jacobs
Timothy Matthew Jacoby
Akil Jahi
Stanley Jalowiec
James Jaynes
Joseph Jean
Willie Jenkins
Robert M. Jennings
Ralph Simon Jeremias
Christopher Johnson
Cory Johnson
Dexter Johnson
Donnie E. Johnson
Donte Johnson
Harve Lamar Johnson
Jesse Lee Johnson

Marcel Johnson
Martin Allen Johnson
Marvin G. Johnson
Matthew Johnson
Nikolaus Johnson
Raymond Eugene Johnson
Roderick Andre Johnson
William Johnson
Aaron C. Jones
Donald Allen Jones
Elwood Jones
Henry Lee Jones
Jared Jones
Julius Darius Jones
Odraye Jones
Phillip L. Jones
Quintin Jones
Shelton D. Jones
Clarence Jordan
David Lynn Jordan
Lewis Jordan
Elijah Dwayne Joubert
Anthony B. Juniper
Jurijus Kadamovas
Jeffrey Kandies
William John Keck
David Keen
Troy Kell
Emanuel Kemp, Jr.
Christopher Kennedy
Donald Ketterer
Joseph Kindler
John William King
Terry King
Juan Kinley
Anthony Kirkland
Marlan Kiser
Melvin Knight
John J. Koehler
Ron Lafferty
Richard Laird
Keith Lamar
Bernard Lamp
Mabry Joseph Landor III
Lawrence Landrum
Eric Lane
Edward L. Lang III
Robert Langley
Robert Lark
Thomas M. Larry
Joseph R. Lave
Mark Lawlor
Daryl Lawrence
Jimmie Lawrence
Wayne A. Laws
Wade Lay
William Lecroy
Daniel Lee
Guy Legrande
Gregory Leonard
Patrick Leonard
William B. Leonard
John Lesko
Emanual Lester
David Lee Lewis
Harlem Harold Lewis III
Armando Leza
Kenneth Jamal Lighty
Antione Ligons
Kim Ly Lim
Carl Lindsey
Marion Lindsey
Kevin James Lisle
Leo Gordon Little III
Emmanuel Littlejohn
Juan Lizcano
Robbie Locklear
Stephen Long
Christian Longo
George Lopez
Manuel Saucedo Lopez
Charles Lorraine
Ernest Lotches
Gregory Lott
Albert Love
Douglas Anderson Lovell
Dwight J. Loving
Jose T. Loza
Melissa Lucio
Joe Michael Luna
David Lynch
Ralph Lynch
Glenn Lyons
Clarence Mack
Michael Madison
Beau Maestas
Floyd Eugene Maestas
Mikal D. Mahdi
Orlando Maisonet
Ricky Ray Malone
James Mammone III
Charles Mamou, Jr.
Darrell Maness
Leroy Elwood Mann
Kevin Marinelli
Gerald Marshall
Jerome Marshall
David Martin
Jeffrey Martin
Jose Noey Martinez
Mica Alexander Martinez
Raymond D. Martinez
Lenwood Mason
Maurice Mason
William Michael Mason
Damon Matthews
Kevin Edward Mattison
Charles Maxwell
Landon May
Lyle May
Randall Mays
Angela D. McAnulty
Jason Duval McCarty
Ernest Paul McCarver
Robert Lee McConnell
Michael McDonnell

George E. McFarland
Larry McKay
Calvin McKelton
Patrick McKenna
Gregory McKnight
Freddie McNeill
John McNeill
Mario McNeill
Charles D. McNelton
David McNish
Thomas Meadows
Anthony Medina
Hector Medina
Rodolfo Medrano
Pablo Melendez
Frederick Mendoza
Moises Mendoza
Ralph Menzies
Jeffrey Meyer
Hubert Lester Michael, Jr.
Donald Middlebrooks
David S. Middleton
Iouri Mikhel
Ronald Mikos
Blaine Milam
Clifford Ray Miller
David Miller
Demontrell Miller
Dennis Miller
Alfred Mitchell
Lezmond Mitchell
Marcus Decarlos Mitchell
Wayne Mitchell
Jonathan D. Monroe
Milton Montalvo
Noel Montalvo
Marco Montez
Caron Montgomery
Lisa Montgomery
William Montgomery
Nelson W. Mooney
Blanche T. Moore
Bobby James Moore
Lee Edward Moore, Jr.
Mikal Moore
Randolph Moore
Richard Bernard Moore
Hector Manuel Morales
Samuel Moreland
James Lewis Morgan
William Morganherring
Farris Morris
William Morva
Carl Stephen Moseley
Errol Duke Moses
Naim Muhammad
Michael Mulder
Travis Mullis
Frederick A. Mundt, Jr.
Eric Murillo
Craig Murphy
Jedediah Murphy
Julius Murphy
Kevin Murphy
Patrick Murphy
Patrick Dwaine Murphy
Harold Murray IV
Jeremy Murrell
Austin Myers
David Lee Myers
Ricardo Natividad
Keith D. Nelson
Marlin E. Nelson
Steven Nelson
Clarence Nesbit
Calvin Neyland, Jr.
Harold Nichols
Avram Vineto Nika
Tyrone L. Noling
Lejames Norman
Michael W. Norris
Clinton Robert Northcutt
Eugene Nunnery
Billy Lee Oatney, Jr.
Denny Obermiller
Abel Ochoa
Richard Odom
Walter Ogrod
James D. O'Neal
Arboleda Ortiz
Gregory Osie
Gary Otte
Freddie Owens
Donyell Paddy
Miguel Padilla
Scott Louis Panetti
Carlette Parker
Johnny Parker
Michael Parrish
Maurice Patterson
Jeffrey Williams Paul
James Pavatt
Pervis Payne
Kevin Pelzer
Albert Perez
Kerry Perez
Louis Perez
Lawrence Peterson
Us Petetan
Tracy Petrocelli
Bortella Philisten
Mario Lynn Phillips
Ronald Phillips
Mark Pickens
Michael Pierce
Christa Pike
Briley Piper
Alexander Polke
Richard Poplawski
Ernest Porter
Thomas A. Porter
Gilbert Postelle
Gregory Powell
Kitrich Powell
Wayne Powell
Gerald Lee Powers

Ted Prevatte
Jeffrey Prevost
Taichin Preyor
Ronald Jeffrey Prible, Jr.
Robert Lynn Pruett
Corinio Pruitt
Michael Pruitt
Joseph Prystash
Wesley Ira Purkey
Derrick Quintero
Syed M. Rabbani
Charles Raby
Derrick Ragan
Walter Raglin
William Raines
Ker'sean Ramey
John Ramirez
Juan Raul Ramirez
Robert M. Ramos
Andrew Darrin Ramseur
Charles Randolph
Samuel B. Randolph IV
William Rayford
Dennis Reed
Rodney Reed
Michael Reeves
Robert Rega
Albert E. Reid
Anthony Reid
David Renteria
Horacio A. Reyes-Camarena
Juan Reynosa
Charles Rhines
Rick Allen Rhoades
Charles Rice
Jonathan Richardson
Martin A. Richardson
Thomas Richardson
Timothy Richardson
Cedric Ricks
Raymond G. Riles
Billy Ray Riley
Michael Rimmer
Britt Ripkowski
Michael Rippo
Angel Rivera
Cletus Rivera
Jose A. Rivera
William Rivera
Warren Rivers
James H. Roane, Jr.
Jason Robb
Robert Roberson
Donna Roberts
Tyree Alfonzo Roberts
James Robertson
Mark Robertson
Charles L. Robins
Antyane Robinson
Cortne Robinson
Eddie Robinson
Gregory Robinson
Harvey Robinson
Julius Robinson
Marcus Robinson
Terry Lamont Robinson
William E. Robinson
Felix Rocha
Kwame Rockwell
Alfonso Rodriguez
Juan Carlos Rodriguez
Pedro Rodriguez
Rosendo Rodriguez
Dayton Rogers
Mark J. Rogers
William Glenn Rogers
Martin Rojas
Richard Norman Rojem, Jr.
Edwin R. Romero
Christopher Roney
Clinton Rose
Christopher Roseboro
Kenneth Rouse
Darlie Lynn Routier
John Allen Rubio
Rolando Ruiz
Wesley Ruiz
Travis Runnels
Eric Walter Running
Larry Rush
Pete Russell, Jr.
Michael Patrick Ryan
James C. Ryder
Victor Saldano
Tarus Sales
Thavirak Sam
Michael Sample
Gary Lee Sampson
Abraham Sanchez
Alfonso Sanchez
Anthony Castillo Sanchez
Ricardo Sanchez
Carlos Sanders
Thomas Sanders
William K. Sapp
Daniel Saranchak
David Allen Sattazahn
Kaboni Savage
Byron Scherf
Conner Schierman
Michael Dean Scott, Jr.
Kevin Scudder
Ricky D. Sechrest
Juan Meza Segundo
Manuel M. Sepulveda
Ricardo Serrano
Bobby T. Sheppard
Erica Sheppard
Donald William Sherman
Michael Wayne Sherrill
Brentt Sherwood
Anthony Allen Shore
Duane A. Short
Tony Sidden
Brad Keith Sigmon
Kenneth Simmons

David Simonsen
Kendrick Simpson
Rasheen L. Simpson
Mitchell Sims
Vincent Sims
Fred Singleton
Michael Singley
George Skatzes
Henry Skinner
Paul Slater
John Amos Small
Christopher Smith
Demetrius Smith
Jamie Smith
Joseph W. Smith
Kenny Smith
Michael Dewayne Smith
Oscar F. Smith
Reche Smith
Roderick Smith
Wayne Smith
Wesley Tobe Smith, Jr.
Ricky Smyrnes
Mark Isaac Snarr
David Sneed
John Oliver Snow
Mark Soliz
Michael H. Sonner
Walter Sorto
Pedro S. Sosa
Anthony Sowell
Jeffrey Sparks
Robert Sparks
Dawud Spaulding
William Speer
Melvin Speight
Warren Spivey
Mark Newton Spotz
Mark L. Squires
Steven Staley
Stephen Stanko
Norman Starnes
Andre Staton
Roland Steele
Patrick Joseph Steen
Davy Stephens
Jonathan Stephenson
John Stojetz
Ralph Stokes
Sammie Louis Stokes
Patrick Jason Stollar
Bobby Wayne Stone
Paul David Storey
Bigler Jobe Stouffer II
Darrell Strickland
John Stumpf
Tony Summers
Brian Suniga
Dennis Wade Suttles
Gary Sutton
Nicholas Sutton
Larry Swearingen
Richard Tabler
David Taylor
Eddie Taylor
Paul Taylor
Rejon Taylor
Rodney Taylor
Ronald Taylor
Von Taylor
Donald Tedford
Ivan Teleguz
James Tench
Bernardo Tercero
Gary Terry
Karl Anthony Terry
Michelle Sue Tharp
Thomas Thibodeaux
Andre Thomas
Andrew Thomas
Donte Thomas
James Edward Thomas
James William Thomas
Joseph Thomas
Kenneth D. Thomas
Marlo Thomas
Steven Thomas
Walic Christopher Thomas
Ashford Thompson
Charles Thompson
Gregory Thompson
John Henry Thompson
Matthew Dwight Thompson
John Thuesen
Raymond Tibbetts
Jeffrey Dale Tiner
Richard Tipton
Chuong Duong Tong
Andres Antonio Torres
Jorge Avila Torrez
Jakeem Lydell Towles
Heck Van Tran
Michael Travaglia
Stephen Treiber
Carlos Trevino
James Earl Trimble
Daniel Troya
Gary Allen Trull
Isaiah Glenndell Tryon
Dzhokhar Tsarnaev
Russell Tucker
Albert Turner
Michael Ray Turner
Bruce Turnidge
Joshua Turnidge
Raymond A. Twyford III
Stacey Tyler
Jose Uderra
Alejandro Umana
Kevin Ray Underwood
David Unyon
Fidencio Valdez
John E. Valerio
James W. Vandivner
Robert Van Hook

Siaosi Vanisi
Richard Vasquez
Christopher Vialva
Jorge Villanueva
Warren Waddy
James Walker
Henry Louis Wallace
Shonda Walter
Christina S. Walters
Billy Joe Wardlow
Faryion Wardrip
Byron Lamar Waring
Leslie Warren
Anthony Washington
Michael Washington
Willie T. Washington
Gerald Watkins
Herbert Watson
John Watson III
James Hollis Watts
Obie Weathers
Michael Webb
Timmy John Weber
Bruce Webster
John Edward Weik
James Were
Herbert Dwayne Wesley
Hersie Wesson
Steven West
Robert Wharton
Daryl K. Wheatfall
Thomas Bart Whitaker
Garcia G. White
Melvin White
Timothy L. White
Keith Dedrick Wiley, Jr.
George Wilkerson
Christopher Wilkins
Phillip E. Wilkinson
Willie Wilks
Robert Gene Will II
Andre Williams
Antoine L. Williams
Arthur Lee Williams
Cary Williams
Charles Christopher Williams
Christopher Williams
Clifford Williams
Clifton Williams
David Kent Williams
Eric Williams
Eugene Johnny Williams
James T. Williams
Jeffrey Williams
Jeremy Williams
John Williams
Perry Eugene Williams
Robert Williams, Jr.
Roy L. Williams
Terrance Williams
Howard Hawk Willis
Edward T. Wilson
James Wilson
Ronell Wilson
Louis Michael Winkler
Andrew Witt
William L. Witter
Jeffrey Wogenstahl
Ernest R. Wolver, Jr.
David L. Wood
Jeffery Wood
John Richard Wood
Termane Wood
Aric Woodard
Robert Woodard
Anthony Woods
Darrell Woods
Dwayne Woods
Vincent Wooten
Charles Wright
William Wright
Raghunandan Yandamuri
Robert Lee Yates
Robert Ybarra, Jr.
Christopher Young
Clinton Young
Leonard Young
Edmund Zagorski

ACKNOWLEDGMENTS

First of all I would like to thank my best friend, Lester, and his wife, Sylvia. Thank you for standing beside me through the good, the bad, and the ugly. Thank you for never judging, and for never giving up on me. You showed up for me for thirty years while I was incarcerated, and you continue to show up for me now that I am free. Thank you both for sharing your time, your laughter, and your endless love. Thank you for brightening up the visiting yard. Thank you for all you have done, all you were willing to do, and all you continue to do. Thank you for working all night and then driving all day to make sure that I had someone to sit down to talk to. Thank you for putting the miles on your car. Most people talk about love, but the two of you show me what true love and friendship really is. I love you not because of what you've done for me, but because of who you are and what you mean to me. If you ever find yourself needing me, the way that I needed you, I will be in your corner just the way you were in mine. Lester, when I think of you, I think of John 15:13: "Greater love hath no man than this, that a man lay down his life for his friends."

I would like to thank Bryan Stevenson for his many sleepless nights working on my case and for believing in me when no one else in the legal system did. Bryan, you are truly the moral voice and compass of the justice system. Thank you for the work you do on behalf of the poor, for being God's greatest lawyer, and for always fighting no matter the odds against you. Thank you for not only being a great lawyer, but a great man. You are my lawyer, my brother, and my friend. If I had a billion dollars, it wouldn't be enough to thank you for all you have done for me. The respect I have for you is immeasurable, and I am thankful to God for bringing you into my life. You have restored my faith in humanity, and taught me that there are good, decent human beings in the world. If I could be half the man you are, I would be all right. I wish more men and women would answer the call given to you to serve the poor and marginalized. Ladies and gentlemen, if you ever find yourself in my position, if you're ever arrested for a crime you did not commit, my advice is first to say a prayer, and then to call Bryan Stevenson. He is your 911.

I would also like to thank the many others at the Equal Justice Initiative who spent long hours and sleepless nights working on my case. Thank you to Charlotte Morrison, Aaryn Urell, Drew Colfax, Cathleen Price, Andrew Childers, Sia Sanneh, Carla Crowder, Stephen Chu, and Ben Harmon. You also saved my life and I am forever grateful.

I would like to thank my literary agent, Doug Abrams, and his team at Idea Architects. Thank you, Doug, for believing in my story and guiding me through the publishing process with endless energy and enthusiasm. Thank you for your commitment to making the world a more just place, and for creating books that touch minds and hearts. No one can agent like you agent, and I am grateful to know you.

I would also like to thank my collaborative writer, Lara Love Hardin. Thank you, Lara, for your amazing gift with words, your understanding, your patience, and your willingness to slog through eight thousand pages of court transcripts and documents. You walked this journey with me every step of the way, and listened to the hard stories and difficult memories, always putting my emotional well-being first before any deadlines. Thank you for getting in my head and helping me condense thirty years on death row into a story that reveals the humanity in all of us.

Thank you to my editor at St. Martin's Press, George Witte, for championing my story and making the book the very best version it could be. Thanks also to the amazing team at St. Martin's: Sara Thwaite, Paul Hochman, Gabrielle Gantz, Martin Quinn, Laura Clark, Tracey Guest, Rafal Gibek, Sara Ensey, and Chris Ensey. A special thanks to Michael Cantwell for his input. Thank you also to Sally Richardson and Jennifer Enderlin for publishing this book.

Since my release I have spoken in front of countless people, and I want to thank all those who have heard my story and given me love and support and inspiration to keep telling my story, even when it's difficult. I would especially like to thank Michael Mouran and his wife, Kathy—a new friendship that I hope will last a lifetime. I hope my story will inspire others to fight for justice, to be a better friend, to love unconditionally, and to recognize that we all have a part to play and work to do to fix a justice system that is not always just.

If you are reading my book and you are on death row or incarcerated for a crime you did not commit or incarcerated for a crime you did commit—my wish is that you will find hope within these pages. Hope to keep on fighting, to keep on living, to believe that you can change or your situation can change. Remember none of us are the worst thing we have done, and right now, wherever you are, whoever you are, you can reach out to your fellow man or woman and bring your own light to the dark places.